Getting the Most Out of Your Consultant

A Guide to Selection Through Implementation

Getting the Most Out of Your Consultant

A Guide to Selection Through Implementation

Gordon W. Fuller
President
G.W. Fuller Associates Ltd.
Food Consulting
Montreal, Quebec, Canada

CRC Press

Boca Raton   Boston   London   New York   Washington, D.C.

Library of Congress Cataloging-in-Publication Data

Fuller, Gordon, W.
   Getting the most out of your consultant: a guide to selection through
implementation / by Gordon W. Fuller.
      p. cm.
   Includes bibliographical references and index.
   ISBN 0-8493-8007-3 (alk. Paper)
   1. Business consultants. I. Title.
HD69.C6F85 1998
658.4′6 — dc21

                                    98-6843
                                     CIP

The Author

Dr. Gordon W. Fuller is President, G. W. Fuller Associates Limited, an international food consulting company headquartered in Montreal, Quebec, Canada. He is also an Associate of the internationally based group Stratecon, comprised of networking food consultants. Dr. Fuller has had experience in industry, academia, and government. He was Vice President, Technical Services, Imasco Foods Ltd for 8 years, where his responsibilities included corporate research and development. He worked in England as Advisory Officer and later as Supervisor of Meat Product Research for the British Food Manufacturing Industries Research Association, which later became the Food Research Association, Leatherhead. His work with the H. J. Heinz Co. in Pittsburgh, PA on tomato products was carried out in association with the Mellon Institute for Industrial Research. He gained experience in chocolate syrups and confectionery products with the Nestle Co., Fulton, NY.

At the University of Guelph, Dr. Fuller was an associate professor in the Department of Poultry Science, where he taught and conducted research on poultry and egg added-value products in addition to his consulting and extension work. He has been an outside lecturer at both McGill University and Concordia University. He was also a research chemist for the Food and Drug Directorate in Ottawa, Canada.

Dr. Fuller is a member of the Institute of Food Technologists (U.S.), a member of the Canadian Institute of Food Science and Technology, a charter member of the Institute for Thermal Processing Specialists (U.S.), and a Fellow of the Institute of Food Science and Technology (U.K.). He is the author or co-author of several papers in scientific journals and trade magazines. He is the author of *New Food Product Development: From Concept to Marketplace,* published by CRC Press in 1994.

Dedication

To my wife and severest critic, Joan, for her patience, understanding, and invaluable assistance with proofreading and helpful suggestions in clarifying my sometimes tortuous text. I am also indebted to my son, Grahame, for his valuable assistance in editing and in getting me into the computer age.

Preface

I have not always been a consultant, although I had always thought I would become one. Daydreaming of such a future occurred more frequently and with greater intensity as a series of rapid senior managerial changes swept through the division of the company I was in. This was the era presaging the great ages of massive downsizing that took place. The changes did not affect me personally, but it became apparent our companies were in a holding pattern. Anything new and exciting was being shelved. Lean and mean became the orders for the day. Frills, including many items such as the technical library that I considered not so frilly, were being dropped. Rumors of a parent company dissatisfied with the return on investment surfaced and ebbed but never really disappeared.

The handwriting appeared brightly on the wall when an individual recognized as a make-over artist and hatchet man appeared in the upper managerial ranks. My golden handshake was not long in coming. I was fortunate in having some three years to prepare for becoming an independent consultant. My preparation came in the form of reading every book on consulting I could find and picking the brains of the many consultants that I, in my position, had hired, met, or just rubbed shoulders with in an activity that is now called networking.

My consulting practice grew nicely. I networked with other consultants and developed a coterie of highly competent and trusted colleagues and friends with whom I shared projects and exchanged information. My work took me to South America, the Far East, and Europe, where I met a number of wonderful, and some not so wonderful, clients all of whom provided me with new product experiences, unique managerial challenges, and problems of such an exciting nature that life was never boring.

But problems did arise. Clients frequently asked me to do chores more easily carried out by their own secretaries which, when I did them, only took my time and their money. I was called in to resolve problems only to find the client did not know or could not explain what the problem was. Some literally did not know what they did not know. It brought to memory a sign that said, "It's not what we don't know that's the problem, it's what we know that ain't so that's the problem." I found I was telling potential clients where assistance could be obtained more readily and freely without going through me.

It began to dawn on me that many companies both large and small do not know how to work with consultants in an efficient and profitable way. There were books written by consultants, sometimes in the most garish fashion, about successful consulting or how to run a consultancy. There were, however, none on guiding those who were seeking help from consultants. There were no books describing how to have a successful relationship with a consultant or how to receive good value for their consulting dollar.

Since I had been a user of consultants and, on the other side of the fence, have worked, and still do work, as a consultant, I decided to put together a book written for companies looking to use a consultant.

Acknowledgments must go to many colleagues who assisted me with this book by discussions, through stories and anecdotes from their own experiences, by comments on issues that I raised, and by general encouragement. These are James Baldwin, Charles Beck, Sylvan Eisenberg, Patricia Fehling, F. J. (Jack) Francis, Terence Higgins, E. S. Idziak, Michel Lenoble, Jean Richard, Richard Swift, Herbert Weinstein, and Richard Whelan. To them my thanks.

Contents

1 Consultants, Specialists, Experts, Advisers, and Gurus: Who and What Are They?

The man we call a specialist today was formerly called a man with a one-track mind.

Endre Balogh

An expert is a man who has made all the mistakes which can be made, in a very narrow field.

Niels Bohr

Guru: someone who gets paid more than a consultant in return for saying less.

Barry Nelson

Quoted in *The Gazette,* Montreal, February 24, 1997

INTRODUCTION

The quotations above describe concisely what this chapter is about. It is a description of those individuals who use their training, knowledge, experience, and, yes, chutzpah to sell their services to others. Such services may include providing advice or knowledge in arcane subjects, applying their organizing skills, conducting training programs or seminars, or applying unique skills in specialized fields of technology. Consultants can provide sophisticated laboratory resources for research activities plus the necessary expertise to guide these investigations. They sell these products to their clients, who need these services for various reasons. In later chapters, the book will deal with understanding these consultants, negotiating with them, getting along with them and, most important, getting one's money's worth from them. For the sake of simplicity, experts, specialists, advisers, authorities in particular fields, mentors, counselors, gurus, and social ecologists will be classified simply as *consultants*. What consultants have to offer for sale will be referred to simply as their *product*. This product may not be a tangible thing but could be a service or some expert advice. The user or seeker of a consultant's product will be the client. Clients may be anything. They range from a government at any of its levels to a prominent personality, e.g., a politician, an entertainer or some other public figure, or they could be an organization or a company which manufactures consumer products or heavy machinery or provides services such as banking, insurance, or legal advice, etc.

Clients feel ambivalent toward consultants. Consultants are revered, respected, and reviled. The respect and reverence owes to consultants' unique skills and apparent ability to resolve their clients' difficulties. The vilification arises because they are seen as feeding off the troubles and adversities of their clients. Their presence suggests to the world at large, and to employees in particular, that their clients were inadequately prepared for whatever task brought the consultants in. In addition, their presence may represent impending change for the clients' staff.

The French satirist, Jean de la Bruyère, provided what might be a motto for consultants: "There are only two ways of getting on in this world: by one's own industry, or by the weaknesses of others." Consultants use both means of getting on in this world but with heavy emphasis on applying their industry to the latter. That is, a client's inability (weakness) to resolve some issue with in-house resources forces him to resort to consultants. The consultant profits by this weakness.

This book is for the clients. It is meant to guide clients on how to use consultants, specialists, experts, advisers, and gurus to best advantage, for experience has taught me that we who sell our skills are frequently poorly used. Clients have learned to manage the resources within their own organizations. They should learn to manage their consultants.

The cynicism, perhaps malice, couched in the quotations that began this chapter should serve as a warning that consultants and their products should always be looked upon with healthy skepticism. Consultants are neither omniscient nor omnipotent, though some would like clients to think so. To get the best out of them, clients must be critical and demanding.

HOW THE LATEST PLETHORA OF CONSULTANTS BEGAN

There has been a recent burgeoning of not only the numbers of consultants but also the variety of fields in which they consult — or certainly so it seems as one glances in the business and trade publications. It should not be assumed, however, that the use of consultants began recently. Consultants have been around for many hundreds of years. They have advised leaders of the most propitious action to take, when to plant crops, or where to hunt. In those earlier days they based their advice on good common sense and their own skills of observation, with some hocus pocus. Today's consultants may be more sophisticated in the methodologies supporting their services, but the results are not necessarily more accurate and can be as mysterious as those in historical times.

Beginning in the 1960s and increasingly in the '70s and '80s, there has been a growing turmoil in industry as companies downsized. This is a comparatively new euphemism for reducing staff requirements. Re-engineering, a new management technique, had arrived.

Some companies, oddly enough, upsized. But the era of never-ending growth for the sake of growth certainly had come to an end. In the food industry where I am most acquainted with activities, this turmoil has continued into the '90s, with large food companies letting people go and selling off some of their unprofitable divisions. For example, Quaker Oats released several hundreds of its staff in the mid

1990s. McCormick and Company downsized in 1994, eliminating some 600 positions. A very small sampling of other mergers and sell-offs reported in *Food Technology*, the house organ of the Institute of Food Technologists, in 1995 lists:

- Cadbury Schweppes acquired control of Dr. Pepper/Seven-Up. H. J. Heinz Company bought the Quaker Oats Company's pet food business. Bayer AG, Leverkusen, Germany, purchased the flavor company, Florasynth. These announcements can all be found in the May issue.
- Quest International acquired Gunther Products from Staley (April issue).
- Sanofi BioIndustries, Inc., was sold to SKW Trostberg, AG, a division of VIAG, Germany (February issue).

This is by no means a complete listing of the mergers and acquisitions that went on during 1995, and these activities represent only those in the food industry. Mergers and acquisitions continue to this day: Haarmann and Reimer Group, a subsidiary of Bayer Corporation is reportedly looking to sell its Food Ingredients Division (Baird, 1997). This sale will include manufacturing facilities in three countries and include over 1,200 employees. These activities continue in other industries: Milner (1997) reported the buyout offer of WorldCom Inc., considered the fourth largest long-distance communication company, for MCI Communications Corp., the third largest communication giant. This is considered the largest take-over ever, even larger than the merger of the pharmaceutical giants Sandoz AG and Ciba-Geigy AG in 1996 (Milner, 1997). Each merger results in a duplication of services, and layoffs ensue.

The result of all this turmoil was, in short, rather chaotic itself:

- Some companies got bigger. They gobbled up other companies which had been cast adrift by their parent companies as these had downsized.
- Some new companies were spawned as the cast-off companies became separate entities under new management and filled niche or local markets.

But there was more change to come. The new companies, really now newly formed megacompanies after their buying sprees, began to divest themselves of unprofitable brands and divisional companies that they now found within their control. The reasons for these divestitures are tabulated (Table 1.1). With these divestitures came the release of hundreds of employees. This loss of personnel was referred to euphemistically as strategically managing personnel resources. A new executive position was coined: added to the roster of positions there was now the new post of the CEH, the chief executive hatchet man (Bruce, 1996). The cynicism of the times was apparent. Certainly, one gets the impression that companies seemed not to want to invest in people. Thus there were two secondary results of this upheaval in the industry:

- Skilled and experienced people were available on the work market.
- Manufacturing and other facilities, as well as unwanted labels and brands, were up for grabs for those desiring small business opportunities.

TABLE 1.1
Reasons for the Divestiture of Products and Companies

Category for Consideration	Reason for Rethinking Value of Category
Products	• Regional in distribution
	• Seasonal demand
	• Limited or ill-defined market
	• Competing with those products of take-over company
	• Noncomplementary to other products of take-over company
	• Special distribution, handling, or storage required
	• Profit margins too low
	• Ethical, moral, or environmental concerns
Brands	• Do not fit with brand image of take-over company
	• Require special marketing strategies
	• Noncomplementary to core business of take-over company
Companies and Plants	• Inefficient, outdated plant or equipment
	• Small production runs require too much retooling and hence too much downtime
	• Labor-intensive operations
	• High energy or water costs at plant location
	• Local zoning regulations restrict expansion or operations
	• Waste, effluent disposal costs too high
	• Skilled labor either scarce or too costly

The latter created opportunities for many of the displaced personnel to become entrepreneurs. Frequently the displaced personnel themselves took advantage of these opportunities with financial support from the parent company. The former employees took over orphaned product lines and manufacturing facilities. From these they built regional markets or developed niche markets for specialty products.

The outcome has been interesting in many ways in that it resulted in the curious situation alluded to earlier: the upsizing of some companies, the downsizing of others; a reshuffling of product mixes as companies changed hands; and, remarkably, a growth of entrepreneurship. Those companies that were spun off for unprofitability with the parent company's core business were bought by smaller companies wishing to broaden their product lines. Some of the spinoff companies were bought by the very workers who would have been displaced. Nevertheless, despite the opportunities for employment that were created, many people remained without jobs because of this downsizing.

Some of those who did not, or could not, take advantage of these opportunities are part of the subject of this book. Many became consultants to the megacompanies that orphaned them and to the neophyte companies that were formed by the new entrepreneurs. The very companies that set them on their own and those that developed in this growth of small niche manufacturers found they needed some of the resources and skills that these "outplaced" (to use the current jargon) workers represented. These people had the experience, the knowledge of the markets, and the technical skills that the new owners needed. They are many of today's consultants.

The skills possessed by such people can be very impressive; indeed, so much so that now many companies try to rescue the skills of those lost in downsizing or in early retirements by tapping into their experience and knowledge. This is done by interviewing those with work histories in unique skill areas and putting their experiences into computer memory to use either as training programs for new employees or as simple, catalogued repositories of knowledge. Bush (1989), McLellan (1989), and Herrod (1989) provide further information on these so-called expert systems and their development as tools for troubleshooting production problems and training new employees.

Turmoil from downsizing was not the only impetus in the abundance of consultants. Management techniques were being developed as universities applied their skills to the science of managing mega-organizations. Each daily newspaper's business section brings news of revisions to traditional ways of managing people in large companies. Disciples of these new techniques have rushed into the marketplace as the new gurus of re-engineering old organizations.

Even the newly downsized operations suddenly found themselves needing consultants. They were without their tiers of experienced middle management who possessed that elusive entity, the corporate memory or knowledge. The ranks of middle management are the heart of most companies. Whatever has befallen a company, it is the faceless middle managers who have seen the problems, a similar crisis, or comparable situation happen before. They know what action remedied the situation. They know who the customers are. Not only that, they know the names of their customers' secretaries and their customers' birthdays and the names of their customers' children. These are assets in oiling the wheels of business. They know, too, who the best sources of raw materials or reliable parts are. They know the correct person to coax and cajole to get something done.

A classic example of the importance of this resident knowledge is used by N. Vanderstoep in his management seminars (Livesey, 1997). Vanderstoep relates the story of the General Motors of Canada Ltd. employee who regularly spent his time giving the message that certain freezable chemicals must be shipped in heated trucks during the winter in Canada. The employee retired. Shortly thereafter, depots across Canada were swamped with calls of complaints of frozen chemicals. No one knew this aspect of this employee's job — that he ensured that chemicals were properly transported. Total cost to the company for this lack of awareness of a job description: $1.5 million.

The new clients, the newly formed companies, lack these skills. Even the larger companies were bereft of these skills as whole layers of these middle management bodies were cast aside. Suddenly these new companies found that they needed guidance in their daily operations. They needed the expertise that had previously been supplied by those downsized. This created an obvious demand for expertise of all sorts, and this meant a demand for consultants. But more important, they also needed help in using consultants wisely, effectively, and efficiently. The abundance of consultants with their promotional skills touting all sorts of snake-oil remedies for a company's ills has made working with consultants something the potential client should study carefully before selecting one.

Outsourcing developed. Outsourcing for a company is, very simply, the employment of outside companies to provide services, parts, or perform activities that were once performed in-house. Outsourcing is similar to the service-providing side of consulting and is better known as subcontracting. It is a subject that will be discussed later.

WHO ARE THESE CONSULTANTS?

Some definition of what a consultant is and some explanation of consulting is in order. In a delightful spoof of consultants, Shahin (1995) describes them as "... modern-day alchemists... (who)... dazzle their clients with "action plans," which the clients, having invested bundles of money and ego on this wizardry, accept much as the king would take a sorcerer's advice in the Middle Ages." Shahin continues, "If (the consultant) were a car, he'd be a Lexus. On cruise control." Clients' egos, which Shahin refers to, will be discussed later when the reasons for employing consultants are examined.

Another old chestnut describes experts required for specialized tasks as a combination of "x," an unknown quantity, plus a spurt, which is a drip under pressure. Neither Shahin's remarks nor this definition suggests that all people have a high regard for consultants.

Consultants have also derisively been referred to as executives-between-jobs. I first heard this devastating definition from a colleague several years ago during a very active period of downsizing by a number of companies. It was made in exasperation after he, while pursuing a potential client, had been told that his potential client was being deluged with proposals from other consultants for a multitude of services. This same comment recently reappeared, however, when an inquiry from a large food company requested information from a consulting firm; this inquirer actually asked whether the associates of this consulting group were really "consultants" or merely executives-between-jobs. After all, "consultant" is a nicer word to put on one's résumé than "fired" or "unemployed." It is very true, however, that many executives and senior technical people who have been released by their companies do have a stint as consultants before being relocated. It provides a pleasant interlude between their last job and the one they hope to find.

Consultants are providers of specialized services for which they charge a fee to the client who needs these services. But this broad definition categorizes as consultants all who provide specialized services for a fee, and this embraces all purveyors of specialized services — painters, plumbers, lawyers, architects, engineers, analytical laboratories, food technologists, caterers, public relations firms, forensic accountants, and so on — that any company may require in the course of its daily business or in its more extraordinary ventures.

Obviously, all people providing specialized services are not, and do not, consider themselves consultants, even though these people may be consulted and asked for opinions at some time in their working relationship with a client. For example, neither an accounting firm hired to audit the books of a company nor a client's bank manager would consider themselves to be consultants. Consulting is not their primary business, not their sole activity nor source of income. Provision of financial services is their core business, yet both would provide financial advice.

It can be seen that consultants provide a service which makes them not unlike many others who provide a service. But, in addition to providing a specialized service, consultants also serve as advisors in areas where their knowledge, even arcane knowledge, is bought by clients requiring this information. The information is used to guide companies undertaking some new venture where the companies feel their own skills are lacking or require complementing. Again, this is not unlike the bankers and accountants "consulted" by clients, except that bankers and accountants provide advice incidental to their core business. Consultants bring advice based on their experience and training, and conversely, consultants gain experience through their advice to other clients and their ability to learn from these encounters. Their experience begets advice and their advice begets experience.

Figure 1.1 is an effort to depict this blurriness between consultants and service providers more clearly. The vertical axis to the left of Figure 1.1 is an arbitrary measure (on a 0 to 100 scale) of the broadness of the spectrum of services provided. The vertical scale to the right is also an arbitrary measure of the similar advisory services provided. The horizontal axis has a two-directional scale, going from 0 to 100% in each direction. That scale increasing from left to right (i.e., from only a service provider, with 0% advisory services, to primarily a 100% provider of advice) is a crude measure of how much advice the consultant provides. The second horizontal scale, from 0% service on the right to 100% service on the left, measures the proportion of largely service work that is provided.

An examination of Figure 1.1 suggests there is not a startling difference between consultants and service providers. To the left of the diagram (within the oval) are represented those who are primarily providers of a service. For example, here one might include testing and analytical laboratories, new food product developers, specialist lawyers (patent lawyers, arbitration lawyers, etc.), accountants in the many specialized fields of financial services, public relations firms, translators and technical editors, painters and plumbers, laundry service, and the list could go on. These specialists provide services. This is their core business. Certainly they might do some advising: painters and plumbers may be far to the left; security providers moving to the right, and lawyers may be toward the center. But there will not be the closeness of a working relationship that is usually characteristic of that relationship between consultants and clients. These on the left usually have a more arm's-length, contractual relationship with their clients.

Within the ellipse on the right of Figure 1.1 are those who provide largely advice or expertise, i.e., knowledge, to those who need it. Here one might find marketing consultants, management consultants, or even consulting food technologists. They assist, coax, cajole, and guide their clients by providing not so much a service (although training programs can probably be considered a service) as wisdom and advice in a multitude of fields. Their relationships with their clients are usually closer than those with service providers, but this depends on the individuals.

Most consultancies are a blend of service and advice. That is, consultants are somewhere in the center of Figure 1.1 between the 100% service provider and the

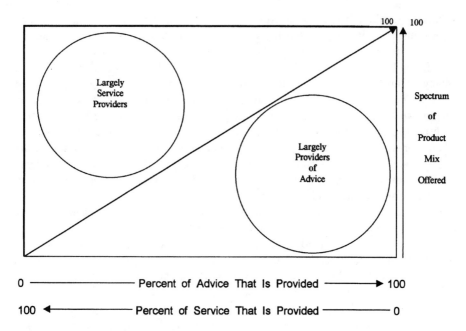

FIGURE 1.1 Distinctions between service providers and advice providers. Consultants tend to the right side of the diagram.

100% advisor. But as pointed out earlier, *only* service providers or *only* advisors are fictitious characters. For example, those who provide security for a client's manufacturing operation will also provide advice and suggestions on making the client's premises more secure, on restricting or controlling access to sensitive manufacturing areas, on employee screening and on providing guidance for the security of key senior personnel as they travel in foreign lands. Such an activity is hard to categorize as either primarily service or advisory.

Most consultants, whether they are individuals or multinational companies, are somewhere in the middle of Figure 1.1. They provide both a unique service, advice, and specialized information.

A CLASSIFICATION FOR CONSULTANTS

Consultants are ubiquitous. They can be found in all fields of activity. Their activities range from gift selection for a client's premier customers — they actually advertise themselves as gift consultants — to developing incentive programs for employees, to designing esthetically pleasing decors to boost worker satisfaction, productivity, and safety. Their specialties range from the mundane to the obscure. I was introduced to a policy consultant and even after she explained what she did I remained none the wiser. Consultants also specialize as troubleshooters or to use the current euphemism, crisis managers, assisting their clients in containing a crisis and in initiating both remedial and preventive action. Where possible, they help their clients benefit from whatever opportunity the crisis may bring.

TABLE 1.2
A General Classification of Consultants

Class	Subclass
Amateurs	• Executives-between-jobs
	• Retirees
	• Academics
	Individual
	Extension departments
	Student programs
	(Some) Research institutes
Professionals	• Individual
	• Independent companies
	• Specialized service providers
	• Research institutes/associations
	• Government agencies
	• Trade associations/quasi-governmental agencies giving assistance to fledgling companies

Consultants try hard in many ways to keep their names in the forefront in what has become a highly competitive field. The competition has forced diversification of their activities. Clients seeking a consultant for the first time are understandably confused by this profusion.

Any attempt to classify service providers and advisers founders in the gray area of those who are purely service providers and those who are primarily advisers, between those whose primary business is derived from supplying a service and those whose primary business is providing advice and expertise.

AN INCOME-BASED CLASSIFICATION

A much simpler classification can begin by splitting consultants into two subgroups: amateurs and professionals. This is shown in Table 1.2, which presents a broad classification of the resources from which any client can choose to obtain assistance.

The major difference between amateurs and professionals is based quite arbitrarily on income from consulting. Where the major or only source of income is through consulting, that consultant will be deemed, in this classification scheme, a professional. Where the consultant has an independent source of income such as a pension, or is currently employed or under contract (as many academics are) with a regular income from a nonconsultative source, then that consultant is considered an amateur.

The Amateurs

The amateurs — let it be quite clear that these are not amateurs in a pejorative sense — do not rely on their consultancy practice for their main source of income. Consulting is, for some listed in Table 1.2, an avocation, a diversion that many of them seek from the boredom of retirement. Also in this category are the "moonlighters," who consult in their spare time to supplement their main source of income.

Executives-between-jobs

Executives-between-jobs can be further classified or more properly recognized by the type of projects they undertake. These are usually short-term projects requiring senior managerial skills where organizing, negotiating, or restructuring abilities are required. Executives-between-jobs act as mentors to inexperienced staff in labor negotiations, assist in the development of business plans, or provide guidance in acquisition studies. They rarely do hands-on work on the plant floor, at the drafting board, or at the laboratory bench.

These assignments serve two major functions. First, executives-between-jobs may use these consulting assignments both to look for a new executive/managerial position and to be screened for such a position. It provides an opportunity for displaced executives to get an insider's view of their client's organizations, to review their problems and their people while at the same time establishing, legitimately, their worth within the organization. Clients then have an opportunity to assess the personalities, the abilities, and the suitability of these executives within their organizations. Typical of this is the example of the director of quality control for a national food company who was let go when his company was taken over by a large multinational company. This person worked successfully under short-term contracts while seeking permanent employment and found a job with a young company requiring an experienced quality control leader for its greatly expanded technical facilities. Many consultants are taken on permanently after successful short-term service.

The second, and more important, function served is that these displaced executives provide a real service to the client by supplying guidance to the client's staff. Their maturity and experience can be very beneficial to a client's young management facing crises for the first time. It results in a win-win situation for all: the client is helped and the executive may have found another position.

Retirees

Retirees are quintessential dilettantes, pursuers of their arts for the love of it, very much like the dilettantes of earlier ages. While enjoying a pension they keep active with projects, often undertaken for the same companies that had pushed them into early retirement. Conditions of their separation packages from their former employers may limit their consulting activities to their former employer only or to subsidiaries of this employer.

Early retirees have many productive years left to contribute their skills. Consequently, they pursue the careers interrupted by such forced retirement. The result is that many see self-employment as an answer to the question of how to utilize their skills and continue their careers. An obvious route to self-employment is to become a consultant. Consulting becomes a means to supplement their separation packages until full retirement benefits begin, to continue to apply their very marketable skills with other companies, and to pursue their interrupted careers.

The many opportunities open to retirees include:

- Teaching undergraduates or graduate students either as external lecturers or as discussion leaders in seminars at universities. Here they are able to introduce a new this-is-real-life approach to many courses in management and other applied sciences.
- Consulting for volunteer organizations such as the International Executive Service Corps (IESC) or the Canadian Executive Service Organization (CESO). These organizations send executives to companies in third-world nations or to needy companies run by ethnic minorities (e.g., craft or native industries run by Indians).
- *Pro bono* work with government, social or fraternal organizations which may provide the retirees with only recovery of expenses.
- Individual consulting work with private companies and organizations such as the World Bank.

Each of these endeavors allows retirees to be active by applying the skills they have acquired during their lifetime. At the same time, they can develop novel applications for their skills as they venture into new fields.

Retirees and other employees displaced by downsizing may find what might be called consulting work for their old employers, who find they over-downsized, in two manners. First, they may be asked to return to train younger, inexperienced staff, or they may take part in the development of artificial intelligence programs (the expert systems mentioned earlier) used both to document existing technology and to train new staff. Participation in these exercises allows their ex-employer to take advantage of their years of experience by cataloguing this experience in the form of either a training program for new employees or an encyclopedic compendium of experience and knowledge to be used as a manual for solving ticklish problems that companies may encounter. Some are asked by their former employers to return to pursue on a part-time basis those wouldn't-it-be-nice-to-study projects that all companies have but are forced to ignore for lack of personnel.

Second, many downsized employees and early retirees return to work with their old companies on a contractual basis. Their ex-employers outsource their manpower needs to the very people they let go. Who better to outsource work to than the very people who are familiar with the companies' operations?

Academics

Academic consultants in the technical, management, and liberal arts departments in universities bring a formidable array of skills to any client requiring advisory services, investigative research, or technical assistance. Their strengths are twofold:

- They possess knowledge in specialized subjects and technologies and are aware of new and advanced concepts and developments in these fields.
- They have the temperament, skills, and resources that small, medium-sized, and even large companies lack to conduct basic investigations and

research. Not the least of these resources is expensive equipment beyond the reach of most organizations, and skilled manpower in the persons of young graduates who may become a source of future skilled employees for clients.

These strengths are valuable to those clients with a heavy commitment to long-term basic research and development. They may be less valuable to critical short-term projects, such as new product development, troubleshooting some manufacturing or marketing problem, or analyzing some product breakdown in the marketplace.

In very general ways, consulting by academics can serve as a reconnaissance by universities for establishing links with industry. This, in its turn, can encourage greater cooperation between universities and industry. The snowball effect is this: with the greater interest and participation of industry in the research of universities, the efforts of academics are encouraged either by monies and equipment supplied by industry or by joint research efforts with industry. The universities can then build "the better mousetrap" with which industry can develop, manufacture, market, and serve its customers better.

Among the university community one can distinguish several categories of consultants:

Individual academics: These are academics who are permitted a limited amount of their time for personal consulting;

Extension departments: These are departments within a university staffed by academics and assisted by graduate students who can provide assistance to regional companies, especially those that have an agricultural base. These are part of the USDA Cooperative Extension Service;

Student teams: Many schools or departments within universities provide senior and graduate students with practical experience by organizing them into teams which then can be used by companies to analyze business or administrative problems. This is particularly true of schools of business administration that use the technique as a teaching tool;

Research institutes: These are specialized services within a university that may embrace several departments. These may combine their skills to form a quasi-independent institute devoted to a particular expertise.

Consortia: Universities cooperatively combine their resources with state or federal governments or private companies to form research associations.

The latter two groups, research institutes and consortia, differ in that the research institutes are wholly within the organization of the university, while the consortia frequently involve only one department (for example, the department of Food Sciences) and food companies with government support.

Cash-strapped universities have realized the great potential represented by the intellectual talent within their walls. Crudely put, it provides an opportunity for earning much-needed income when government funding for universities is being reduced in many countries. Additionally, it serves a learning function by permitting universities the opportunity to understand the needs of industry, to study the ways to transfer technology successfully and to appreciate the constraints facing industry respecting research.

Some of these constraints that industry faces can be the cause of irritation between academics and industry. Time is one constraint in the marketplace that universities must respect if they wish the support of industry. Industry must get innovation into the marketplace in the form of desirable products before its competition gets there. It cannot let technocrats tinker and tinker with innovative projects to fully understand them and "get all the kinks out."

Conversely, this interfacing presents the opportunity for industry to appreciate the skills represented by academics and to understand how these skills can complement their needs. To this end, many universities created offices of technology transfer (OTTs). The objectives of these OTTs are primarily to find uses for the resources of the university so that these can become business assets. This can be done in several ways:

- These offices can assess the research projects which have been undertaken by academics to determine whether they have any commercial viability or patentability. Patenting protects the project but may scare away the investors who might also feel that if they provided the money, then the patent belongs with them. Questions about the ownership of intellectual property can be a hindrance to industry support.
- They search out likely industrial firms that would be interested in supporting the development of particular research projects already in progress or who would continue to provide support for those projects at the laboratory stage to bring these to industrial fruition. It is with the latter development from a laboratory stage to a marketable product that difficulties of ownership may arise.
- These OTTs canvas companies that would be interested in applying any patents that had already been obtained for the payment of a royalty.
- These OTTs also assist academics in finding research monies from industries, from governments, and from research fund-granting agencies to initiate new projects.

The OTTs act much like agents or brokers would: OTTs put interested parties together for their mutual benefit. The sole difference is that the broker's fee, so to speak, is the financial support the university receives.

There are many examples of the cooperation that can be had between universities, industry, and government. One such cooperative program was described by Bagnall (1996). The development was for a foot prosthesis that permitted a more natural gait, allowing a lateral movement when walking. A small piece of plastic was geometrically designed to imitate a normal walking motion more naturally, and then inserted into a plastic artificial foot. The cooperating parties were the Université de Montréal's engineering school, École Polytechnique, and the private Quebec medical equipment company, Medicus Ltée. Funding was supplied by two government bodies through a particular funding program called Synergie. This program included funds from the Natural Sciences and Engineering Research Council of Canada, the Quebec provincial government, and Medicus Ltée. Medicus could then develop the prosthesis for commercial use.

Industry/university cooperative research programs (governments may supply some of the research funding) for food research,* in particular, are discussed at length in a series of papers (Walters, 1987; Swartzel and Gray, 1987; Krueger and Walker, 1987; Rossen and Solberg, 1987; Danzig, 1987; and Mason, 1987). Swartzel and Gray (1987) discuss the North Carolina State University's Center for Aseptic Processing and Packaging Studies. Krueger and Walker (1987) describe the University of Nebraska's Food Processing Center. Rutgers University's Center for Advanced Food Technology is discussed by Rossen and Solberg (1987). Walters (1987) and Mason (1987) present the benefits of such programs. Danzig (1987) elaborates upon pitfalls in such programs and puts forward his thesis that government, industry, and universities must fulfill their respective goals before such ventures will bring forth the values industry seeks. Universities, he feels, may focus their research too narrowly at the expense of providing education. Consequently, they may graduate supertechnicians instead of well-trained scientists who have a love of learning and scholarship. There are other problems, including the politicization of research and the undertaking of popular research, i.e., research projects that get the grant money, but these are topics beyond the scope of this book. Giese (1997) provides an update on the above technical centers and describes several more which food companies can use to assist with technical problems.

Many academics have mixed feelings about getting too close to industry. The attitude toward companies can be mixed, ranging from cool, perhaps even reactionary, to very enthusiastic. The Biotechnology and Biological Sciences Research Council (U.K.) commissioned a study of commercial funding at four research institutes. This study classified 65 respondents into five response groups according to their enthusiasm for working with industry (Coghlan, 1995). These groupings were:

- 10% who were considered to be enthusiastic about working with industry.
- 35% who were less than enthusiastic but nevertheless still interested in working with industry.
- 35% who were even cooler about collaboration but still willing to work with industry's money.
- 10% described as academic high-grounders who would accept industrial money but were not about to sacrifice their research goals for a pursuit of applied research for itself.
- 10% who were averse to any cooperation with industry.

Oddly enough, the study found that it was the academic high-grounders who were most effective at obtaining funding from industry. This small sample size provides no more than a suggestion that industry, at least in the U.K., does value pure research and the so-called academic high-grounders were willing to, and do, provide a valuable service to industry. On a broader scale, it demonstrates that universities

---

* The reader must forgive me for the use of references to largely food sources and for using anecdotes based on food experiences. That, however, is the nature of the beast. I am a food consultant.

may provide opportunities that can have immense value to research-oriented companies.

Another tool supplied by universities that industry can use is students. Students can be organized into teams to visit small businesses, study the problems these businesses are having, and plot out courses of action under the guidance of senior academic staff. In short, they act as consultants. Small companies may be very interested in using these services.

Some universities have so-called sandwich courses in which students work to gain industrial experience but, at the same time, they can provide expert assistance gained through their schooling. Students represent skilled labor.

Three purposes are served. First, small businesses, and even some larger companies, are served with a source of genuine expert assistance by competent people provided at a reasonable cost. Second, the students who provide this assistance get valuable training in working to resolve problems that real companies face. If some companies shy away from having such inexperienced assistance, one need only remember how glad we are to be assisted in life-threatening situations by nurses-in-training and doctors-in-training. A third advantage can be seen: the company using such assistance may find the young employee that they need in the future.

The Professionals

Professional consultants are those whose main livelihood is their consulting practice. However, a further distinction must be made: it must be made abundantly clear that the word "professional" does not imply a skill level nor any standard or code of performance. I know of no professional governing body for consultants, such as the professional bodies for medical doctors, engineers, or lawyers, with laws to punish or otherwise reprimand its members.

It follows, then, that there are no tests, standards, or entrance requirements, nor even a need for experience in any particular area of activity in order to become a consultant. Indeed, I know of at least one group of young graduates at the baccalaureate level, with no industrial experience, who formed a consulting company upon graduation. This was a private company, not to be confused with the teams of senior students working under the guidance of their professors as described earlier. Mercifully, it failed. Knowledge is important, but it must be tempered by experience.

It is more than possible that a consultant may also be a member of a professional society. But potential clients must be very clear that membership in a professional society does not make consultants "professional consultants." Anyone can put up a sign advertising consulting or other advisory services. For instance, the IFST(U.K.) publishes a list of food consultants, but they also place on this list a demurrer, to wit,

> "… where a member undertakes work resulting from the appearance of his name on
> these lists… he does so … in no sense representing the Institute."

This is a clear *caveat emptor* for the potential client. This U.K. Food Institute has also adopted and does publish for its members, all its members, not just consultants, a code of conduct (IFST(U.K.), 1991). Complementing this code are a series of guidelines which explain in greater detail issues raised in the Code itself. While other societies may have codes of conduct such as these, it must be emphasized that while consultants may be members of these societies and conduct themselves according to the codes of ethics of their organization, consultants *per se* do not have such a code of conduct.

Networking Consultants

Networking is a word that has crept into the vocabulary via the computer and is now used in many disciplines with slightly different meanings. With computers, it simply refers to computers that "talk" to one another, i.e., that are connected. In public relations and management terms, it means making "contacts" — that is, the creation of an informal complex of influential or knowledgeable persons who can be contacted in order to find something out, get something done, or meet someone. In brief, networking is the formation of loose associations or channels of communication to be used in times of need.

Most consultants network. They have channels of communication to colleagues on whom they can call for assistance. That is, they work in loose alliances with other consultants. A diverse group of consultants in different locations within a country or in different countries agree to cooperate. They can combine their expertise in different areas of abilities to undertake large projects. Thus, an alliance comprising unique specialist skills can eventually be built up that is, or could be, international in scope. This alliance permits a small consultancy to have a modicum of international stature. Such networking alliances are becoming the norm.

These networks can be used by one of the members to search equipment or raw material suppliers in different countries where there are other associates. They can allow a consultant in one country to investigate for a local client the market conditions for a product in another country where a networking colleague resides who will undertake the work. Further, it allows an individual consultant to pull together through the resources of the network those unique skills better suited for a particular project, thus expanding the resource base over that which any individual consultant could possess.

Such a network is described in *Food Technology* (Anon., 1994). This network, called Stratecon EuroBEST, has associates in Europe (England and Belgium), in Canada, in several locations across the U.S., in Mexico, and in the Pacific rim countries. The talents of the associates are in planning business strategies, regulatory affairs, ingredient technology, food intelligence and information, technical translations, and technology transfer. What an alliance such as Stratecon EuroBEST does not have, which separates it from the large formally structured consulting companies, is its own research and development facilities with its attendant support staff. This is not a hindrance, as it might seem at first. Members generally have access to laboratory facilities and to rented pilot plant facilities where any studies can be carried out. An advantage is that these alliances do not have high overhead costs to support their resources.

Clients who are in the preliminary stages of investigating consultants should not be dismayed if their initial contact is only with an individual. That individual may have ready access to several other consultants strategically positioned around the country or the world who can be formed rapidly into a team to move quickly and efficiently with a minimum of travel expense or disruption caused by time zone differences.

Individual Companies and Specialized Services

Many small companies can offer specialized services such as information retrieval (a favorite of retired librarians with a computer), statistical analyses, product pick-ups, translation services, or chemical and microbiological analyses. There are even pilot plants for small-scale manufacturing, as well as contract packing facilities. By subcontracting parts of projects to these readily available resources, individual consultants can undertake some formidable projects with the confidence one formerly expected only of larger firms.

Large consulting companies, on the other hand, are one-stop consulting and development companies able to provide a broad range of services to their clients from in-house resources. They can provide financial and accounting services (forensic accounting, for one), legal services, security for executives as they travel, security for plants manufacturing sensitive items and "debugging" operations to avoid industrial espionage, research and development, marketing studies, business re-organization and management, and so on. The price they pay is, of course, the need to keep this formal organization and the associated overheads supported. They are faced with office rental in foreign countries for their field operators, expensive laboratory and pilot plant facilities, and support staff which must be kept fully occupied. As a result, their marketing programs can be aggressive, with exhibits at trade shows and heavy advertising. Their overheads are much higher than those of smaller consulting firms or the alliances discussed earlier. Relying as they do on larger projects, the nature of the projects they undertake is different and their fees are correspondingly higher.

Research Associations and Institutes

Overseas research associations, such as the Leatherhead Food Research Association (LFRA) or the Swedish Food Institute (SIK), provide consulting services including new product development, technical information, worldwide market information, analytical services, and foreign and international food legislation. They are, in essence, also one-stop consulting firms, albeit offering a broad range of services in the narrow discipline of food. Areas of management or finance are not strong specialties of these associations.

LFRA's basic membership fee provides access to food legislation of over 140 countries, including such international standards as *Codex Alimentarius,* as well as access to market intelligence and commercial data on uses and acceptability of food additives worldwide, new products and novel foods introductions, food company data, and ingredient and machinery suppliers. The technical resources available at LFRA is invaluable to food companies planning new ventures in foreign markets, where knowledge of the regulations governing foods, the permissibility of additives and ingredients, and the regional competitive products would be essential.

Companies join these associations by paying a fee, usually a sliding fee, based on some financial or production criteria, e.g., net profit, production volume, etc.

However, terms of membership and servicing fees vary with each organization, and companies seeking membership in any such research organization are well advised to negotiate their fees. These fees then become the basis for funding the services and research the association performs for its members. Further research monies come from patents, sales of analytical, advisory and information retrieval services, and contract research from governments, industries, and companies wishing private and confidential research.

The pooled research funds are used to support large research projects for the members of the organizations. For example, at LFRA, members who manufacture meat products will pool a portion of their fees to undertake, perhaps, a cooperative project on meat binding. This project would be agreed upon by all those with a meat interest. The members contributing to this project would share the results.

Other associations in fields other than food provide similar benefits for their members. In general, membership in these associations gives a company access to the resources of that association and to its research programs. Confidential research can be undertaken for members at very competitive rates.

There are many other food research associations; Campden Food and Drink Research Association (CFDRA), also in the U.K., the Norwegian Food Research Institute, and the Food Processors Institute in the U.S., to mention only those whose work I am familiar with. Even these associations network. Recently SIK and CFDRA combined their services, and LFRA has alliances with the Packaging Industries Research Association, the Institute of Food Research, and the American Institute of Baking.

Free Assistance

There is much advisory and service help that is freely available for clients, but clients must remember that nothing is absolutely free. There are usually some conditions or restrictions that prevail. Nevertheless, clients should not overlook such assistance and should explore all such free resources before spending money on consultants. These resources are:

- Extension departments at universities, which can provide a wealth of skills, although these are primarily confined to the food and agricultural fields or to other industries important to the local state or provincial economies
- Technical sales representatives of companies such as those selling machinery or supplying parts or raw materials can be sources of useful information and technical assistance

Clients can face problems using the assistance of technical sales representatives — and here is one of the strings found attached to "free" assistance. Clients must respect the bias such help or knowledge may contain. Obviously, such consulting services from technical representatives are designed to promote the products that these representatives wish to sell. Clients would be very naive to think that any trial carried out using the technical resources of any sales representative's company would put that company's products or equipment in a bad light.

A company received unexpected benefits by working with one technical service agent. This representative for a food ingredient supplier saved the company a great deal of development monies. He provided a readily available formulation book published by his company. In this were many product formulations using, of course, ingredients distributed and manufactured by his company. Recipes in this collection were disturbingly similar to those supplied by a new product development group the company was currently employing. The development group was soon dismissed.

Not all associations with technical service representatives are as fruitful as this. Nevertheless, companies seeking assistance can be pleasantly surprised by the amount of advice and assistance that is available from suppliers.

Giese (1997) describes the many services for food processors that are provided by suppliers and equipment manufacturers.

Government Assistance

This assistance, which is available to all, is hard to classify in the simplistic dualism of "amateur" and "professional." Neither definition holds when applied to work assistance available through the government.

Such an example, albeit primarily for agricultural or agriculturally based products for the U.S., would be the technology transfer opportunities available from government research centers such as the Eastern Regional Research Center (ERRC) of the U.S. Department of Agriculture's Agricultural Research Service (Anon. 1993). The (U.S.) Federal Technology Transfer Act (1986) encouraged the cooperation between U.S. industry and government research centers to apply government-sponsored research and develop new products and practical applications based on this research.

Close cooperative liaison between private industry and ERRC staff is maintained through agreements (Cooperative Research and Development Agreements) that permit companies exclusivity to patented inventions. There is also a USDA Patent License Program available, through which interested companies can negotiate license fees on various bases and receive assistance for commercialization.

Many countries have programs to assist their industries and in particular to assist agricultural, forestry, and fishing industries. In Canada, there are cooperative federal/provincial government programs to assist industry. There are research stations across Canada with equipment and staff available to companies for product development. Another government body in the U.S. from which companies can get assistance is the National Center for Agricultural Utilization Research (Giese 1997).

OUTSOURCING

Outsourcing has rapidly become a new buzz word in the language of business and deserves some further explanation here. It is somewhat of a deceit to discuss outsourcing as if it were a new phenomenon. Outsourcing has been around for many years. The name may be new, but companies have for many years contracted out, for example, their legal, accounting, cleaning, and laundry services.

Outsourcing is an activity whereby a company farms out some of its activities to other companies more expert in that activity. The activities that are farmed out to others are those not pertinent to the company's core business. That is, the support or peripheral functions of the organization are contracted out to others. Security is one service that can be readily outsourced. Many companies once supplied their own security for their manufacturing plants, but security firms can provide a range of services (from trained guard dogs, to voice and fingerprint recognition devices for access to secured areas, to hidden cameras for the detection of pilfering, to protection of senior management in their travels) more cost effectively than clients could themselves. Clients transferred their security concerns to these firms. This was especially the case when industrial espionage itself became more sophisticated.

Some other examples of requirements that might be outsourced are accounting, auditing, pension planning, executive remuneration, and benefits activities. These could be given to an accounting firm. Similarly, distribution and warehousing might be given to a specialist transportation company whose only activity is warehousing and distribution. Sanitation and packaging are also activities that have been outsourced.

Many food companies have found that activities, such as general cleaning, especially grounds maintenance, plant sanitation, and preventive maintenance, could be handled more cheaply and effectively by companies specializing in these services. This eliminated the need for janitorial services. Even the services of law offices and chartered accountancy agencies can be looked upon as examples of outsourcing. Such divesting of the more unusual and uncommon requirements of a company relieves that company of supporting such expensive staff on their payrolls.

Companies discovered that for many activities it was far cheaper to hire outside resources than it was to own these resources. The logic behind outsourcing is simply one of economics and efficiencies. The specialist company to whom the support activity is contracted is presumed to be able to do the activity more efficiently and hence more economically than the company farming that activity out. Clients can stick to the core businesses that they know so well and lease those services that other specialist companies supply more adroitly.

Outsourcing has many similarities to consulting. One could be considered a variant form of the other (see Figure 1.1). Much depends on how tightly one wishes to define each. Any differences are ones of degree. In outsourcing, a client relies on the expertise of the supplier or servicing company to provide an appropriate service. The service or product is to be produced or carried out to very specific standards of performance. These are not quite the demands that are made upon a consultant. Consultants are not required to work to a standard.

The employment of a consultant is generally for a short period. The consultant comes when needed and goes when the task is finished. Consulting is often a one-time activity. Only when the consultant is on a retainer is the period of employment longer. Retainerships may last for many years. Outsourcing differs somewhat in that the contract for whatever service is needed is for a longer term, such as a year or more, and is frequently renewable — even permanent. However, an organization can switch, for example, its laundry from one cleaning company to another depending on which provides better service. It is rare, however, that the client will take up doing its own laundry again.

There are other minor differences that are hard to generalize. Outsourcing frequently sees the client and the service supplier being at arm's length. In a laundry service, the dirty linen is picked up, cleaned, and dropped off. There is no, or little, interaction. The closeness that prevails with a client/consultant relationship is not there.

Companies may outsource with several different service suppliers. In some industries one therefore finds not a self-contained company but a tree of suppliers, at the end of which is a shell of a company putting together the pieces brought by suppliers. Each, much like networking consultants, supplies skills and technology to assist the next supplier down the chain. At the end of that chain is a finished product. A company then simply becomes a chain of suppliers with its advertising and promotions, manufacturing, distribution, and sales all outsourced to different companies. The result is a one-person-company selling a product with city-wide or state-wide distribution. That one person simply coordinates the various activities of its service suppliers. Everything else is outsourced.

Figure 1.1 can be used to greater effectiveness here to explain what is happening. As the percentage of service increases (and the duration of time the services are used increases), the left side of this figure really becomes a measure of outsourcing. Regular use of service suppliers is in essence, outsourcing, much like retainerships for consultants.

Outsourcing has brought its own problems: labor. Unions at the large auto manufacturers, for example, are concerned at the growth of outsourcing. At one time, the auto makers manufactured all the parts that were used in cars. Many of these jobs are disappearing as the auto companies move to using parts manufactured by suppliers, some of whom are non-unionized with cheaper labor. As more companies took to outsourcing as a method to support their efforts to downsize, outsourcing became anathema to workers and their unions.

In a similar vein, some companies let salaried employees go. Then they rehired them not as salaried employees but as contract workers. That is, these people were brought in as workers on a contract — no benefits, no security. The companies outsourced the same work to the same now ex-employees. Workers and unions alike are very concerned with this trend.

This book will not be a discussion of outsourcing. Inevitably, the short-term use of outsourced resources may, however, involve the use of consultants. It will be difficult at times to distinguish between a client's use of consultants and a client outsourcing certain activities to more efficient and expert service suppliers. Any attempt to bring a sharper definition conjures up the statement made by someone about pornography with words to the effect — "I don't know how to describe it, but I know it when I see it." Likewise, the client will recognize outsourcing when it appears.

2 What Services Do Consultants Provide?

It isn't that they can't see the solution. It is that they can't see the problem.

G. K. Chesterton

That man is great who can use the brains of others to carry out his work.

Donn Platt

INTRODUCTION

The simple, facetious, and perhaps even irreverent, answer to the question heading this chapter is this: consultants provide comfort, handholding, and moral justification for their clients. A more serious rephrasing of this answer might be: consultants provide guidance, leadership (or direction), technical or managerial support, and sound advice based on experience. Either of these answers, the cynical or the more staid one, reveals the real value that consultants offer. Consultants, in general, provide some desired service for their clients.

Also, both the sayings that preface this chapter provide some insight into the services that consultants can provide. That is, consultants provide clarification of issues facing clients as well as expertise in resolving them — and a little something else hinted at in Platt's quotation and which will be discussed later.

THE SERVICES

Chesterton's words, in particular, ring very true. Consultants provide clarification of perplexing situations existing within the organizations, the business environments, communities, and for customers of their clients — in other words, the ecosystem of the client. Clients may recognize in an unfocused fashion that something is wrong, but cannot exactly pinpoint the what, where, and why of the problem, or they may misconstrue its cause. The illumination of the issues by consultants facilitates the resolution of these problems. Priorities can be sorted by clients on the basis of this clarification, and tackled in a logical fashion. Clients often see only the trees and cannot determine where the forest is, so to speak. Consultants provide definition to issues facing their clients so their clients can undertake a more concerted approach to their problems. Consultants bring analytical skills their clients need to help them focus on the resolution of issues rather than on the problems those issues might have caused. Consultants are tools to be used by their clients to resolve issues that clients face.

An example of what consultants can provide in defining problems might be the following:

> A public figure is suffering from a poor image. The individual, as well as his organization and his supporters, are at a loss to understand why the candidate just does not "hit it off" in the popularity polls. A consultant, usually from a public relations firm, is brought in. This consultant will analyze both the image this public figure portrays and the message this public figure conveys. Both tasks will be carried out by surveying the audiences this individual seeks to motivate. The consultant searches for audience reactions to both the image and the message. After a careful analysis of the responses of the target audience, the consulting firm will then recommend a remake of the individual's image and message. This remake may include:
>
> • voice changes. They recommend the individual pitch the voice lower, become less strident, and eliminate all distracting speech mannerisms;
>
> • cosmetic changes. Wearing glasses is eliminated either by contact lenses or laser eye surgery. Clothing styles may be altered to produce a more casual appearance. The individual's hair color and style may be changed; and
>
> • the elimination of irritating or offensive mannerisms or body language.

Et voilà, the public figure emerges like a butterfly from a cocoon with a new persona. The consultant has rebuilt the public figure's image in accordance with the preferences of the target audience. Others in the public relations firm will work on the message, which may be modified to be less strident and vicious to one that is more positive, conciliatory, and cooperative in tone.

POLITICAL USES OF CONSULTANTS

Platt's *bon mot*, on the other hand, implies the "little something else" hinted at earlier in this chapter with regard to the services provided by consultants. In its simplest interpretation Platt's remark would appear to suggest that individuals can benefit by using the skills and knowledge of others (in this context) consultants, to ensure that certain tasks are accomplished. Consultants serve as devices to accomplish something that clients wish to be done tactfully, surreptitiously, or discreetly.

Thus, there is revealed a darker side of the use of consultants by clients. This dark side is the political or tactical use of consultants: that is, using or selecting consultants to have one's views confirmed or wishes carried out, or using a consultant as a foil to undertake some difficult, unpopular, unpleasant, even clandestine task. When the task is accomplished, any fallout can be directed to the consultant. No fault is leveled at the client. Clients can always point to the recommendations in the report submitted by the consultants as justification for the action that was taken. That action, however, supported the views, opinions, or desires of the client.

Qui facit per alium facit per se.

(He who does (anything) through another does it through himself.)

To some, this use of the consultant might be described as devious; to others, it is the judicious use of resources and a demonstration of good tactics and leadership. The important issue is that the use of consultants served to accomplish the task with limited repercussions and recriminations against those within the client's organization. This is clearly a political use of consultants.

Two illustrations describe this political use of consultants more clearly. The first is hypothetical but draws heavily on the personal experiences of fellow consultants:

> Mature companies have often peaked in their growth. They need help to rejuvenate themselves. Their products have lost appeal; quality has fallen compared to the competition. Their markets are disappearing as customers change. Old products, bell-ringers in their day, need to be discarded or redesigned — much to the annoyance or resistance of those who originally developed them. Innovative products are needed but resisted. A rethinking of the direction of the company is required. Old companies, set in patterns of operation and thinking ordained in the mists of time, require reawakening, sometimes a rude reawakening, to recover the strengths they once had. Who better to "stir the pot," "ruffle feathers," "step on toes," than the outsider, the consultant?

Recommendations and guidance from outside the company may provide the wisest counsel for future courses of action, with the least amount of ill-will or finger-pointing among the ranks of the client's management.

A factual example points up how consultants can be used by a client to manipulate:

> A company produced a broad range of consumer products. Among these was one particular bell-ringer product, the flagship product for which the company was well known. Defects began to appear in this product and the number of complaints rose. Investigations began, but Research and Development could find no answers to the problem. Suppliers were canvassed, but there had been no changes in any of their products. On the basis of his department's work, the R&D director realized the enormity of the problem. This was major, something which would involve extensive, expensive, and time-consuming investigations beyond his in-house physical and financial resources. Management, however, were making threatening noises and were very impatient with the lack of progress. The director contracted the project to a very reputable consulting firm. In the meantime, the director, with his staff, redesigned the product and developed an equally high-quality, alternative formulation. The consulting firm failed in its attempts to solve the problem, as the director had expected. The R&D director presented a satisfactory solution to senior management, emphasizing his group's resourcefulness, justified his group's inability to resolve the problem by presenting the failure of the much better-equipped consulting firm, and protected his staff from management's wrath. Management's displeasure fell upon the consulting firm. Not only had the consultant not solved the problem, but the client had nothing to show for the expense of the exercise.

A resourceful client can use consultants to serve many purposes.

Consultants, then, bring those skills and services that are not available in their clients' organizations at a time when those services are needed. Even if the services are present in-house, clients may have already committed these skills elsewhere in their organizations to other critical tasks. It may also be more politic for clients to use outside resources in some circumstances. To summarize, consultants provide skills when it is tactically and politically opportune for clients to use them.

CLASSIFYING THE SERVICES

The services that consultants give to clients are diverse. They defy classification without such vague listings as "miscellaneous" to include the more unusual of these services. In addition, consultants provide, or should provide, unbiased, objective, third-party approaches or solutions for those organizations that find themselves facing difficult decisions. The skilled consultant will direct all clients dispassionately and objectively to rational programs of action to resolve issues that threaten their organizations.

There are two fundamental ways to describe the services offered by consultants. By doing so, one can avoid the dangers inherent in trying to classify all the diverse products offered by consultants into one unwieldy system, while also illustrating some problems to be anticipated in working with consultants. The services can be described as follows:

- *Services described from the viewpoint of the client.* This description recounts what clients believe they need or want to do. That is, they reflect the clients' interpretations of their needs and, as such, guide clients to what consulting services are offered; or
- *Services looked at from the consultants' viewpoint,* the obverse side of this question. How do consultants describe the services they are being asked to provide for their clients?

Tables 2.1 and 2.2 present these disparate views somewhat more fully. The descriptions as seen by clients are soft, more diffuse, with all, or certainly many, departments within their organizations involved, however peripherally. Those of the consultants are more direct, focused, task-oriented. These differences and their implications will be discussed further.

HOW CLIENTS DESCRIBE THEIR REQUIREMENTS

Table 2.1 presents the services as clients might classify them. Clients are likely to rationalize their needs according to those compartmentalized elements that make up their organizations, or according to those elements outside their organizations that they are involved with, or that they wish to be involved with. In broad, general terms these elements are:

- Possession of something such as a product, service, or image, to sell or promote. This *something* is believed by clients to be desired by some segment of the public or by the public in general. This public can be found in either a very broad marketplace or in some very narrow, specialized market.

TABLE 2.1
A Client's Classification of Activities in which Consulting Services May Be Required

Classification According to Clients	Specific Consulting Activity

Product-Related	Quality Maintenance
	    quality control programs
	    audits
	Design and Development
	    new product development
	    image development
	Audience/Customer Investigation

Plant or Process Related	Engineering
	    plant design and layout, equipment design (ergonomics), new technologies
	Process Optimization
	    waste management and control, process control
	Employee Relations
	    training programs

Business	Administrative
	    management reorganization, financial affairs, communications, computer technology
	Employee Relations
	    remuneration, reward systems, pension plans, profit sharing plans, labor and union negotiations, training programs
	Strategic Planning
	    long range research planning

Marketing/Sales	Audience/Customer Investigations
	Promotional Activities
	    labels, packaging design, trade literature, all media advertising, trade shows, contests
	Selling Activities
	    pricing policies, institutional sales, export sales, agents, distributors

- An ability to produce, promote, maintain, or present that *something* efficiently, safely, economically, and at a consistently high level of quality. This ability can have its physical representation as a manufacturing plant, or it may be seen as the intangible charisma of a politician, the talent to entertain, or the skill to create.
- A means of getting that desirable something into the hands of those to whom it is considered desirable (their target audience), and a desire to encourage others to want it also. Clients will either broadcast the products to a wide audience or narrowcast the products to a more select audience.

TABLE 2.2
How Consultants Classify the Demands Arising from Clients

Nature of the Demands	Examples of Tasks
Problem Solving	Crisis Management correct, protect, limit damage, recall programs, public statements Product Redesign

Investigative Studies	Basic Research
	    fundamental research in novel technologies
	Applied Research
	    product improvement, new product development

Assessments	Evaluations
	    staff evaluation, efficiency of internal systems (QC, R&D, Distribution, etc.)
	Audits
	    products, services
	Surveys
	    consumer opinions, focus groups
	Market Analysis
	    consumer demographics and psychographics, competitor studies

Advisory	Financial/Business
	    market expansion, acquisition studies, investment opportunities, financial
	        planning, venture capital
	Technical
	    specialized technical information
	Negotiative
	    labor negotiations, third-party opinions, arbitration

Administrative	Management Technology
	    re-engineering, restructuring
	Communication Technology
	    computerization

Specialized Services	Professional Services
	    chartered accountancy, legal needs, architectural services, engineering, etc.
	Training Programs
	    specific skills (e.g., computer use), educational courses, information retrieval
	Unique Services
	    linguistic experts (translators), cultural/social experts

- The creation or maintenance of a functional organization incorporating the whole of the above as a stable, financially sound, well-managed entity employing competent people and capable of growth.

The above list describes, in a very general way, the bases upon which clients might see the elements of their organizations, as well as how or where their requirements for outside resources might be found. All attempts to focus on a single need founders, because it is necessary to shift from one element to another. For instance, improving a product's sales requires involvement in all elements. Are sales down because the product is inferior to the competition's product, or because marketing is poorly handled, or because production cannot maintain volume to feed distribution?

A means of getting a desirable *something* to the desired target audience involves production and scheduling, marketing programs with supporting advertising and promotions, a sales staff, warehousing and distribution, and a comprehensive business plan directing all this. For example, the activities to get a new product on the market involve, first, the company's marketing department. They start with the consumer to determine the consumers' needs or what they *think* they might need. Marketing researches the marketplace to explore the strengths and weaknesses of the competition's products, and to determine promotional and pricing strategies.

When all this information about the marketplace, the target audience, and the competition has been collated, needs of the targeted customers can be described in a concept statement developed by the marketing department. Using this statement, the research and development group creates the product, the "something desirable." This is ultimately refined to contain those features the target audience desires most.

In the more specific terms of the new product developer, R&D develops a product that satisfies the perceived needs of consumers at a price the marketing department foresaw in its research and is one the consumer will be willing to pay. Management has budgeted to provide financing for the raw materials, parts, equipment, and packaging for the new product. Production will manufacture the product to the quality standards demanded at the cost determined as acceptable and in the volumes projected by the marketing department. The sales department has developed promotional materials in preparation for the launch into the designated test markets.

If the issues concern a service or image, these are also seen by clients as involving many elements in their organizations working in concert. Therefore, clients see the need for consultants to cut across many elements in their organizations regardless of the nature of the service or image presented. In the minds of clients, activities in one division of an organization are rarely independent or without some impact on activities in other sections. Cooperation between the departments is essential for the smooth functioning of that organization.

Clients, therefore, think of the activities of consultants in a similar manner — that is, as diffused over many different elements in their organizations. This diffusion of activity may not be, indeed seldom is, shared by consultants, who are likely to view an assignment as very specific and direct (compare Table 2.2) with respect to tasks. Consultants are prone to take very insular approaches to assignments — go to the problem, analyze the problem, make recommendations for the problem's resolution, follow up, then leave. Frequently this blinkered view on the part of consultants is desired by clients — mind your own business, do your job, and get out.

However, this dichotomy between the understanding and interpretation of assignments by clients and by their consultants can be both the source and the result of fuzzy dialogue between them. Consultants can be misled by how clients describe the assignments, so much so that they do not know what their clients want or, more to the point, where their client's needs are truly centered. Clients, on the other hand, can be understandably confused by what their consultants propose to do, and much later by what their consultants are actually doing or what they have done.

Clients should not interpret the foregoing observation as suggesting that consultants are not influenced by the descriptions clients give them of situations within the clients' organizations. Consultants do not disregard the descriptions, but they may misinterpret them.

Nevertheless, clients must recognize there can be a difference in how clients and consultants understand the issues. Consultants are more direct in their approach and description of tasks. Clients have greater recognition of the many side elements within their organizations that may influence the task. Acknowledgment of this difference in outlook can ease any difficulties that arise later.

PRODUCT-RELATED SERVICES

Clients depend for their survival upon the products, including services or images, they sell and the public demands. This truism holds regardless of the nature of the products or the client. If the targeted audiences tire of the product, then that client will encounter a loss of influence, prestige, or market share. This loss foretells disaster; new products are required.

All products have finite life cycles (see for example, Fuller, 1994), but companies have indefinitely long life cycles (or so their owners and shareholders hope). It benefits companies, therefore, to be constantly looking for and researching new products. Consultants satisfy this search for new products by providing:

- Knowledge and understanding of the habits of the targeted segment of the public. There is a need for knowledge about the target's preferences in flavors, colors, designs, and functionality, as well as their social attitudes toward products and images. Knowing what elements motivate their audiences to make certain decisions about products is important to clients.
- Assistance in new-product development and ancillary fields of raw material or parts specification, processing technology, packaging and package design, and perhaps sourcing co-packer arrangements or parts manufacturers. Assistance in such diverse fields as psychology, speech therapy, cosmetics, dietetics, and behavior modification for reshaping images may be called upon.
- Support systems for the production, maintenance, and promotion of safe, wholesome, durable, desirable, accepted, and believable products.

Marketing, with its closely associated promotional, sales, and distribution functions, can operate best only with the confidence that it has the best product or service for its price and quality. Certainly it is important that the marketing department and its associated departments believe that they have a product that is better than the competition's. To this end, consultants can serve their clients effectively by assisting in the development of the new product and by demonstrating how quality can be designed into that product. They can help their clients with advice on more efficient manufacturing procedures and institute guidelines for improving quality-control systems. The introduction of such simple applications as statistical quality control can help reduce product defects. Redesigning quality into old, mature products, or building quality into new products, plus a sound QC program, can bring about an impressive reduction in the number of product failures that reach customers.

Consultants, therefore, can provide these new products for clients who prefer to outsource the task entirely, or they can assist clients who prefer to supplement their own research and development resources. The assistance can range from providing market and customer information to establishing specifications for raw materials, parts, or equipment or to sourcing these requirements.

New product development is poorly fitted into any pigeon-hole in Table 2.1. Development of a tangible new product spreads across several areas within an organization:

- First, there is the period of technical development. This may, for an innovative product, require extensive research spanning several years. This is the trying-to-build-a-better-mousetrap phase of product development. For software development, it will involve the development of the program and then test marketing, which would include beta-testing with constant feedback, ever improving the program for the end user.
- Contemporary with this technical research there is exhaustive sales projections and consumer contacts, as well as market research and analysis. Dependable sources of suppliers of parts and materials are investigated.
- The next part of the process begins with the hand-over of the product to the production department for full-scale production trials and test marketing. There may be further refinements after test marketing has been completed.
- Finally, mass production will begin in earnest. Sales, distribution, and promotion take over.

Each phase in this continuum from concept to product is vastly different, with problems unique to each stage. Consultants with skills appropriate to each stage can assist clients. For instance, once a software program has been written, it needs documentation. Clients require skilled technical writers and editors to prepare instructions for the proper use of the software program.

Consultants can also build images for their clients. Where clients want to create an image or simply to make an impression, whether these are personal ones or images for their organizations, the roles of consultants can require many skills. Where organizations are the concern, clients want their employees, their premises, and their locations to be impressive, to create images of affluence and success. They want to leave impressions that give their customers confidence or pleasure in maintaining relations with them. To impress, art consultants will be asked to fill the reception foyer or the empty stairwell wall with appropriate art pieces that complement the dynamism or innovative qualities of the business activities of their clients.

They create the image that their clients are "patrons of the arts." An important and valuable side benefit is that artists find markets for their work. Art consultants help their clients create impressions. They allow their clients to demonstrate their generosity to the arts, to show themselves to be avant-garde, to display their art knowledge, and to let others see their sense of daring and worldliness. All this creates an image for customers. There is also decorative value: the working environment has been improved. The improvement can have a positive impact on staff moral. Also, good art will grow in value. There is, then, an element of good investment that has been introduced by the art consultant. Clients should not overlook the investment possibilities of art.

Design and decoration consultants also provide services. First, like art consultants, they can design decors to be attractive and impressive, and which convey confidence and success to customers. They can also design for pleasing functionality, creating safe environments which improve staff morale and increase productivity.

Consultants can be found who will plan those special parties and receptions for staff and for customers to enhance their clients' images. There are also those designer/consultants who will create exhibit booths with unique visual impact for trade shows, allowing clients to display their products to best advantage.

PLANT AND PROCESS-RELATED SERVICES

Plant, process, and product-related services supplied by consultants have many common elements. A faulty process, whether it is a manufacturing process or a series of interlocking administrative systems, results in products or services that may not meet expectations. Perhaps there is an unacceptable number of product defects, or services that do not deliver what was promised. The plant or organization where the product was created may be a factor in this poor-quality product. Consulting engineers and management consultants provide services to correct these defects. If new plant processes or innovative processes are required, consultants can assist in the redesign and adaptation of old plants and processes; they can help in the training of the client's staff and in the optimization of the new processes. Where equipment must be designed *de novo* to meet unique requirements in design and fabrication, clients must work with process engineering consultants and provide them all the necessary data on the process and projections. Management consultants can reorganize systems to improve decision-making and communication. Consultants can lessen the negative impact created by the adoption of the new systems on the organizations and physical plant.

Small manufacturing facilities cannot always afford to have all the resources in-house, such as a fully equipped test laboratory or a pilot plant, that larger manufacturing facilities have. Still they need to test products and processes, and this need can be satisfied by organizations such as government testing facilities, university technical research laboratories, and pilot plant facilities, or the technical service personnel and test pilot plants of their suppliers.

A by-product of all manufacturing is waste. Waste can represent a toxic environmental hazard or a blight on the landscape. It is an economic loss to clients because of the expense needed to dispose of the waste. If not properly controlled and contained, waste becomes a pollutant which will arouse public anger, provoke environmentalists, and invoke financial penalties. Environmental regulations for waste disposal or water reclamation can and have been the cause for the shutdown or the relocation of many plants.

At the very least, expenses to meet legislated environmental standards can be appreciable costs for which manufacturers need to take serious account. For example, efforts have been made to reduce the waste caused by discarded packaging, but to do so requires an expenditure for research on techniques to bring about the reduction of packaging. The Dutch government, with the cooperation of its packaging industry, has enacted legislation to ban landfill use for disposal of packaging material by the year 2000 (Akre, 1991). This enactment alone will involve enormous effort by the packaging industry and a great need for consultants to modify existing packaging to make it recyclable. Additionally, a similar effort will be required to develop new recyclable packaging with equivalent product-protective powers. Packaging design consultants will be taxed to produce these new materials for their clients.

Consultants serve their clients by providing advice and skills to reduce the costs of production by reducing waste in all its forms. Consultants demonstrate how to be less wasteful with resources such as water and energy, items which have become expensive and represent appreciable overhead costs. For these tasks, clients need the expert advice of consultants in water reclamation, energy utilization, and conservation.

Another area in waste management where consultants serve useful purposes is in the technology to convert toxic wastes safely into either cash-yielding recyclable by-products or into safely disposable, environmentally friendly landfill.

Many customers demand that their suppliers be ISO (International Standards Organization)-certified, and this has proven to be a bonanza for consultants. This requirement has forced many suppliers to re-examine their QC and process control systems and adapt them to the requirements of the ISO. This has required training suppliers in the requirements of ISO. Training programs are truly the bread-and-butter of many consultants.

Advances in technology have made clients dependent on consultants for guidance in such new fields as biotechnology, cybernetics and robotics, microengineering, and communication. Research into food preservation that maintains the freshness so desired by consumers yet provides extended shelf life has led to some exciting new preservation technologies. Consultants who have worked extensively in these fields can help in developing new processing technologies, such as ohmic heating (Biss et al., 1989), high-pressure processing (Farr, 1990), which has been extensively used in the ceramics industry, and radiation preservation.

The food industry is not the only industry developing new processes based on new technologies. The recent advance in chip manufacture announced by IBM using copper instead of aluminum is one such development that has pushed other chip makers to research the new technique or to develop better ideas. Many companies may be spurred to seek advanced research institutes to consult with experts in obtaining technology that bridges the gap between their present state of technology and those developments that are coming to fruition.

BUSINESS-RELATED SERVICES

Consultants provide much-needed guidance to small, entrepreneurial companies for the administrative functions of their businesses. This includes financial advice with respect to cash-flow, the establishment of compensation levels, salaries and salary contract negotiations, pension plans and profit-sharing, or employee incentive plans. As they grow, companies move beyond simple bookkeeping and require more sophisticated help. Emerging entertainment artists, for example, and neophyte political figures also need financial and managerial guidance in the early stages of their growth.

In their rapid growth, novice entrepreneurial managers of young companies will also have to cope with labor and union negotiations, as well as learn new management techniques for their expanding enterprises. Technological advances in computers and communication require that even large companies resort to outside advice to take full advantage of newer techniques.

Consultants also supply necessary legal services in acquisitions and mergers, in leases, in contracts, and in the inevitable instances of litigation that can arise in business. Cooperative ventures between companies require the guidance of lawyers, financiers, and business administrators. There are many pitfalls in such cooperative ventures, and companies should seek professional advice during negotiations. Companies need to be very clear not only on the advantages and disadvantages of the venture, but on all the contractual obligations, before agreeing. Leases and land purchases, which are never simple agreements, require thorough investigation of zoning regulations, of adjacent business activities, of future planning and zoning by regional governments, and of historical rights-of-way. Items which are more the domain of the marketing and sales departments need to be reviewed for misleading or inaccurate statements. These items include promotional literature and other advertising materials, product guarantees and product liability statements, labels, and even the terms of promotional contests. Errors in these can be sources of irritation to customers.

The value of consultants in providing training and honing the skills of the client's staff has been discussed earlier when it was emphasized that training courses were tasks best left to consultants. The training of employees is important to clients for several reasons:

- It establishes that a client has confidence in the employees being trained and is an overt demonstration of the value the client places on its employees.
- Training is considered a perk by employees, a reward for good work. Employees recognize the opportunity as a statement of the possibility of further growth within the organization.
- It provides clients with a cadre of more skilled employees who might be the nucleus of future senior management.
- It broadens the client's knowledge base.

The value clients see in training staff has encouraged consultants and the training companies they operate to develop technical training courses, certification courses (ISO-certification, for example) and seminars in diverse topics such as the North American Free Trade Agreement or in-house computer communication. These courses range from one-day regular classroom presentations on the premises to week-long retreats in secluded training centers. Also included may be video presentations designed for teams of employees to use on a self-help basis at their workplaces, trainers working side-by-side with employees, and literature and other material to be read by the employee, who will then be tested at a later date.

The most commonly requested courses are technical training for professionals, management development, sales training, and marketing (McFarland, 1996). However, training sessions as esoteric as teaching airline workers how to load thorough-bred horses safely onto airplanes are also available. Clients should be forewarned, however, that many courses frequently tout the particular theories or philosophies or methodologies or services that the consultants themselves have developed. Staff may become trained in less than rigorous techniques with only limited value.

The evaluation and selection of staff is closely allied to staff training. Here again, the client can find consultants who specialize in assessing employee opinions and attitudes. These consultants can also interview potential candidates for senior managerial positions or for positions demanding exceptional personal skills required in high-pressure situations.

MARKETING, SALES, AND DISTRIBUTION

Once local markets become saturated, there is a natural desire to either expand into new geographic markets, or to target new consumer markets by redesigning the product. But novelty brings dangers because it is unknown. No market can be assumed to be the same as any other, nor can any consumer be assumed to react the same as another. As companies venture into new market areas, the assistance of marketing consultants familiar with the new area or the new consumer is important. These consultants can supply market information through their own internal resources, or undertake research to get information that describes the particular market or customer that their clients want. For example, insurance products targeting a young market and a senior's market require very different marketing strategies.

Exportation

Export markets can be even more daunting areas for expansion. Consultants are particularly needed when the new venture is to market products or services in foreign countries, where differences in consumer law, cultures, language, advertising, regulations regarding promotions, and consumer habits can bewilder the neophyte marketer.

Where clients export their products to several countries, the problems are magnified. Each country presents a different challenge regarding the relevant legislation for marketing, distribution, and even manufacturing. In foreign countries, agreements with agents, distributors, and those arrived at in joint ventures need to be carefully investigated by clients with competent lawyers knowledgeable in the pertinent laws and regulations. Many regulations are promulgated by foreign governments to protect their local industries or products, and these can prove a challenge to the unwary. Any move demands a careful investigation by trained, knowledgeable investigators.

There are other needs: the exporting company needs competent translators for all business communications, and foreign market analysts to create suitable promotional materials for each country. Advertisements successful in one culture are not necessarily successful in another.

A move into foreign markets by a company requires all sorts of specialists. Many companies, small ones in particular, rarely have the internal resources to handle all the contingencies that arise in exporting and need specialist companies/consultants. Market expansion also needs reliable distributors and agents. Consultants can help companies by researching and screening reliable, reputable agents, distributors, or manufacturing partners.

Auditing the Sales/Consumer Interface

Market research consultants can provide another interesting service. They furnish "mystery shoppers" for their clients. These are ordinary-appearing customers who will go into stores, banks, restaurants, or any institution serving the public to make purchases, to make inquiries, to register complaints, or generally just to record how they were served. From these data, consultants determine where clients should be concentrating their efforts to maintain their customers. In markets that are becoming very competitive, clients need to know whether there is a diminution of brand or name loyalty. Institutions, such as banks and trust companies, are keen to check that policies are being applied fairly with no bias to any minority group. Not only does this allow these institutions to maintain customer satisfaction, it also averts any litigation that might arise should minority groups consider that they have been unfairly treated or discriminated against.

SIDE BENEFITS: TECHNOLOGICAL OR PROMOTIONAL GAINS?

Consultants can have popular cult followings. The unique skills or knowledge of certain consultants may make these individuals popular figures. Because of their popularity, they write columns in magazines or in daily newspapers, or even become radio or television personalities. Popular skills are in such areas of technology as food (in particular, food cookery), finance and investing, home repairs, or auto repairs. Their skills make them personalities, sought after for their advice and their very promotable personas.

A client may need some expertise — for example, the food preparation skills of a renowned chef — in a particular venture, and so the chef is hired. Two benefits emerge. First is the technological one: the chef develops recipes using the client's products, which the client can use for promotion, or the chef may even develop a line of new products using the client's ingredients. But there is a second advantage: the chefs/consultants are strong attractions when making appearances at trade shows, preparing the dishes using the client's products. They may even allow their images to be used in the client's promotional literature. Clients, therefore, realize some side benefits to using established, well-known consultants where exposure of this fact has promotional value.

Public Relations in the Marketplace

Clients face a dilemma in the matter of countering misinformation or damaging information in the media even when their products are only indirectly involved. They are quite literally and figuratively in a Catch-22 situation, damned if they do and damned if they do not defend their products. If they defend, they are likely to be accused of self-interest; if they do not, the false allegation besmirches them. For example, the appearance in the scientific academic literature (López-Carrillo, 1993) and subsequently in the public press (Cox News Service, 1994) that chili pepper consumption may be a factor in stomach cancer certainly set companies with products based on hot chili peppers scampering for some information and guidance on damage control and how to refute the study. Similarly, electric power companies have been staggered by studies purporting that high-tension power lines cause damage to those living near them.

However, any refutation of such studies must come from qualified spokespersons recognized in their field, prepared with unimpeachable evidence, and known to be unbiased in their outlook. Manufacturers of chili-based products or the power companies would risk the criticism of self-interest in any refutation of the information. They are acting in their own defense and as such are highly biased participants. Consultants serve important roles in steering clients to appropriate experts or even serving as the experts themselves. Being prepared for the inquiries of concerned consumers is wise, and the advice of specialists in this field is particularly needed. When experts are also recognized public figures, the damage control and reassurance can be very comforting for the public.

TASKS FROM THE CONSULTANT'S POINT OF VIEW

Consultants have a different perspective of their clients' assignments. Theirs are usually more focused views, more concerned with getting to the problem. In the eyes of consultants, the clients' demands are classified according to the nature of the work. Neither their clients' products, whether they are substantial or illusory such as a public image, nor their clients' organizations bear heavily on their categorizations. Nevertheless, the products and the organizations do influence how consultants approach problems, but consultants will rarely see the problems as their clients do. A crude example might help to illustrate this better:

> Clients see a new-product development project as cutting across the responsibility areas of several departments. NPD consultants brought in to develop the new products are concerned only in developing the products according to the parameters (cost, for example) established by the client. It is not in the interests of NPD consultants, nor is it their mandate, to be concerned with marketing programs, advertising, financing (except within their own mandate), distribution, consumer research, etc. These are items that occupy clients.

Consultants interpret their clients' demands as one of six general task areas (Table 2.2). These cover most of the problem areas in which clients seek outside resources. Rephrasing and combining the points in Table 2.2, these problem areas become:

- Getting the client out of some awkward, embarrassing, or damaging predicament, then exercising damage control or resolving the problem.
- Supporting or sparing a client's beleaguered resources in the course of certain business activities. This is closer to outsourcing.
- Providing guidance and training to the client's staff in novel ventures or reorganizing administrative systems within the organization (e.g., re-engineering). For individuals, making over an image would be an example of this.
- Supplying unique advisory services based on arcane knowledge possessed by the consultant.
- Third party (anonymous) inquiries in which the consultant will act on behalf of the client.
- Research/investigative/inspection services.

These categories can be further condensed and simplified: the consultant provides a higher level of skills or competency in some art or technology that the client needs but cannot provide in-house.

The differences between Tables 2.1 and 2.2 and the unique viewpoints they represent have been noted earlier. Clients should be cognizant of the disparate views represented by these different functions as understood by consultants and themselves. Clients and consultants see the functions differently. Without understanding the differences, clients may find their expectations are not being met.

WHAT CONSULTANTS SEE THEMSELVES PROVIDING

Many of the services that consultants see themselves providing have already been discussed in the previous section. In that discussion, they were looked at from the client's point of view. Some require further elaboration.

Assessment Services

Here, consultants lump all those activities that involve some quantitative or qualitative evaluation of some aspect of their clients' activities: product audits, consumer intercepts, plant inspections, evaluations of employee morale, etc. These assessments can be internal, involving functions within the business organization generally, or can involve external factors in the marketplace that may influence the client's business.

Many assessments are quantitative ones: they can be measured. Consultants choose some yardstick against which reliable measures can be made. Some evaluations, however, involve both quantitative measurements, e.g., how many defective products were noted during a shift, and qualitative assessments, e.g., what was the severity of the defects?

Consultants may be called upon for entirely judgmental evaluations. Clients may request an evaluation of their promotional materials, of sales techniques and success of the sales personnel, of the efficiency and effectiveness of the research and development group, or of the corporate morale of their organizations. These are all judgmental evaluations and highly qualitative.

Such assignments are challenging to consultants and are fraught with the potential for misinterpretation between clients and consultants. How does this influence the consultants' activities? First, it may not influence the assessment process at all, but consultants may be prompted to look for bogey-men that are not there. Thus, consultants may not present that unbiased and objective assessment by their clients desire because they may be hypercritical and unwittingly conduct a witchhunt to satisfy what they believe to be the goal of the assignment.

Here may be seen how the disparity between the views of clients and consultants might suggest different objectives. In the mindset of consultants there may be two reasons for the assignment:

- First, their clients are not confident that those in their organizations can be relied upon to provide an objective response.
- Second, their clients have deeper, ulterior motives for wishing to bring outsiders in, and they want a third-party assessment of the problem, i.e., the consultant is the foil the client needs to accomplish something else.

To repeat, consultants could be overzealous and lose objectivity.

SUMMARY

Clients requiring a particular service or needing assistance in any field of interest or with any problem can find consultants to provide the advice or service needed. These services can range from the sublime to the ridiculous: from a need to know the food or dietary laws of a group of people in a foreign country, to determining which Christmas gifts are most appropriate to give to their employees or to favored customers.

Seeking a consultant for the first time is understandably a confusing exercise because of the profusion of experts and specialists and the great variety of services offered.

There is a distinction between how consultants describe their activities and how clients classify their needs for a consultant's services. This distinction may cause a warp in communication between clients and consultants. A successful working relationship crystallizes down to communication, through which both clients and consultants understand one another and establish reasonable expectations.

Most organizations will need to employ outside assistance at some time in their growth. Growth produces problems for companies started with the idealism of a young entrepreneur. Too-rapid growth exerts tremendous pressures on management by creating situations well beyond management's skills to resolve.

3 What Benefits Do Consultants Bring Their Clients?

A stander-by may sometimes, perhaps, see more of the game than he that plays it.

Jonathan Swift

ARE THERE ANY ADVANTAGES OR DISADVANTAGES TO USING CONSULTANTS?

The answer to that question depends very much on who the judge is, what the criteria are, and how the judge is affected by the consultant's activities. If the judge benefited, the decision will certainly be that there were advantages to using consultants. If the judge was disadvantaged by the results of the consultant's activities, regardless of whether the consultant's activities were successful or not, then that judge would be likely to have negative opinions.

A good example of the many elements involved is a client who has been advised to downsize with benefits for his organization. Using consultants is considered an advantage. However, if the decision to downsize forced the closing of a plant in one small community and resulted in the consolidation of the work in another, distant community, there will be mixed blessings. Impacts on the community losing a source of employment and the effects on those who have been let go are disadvantages to be entered on the negative side of the ledger. The community that gains is happy and sees only the advantages. Employees who lost jobs are disadvantaged. Employees forced into early retirement have had their careers disrupted and will have mixed emotions, depending on their retirement settlements. Those offered jobs but forced to relocate may be unhappy. Key employees may refuse to move, thus disadvantaging the client.

Any application of the consultant's recommendations prompts the following questions:

- Was it an advantage or disadvantage?
- How was it deemed to be so?
- By whom is it considered as such?

It may have been an unpleasant decision, and there may be some positive and negative repercussions, but the client was benefited. The emotional and economic impact on those who were disadvantaged by the client's decision is felt marginally by the client, if at all. Those who were disadvantaged will look upon the use of consultants unfavorably.

It makes a difference whose ox is gored.

Martin Luther

EVALUATING ADVANTAGES AND DISADVANTAGES

Any discussion of the advantages brings out ambivalences best expressed by statements such as "on the one hand ..." rapidly followed by "but on the other hand." To obtain any desired benefit someone or some group in the client's organization is usually made uneasy at best, or badly disadvantaged at worst (see the example in the preceding section). The adage that one cannot make an omelette without breaking eggs certainly has more than a grain of truth.

WHO IS THE JUDGE?

Clients are the only judge. It is they who will always be balancing the benefits of using consultants against the downsides of doing so. Clients must recognize that every advantage resulting from activities on their behalf may have a dark side as well. Using consultants can, then, be like a two-edged sword cutting two ways, with both advantages and disadvantages.

The criteria upon which to evaluate the results of the consultant's activities, pro or con, are solely determined by clients. They must be the final authorities on what yardsticks are to be applied to the outcomes so that they can be considered advantages. By default, all else becomes a disadvantage *to those clients*. There cannot be any impartial third party to ordain whether steps taken as a result of a client adopting the recommendations of a consultant were advantageous or not.

For clients to refer potential projects to consultants, they must see a distinct, even unique, advantage or certainly more advantages than disadvantages for having done so. Otherwise, why should they undertake such expensive and potentially disruptive exercises? Before committing to any project requiring a consultant, clients should have first analyzed all the consequences. If clients were benefited, then there were advantages, regardless of any secondary repercussions felt peripherally. Clients are the only judges.

WHAT ARE THE CRITERIA?

Simply put, if consultants have been requested it is because someone in the client's organization has decided there is a need for using some outside resources. This may be because:

- A situation has arisen that the client, unaided, cannot resolve efficiently or effectively for whatever reason.
- A situation has arisen that may affect the client's activities in the future, and the client does not want to manage this directly at this time.

- A situation (an opportunity, perhaps) quite alien to the client or the client's present activities has arisen that requires investigation before the client can act prudently.

That is, there has been a change somewhere that affects the client, and help is needed to cope with this change. In a nutshell, clients have assessed the strengths of their groups. They have realized that in certain parts of their structure there are weaknesses that must be shored up before issues they face can be acted upon. Persons within their organizations will decide, rightly or wrongly, for one of the above reasons that consultants can help.

There is yet another advantage to be gained from engaging certain consultants: prestige. Having it known that a certain highly publicized consultant has been hired lends a certain glamour to these clients. The presence of the well-touted guru gives a certain panache, an air of importance, to those clients using the guru's services.

The criteria for evaluating advantages and disadvantages are decided solely by whether one of the above reasons was satisfied. If the *purpose* of hiring a consultant has been served to the advantage of the client, then that is a sufficient criterion. The sole criterion is whether clients have benefited *by having their purposes served in using consultants*.

Whether the issues the consultants were first called to address were successfully resolved or not is not the sole criterion in evaluation. Indeed, success ought *not* to be a criterion. The sole standard that clients should use is whether the action benefited their purposes, not whether the issues were successfully resolved. Success of the assignment and successful fulfillment of the client's purposes are vastly different value judgments based on different concepts, though they may be coincidentally the same. Satisfying their goals is, nevertheless, the only criterion for judging an action taken as a result of their consultants' recommendations to be an advantage. All else are criteria to be labeled disadvantages.

Any confusion about the above can be clarified by this example:

> The president of a company is pushed by elements within his company to expand into a certain high-risk venture that he feels is unsuitable at this moment, but the circumstances force him to start some effort at undertaking the venture. A consultant is requested to provide an in-depth study of the venture and its possible consequences for the company. The outcome is that the project is, indeed, unsuitable. The client was benefited. The proponents favoring the project were disadvantaged.

Had the project shown the venture to have a remote chance of success, the president would have been disadvantaged and his leadership would have been challenged.

THE ADVANTAGES

With the preceding criterion clearly understood, the highly individual nature of judging advantages and disadvantages becomes apparent. Advantages and disadvantages are specific to clients and the nature, even purposes perhaps, of the projects they commissioned. Either can only be discussed in generalities. A successful new product development or a new image, for instance, will bring vastly different advantages to its client than will a successful training program. The introduction of a more efficient accounts payable program will bring even different benefits. Each will bring positive results if it serves the client's purposes, and maybe additional side benefits.

OBJECTIVITY

Objectivity in the work of consultants is usually a characteristic to be desired. Consultants do bring objectivity, being unbiased (usually) third parties to an evaluation of issues. Jonathan Swift, whose remark prefaced this chapter, saw it clearly. His comment pithily describes the potential value of consultants. Consultants, as standers-by, frequently see what their clients and their organizations, who have been "playing the game," do not see. Consultants see the entire playing field. They have more opportunity to observe. They are on the sidelines, at arm's length from the activity. They are not diverted from their observations by having to actually play the game.

Players rarely see the entire game. They see only what is before their eyes; they are centered on the action of their opponent. So it is with the client's staff. The game is being played around them, but their narrow focus permits them to see only their own section of the field, their own departments. They fail to see all their individual pieces put together as the game they are trying to win. The game plan has fallen apart — their plays are wrong, their defense is inappropriate. The coaching staff, the CEO and the COO, need new plays, new ideas, assistance.

Consultants as the by-standers see more of the client's activities than do those who are more deeply involved in day-to-day details. Tritely put, consultants bring fresh eyes and no preconceived notions, or in the jargon of the day, "no baggage," to an examination of the issues facing clients. Divorced from the hectic pace that prevails within organizations, they have the uncluttered time to assist these organizations in rethinking their situations or in using their resources better.

Novelty

Akin to objectivity by seeing with a new set of eyes is the element of novelty that consultants bring to the viewing of issues facing clients. Consultants do bring new perspectives to attitudes within their clients' organizations, perspectives enriched by different experiences and skills. They bring the novelty of experience to their clients. Where the organizations are mature, well established, and perhaps a bit stodgy in their managerial outlook, this novelty of approach can be very refreshing indeed or, perhaps, daunting and antagonistic. Where organizations are young and entrepreneurial, consultants provide the necessary leveling hand, acting as cautionary *eminences grises* to advise management in such matters as business planning, marketing ventures, cash flow, and inventory control.

EXPERTISE

When clients wish to explore the possibilities that might be gained from new technologies, there are distinct advantages for clients in being introduced to these first by consultants with expertise in those fields. This initial exploration is more cheaply and more expertly done with the resources consultants possess. Using these resources, clients can save themselves time, gain knowledge, and determine whether the new technology has any promise for them, be it in the "soft" sciences (management sciences, psychology, economics, etc.) or the "hard" sciences (chemistry, physics, mathematics, etc.).

For instance, government legislation in several countries has encouraged industries, sometimes forcefully, to reduce waste, and reduce pollution, redesign processes to be more environmentally friendly. This created new growth industries in such areas as waste recycling, the development of valuable products using recycled materials, water reclamation, and disposal or conversion techniques for hazardous wastes. However, these activities require expertise in the conversion of waste to valuable products or to nontoxic materials. The expertise offered by consultants in these fields has allowed clients to meet the new environmental laws quickly. This knowledge transfer has allowed clients to create valuable by-products from waste, reduce overhead costs associated with waste disposal, and to present themselves as good corporate citizens.

Similarly, new industries were created out of advances in technology, new materials, and new techniques in fields such as electronics, computing, communications, and biotechnology. The technology transferred through training by consultants provides leap-frogging into new products and services. Clients receive a headstart.

ECONOMIC ADVANTAGES

Consultants represent a bottom line expense. They are a cost of doing business. When clients wish to explore innovative ventures, they are disinclined to invest in added staff that may be needed for what may ultimately prove to be an unwise venture. They have obvious misgivings about financing unproven ventures. Clients will find it to their advantage to work with consultants in what may be risky ventures rather than invest time, their own physical resources, and the additional people and equipment that may be needed. There are advantages to utilizing the resources of consultants (especially, for example, the sophisticated resources found in universities, research associations, research institutes) for investigating novel but unproven enterprises. In many instances, the expenses can be written off as deductions for tax purposes through some government programs to encourage research.

Buying services from outside resources avoids many employment obligations that hiring staff with those same skills would have incurred. Items such as vacation pay, workers' compensation, unemployment insurance, pension plan contributions, medical and dental plans, federal, state, or provincial tax withholdings, all of which may be deducted from payroll, can be avoided. These obligations contribute significantly to overhead expenses. Furthermore, the paperwork and the time to complete these administrative obligations is significantly reduced by hiring consultants. So too are obligations such as termination and layoff notices; pay and employment equity programs are reduced. Further, there are no emotional problems for clients when terminating employees who had been taken on for a venture that failed. Using consultants for exploring ventures for their viability results in no unpleasant employee terminations.

POLITICAL ADVANTAGES

There are political, or tactical, advantages in the use of consultants. This usefulness has been mentioned earlier several times.

A common criticism leveled at consultants by staffs can be summed up as follows: "There was nothing new in the consultant's report. He told us what we already knew." In many instances that is what the consultant did. That was what the consultant was supposed to do. Staff cannot blame the consultant for recording what was already known but which no one had dared to put in writing or bring to management's attention. In effect, the consultant figuratively let the dirty laundry hang out for viewing.

The people responsible may already have known the situation, and probably did. The client's staff had access to the same facts and observations as the consultant had. Why then, did no one in the client's organization use or want to use the knowledge to draw his own conclusions? Was he or she too embroiled in day-to-day activities? Where was the blind spot? More important, *why* was there a blind spot? Why was it found advantageous to call outside resources in to tell "...us what we already knew."

Such a rhetorical question can be answered cynically. It was better (i.e., politically or diplomatically) that an outsider present the obvious and perhaps unpleasant reasons for the problem. This is especially true if the problem is an internal one, such as managerial failure or incompetence.

The political value of consultants can be seen to advantage here as it was in Chapter 2 where the research director used a consultant to protect his research team. Consultants may be needed both to make public that which was known to all and to be the instrument to correct the situation. When the self-evident comes from someone outside the client's circle, it is often accepted and acted upon more easily.

It is true that many clients do seem to waste money hiring consultants to tell them the obvious, or what becomes obvious after the consultants have drawn some observations together. But is this really a waste? If the reports of the consultants clear the way for some positive action or serve their clients' purposes without embarrassing upheavals or losses of face, then great value has been gained.

THE DISADVANTAGES

When clients employ consultants, there can be significant repercussions throughout their organizations. These can reverberate throughout the communities of these clients and possibly into their markets. Clients must expect these repercussions and carefully weigh their ramifications before they finally agree to use an outside resource or to implement any of the recommendations consultants make. If these repercussions are anticipated, clients can be alert to subtle signs of their appearance and take steps to minimize their effects within their organizations.

LOSING FACE

First, any decisions to use outside resources reflect on the collective capabilities and skills within an organization. It may seem to some within the client's organization that the need for a consultant reflects negatively on the ability of someone within the organization. In fact, it may only reflect an honest admission that the depth of skills in those organizations is not adequate in particular areas. This negative reflection on internal abilities may be strongly resented by those who feel it is a reflection on their own capabilities; they feel a loss of face among their colleagues. Insecurity among the ranks can result from this apparent lack of confidence by their employers. Staff can be fearful for their future, believing their employers consider them inadequate for their positions within their organizations. Senior management may feel some embarrassment at having their management styles or structures criticized or restructured. It might appear to others that their management abilities are faulty or are being criticized.

A corollary disadvantage of engaging consultants is the poor reflection it might cast on the managerial skills and judgment of those who approved the use of consultants. If there were doubts about the need to use consultants, then the credibility of the individuals who hired them is seriously eroded. If the outcomes of adopting the recommendations put forward by the consultants are disastrous for the clients — and consultants are not always right — then those responsible for the decision are especially vulnerable to criticism. Even if the outcome of the consultant's work and its implementation are beneficial, there may still be a negative impact in some quarters of the organization. It is a sad commentary on human nature, but those in management who were disadvantaged by, or had been opposed to, the work will be unhappy and will be looking for their moment to retaliate. It can be a no-win situation.

Lost Opportunities for Employee Growth

Using consultants deprives employees of accepting challenges, of decision-making, of showing leadership and initiative. It limits their learning and development when they are not permitted to face challenges that are turned over to consultants. It saps their confidence in their abilities to handle the business of the organization. Furthermore, clients are deprived of an effective means of assessing the capabilities of their own young staff for future management positions. When clients do not allow their staff to show their mettle by tackling challenging problems, they lose an effective tool for evaluating individual capabilities.

Dissension in the Ranks

There will certainly be those who are frustrated by, and antagonistic to, the presence or activities of consultants. Consultants arouse a sense of frustration and irritation in workers whose day will be interrupted because of the activity of consultants, or because they must assist these consultants while somehow also managing to complete their own work.

The interplay between consultants and staff can stir up feelings of fear, enmity, and resentment: fear because of what changes in accepted routines this outsider's presence might bring in the future. Enmity arises because the end result of the consultant's activities might represent the end of one's security within the organization. The feeling that "I could have done that just as well as the consultant had they asked me" may bring resentment. These feelings can hinder internal work schedules, blunt the effectiveness of consultants, and dilute any benefits that were expected by the clients. Such reactions are the seeds for dissension. Therefore, clients must recognize that the employment of consultants might be construed as an action from which conflict, jealousies, however petty, and irritations could arise.

UNBIASEDNESS: A DISADVANTAGE, PERHAPS?

Earlier in this chapter, the unbiased outlook that consultants bring to an assessment of the circumstances of their clients was argued as a distinct advantage. The value of consultants as detached objective observers cannot be underestimated, but unbiased observers may not always be what is desired. Clients may want someone to see their problems as they do and through their eyes. It may be disadvantageous to the client to have a dispassionate observer. Clients may need someone who understands the ethos of their organizations enough to preserve the nature of their organizations. Clients need consultants who can work effectively from within their organizations, building on their strengths rather than tearing them down to rebuild. Clients are the best judges of what their strengths are.

Objectivity of consultants is not always welcomed by, nor helpful to, their clients. In my early days as a consultant, I visited a factory that was old and very run-down. My objective report was scathing. I was brought up short by the plant manager who told me simply not to tell him the obvious. He knew the plant was old and run-down, but he also knew they produced a quality product; they even co-packed for other companies; and they had never had a recall of their product. He wanted an understanding of their difficulties so that they could protect their company and the quality of their products from the deficiencies of their facilities. He wanted assistance in developing sound HACCP (hazard analysis critical control point) programs, an audit of their QC systems, and recommendations for improvement to overcome their obvious physical difficulties. He wanted advice to make the plant safe for workers and products.

EXPOSURE

The use of consultants does open up the possibilities that the internal affairs of the client will be exposed to outsiders, not only to the consultants, but also to a wider audience. No matter what efforts consultants take to ensure confidentiality, leaks can occur either through an act of unintended carelessness on the part of someone with the consultants or by deductive reasoning on the part of competitors. The following anecdote is an example of a very innocent bit of leaked information:

> A container sales representative asked casually during a routine visit to a company I was associated with whether there was any interest in low-profile containers. There was, but we needed a sealer for them. The representative reported we were lucky because it was in the area, and we could have it after another company across town was finished testing this equipment. We were then aware of the new packaging and the products that the competitor was researching.

TABLE 3.1
Some Advantages of Using Consultants

External Advantages	Internal Advantages
• A source of diagnostic skills in crises, e.g., product failures	• Advice in managerial decision-making
• Advice and guidance in new ventures in marketing or export markets	• Expertise in R&D, novel processing technologies
• Acting as a proxy, agent or tool where sensitive inquiries or activities are required	• Ability to explore new ventures with minimum of overhead and no increase in staff
• Availability of resources (laboratory or pilot plant)	

Confidentiality can also suffer when using academics on sensitive projects. The following occurred to me on a visit to an American midwestern university to discuss with a professor the possibility of placing a research project with him:

> I was passed to a graduate student for a tour of the departmental facilities while the professor conducted a lecture and seminar, even though my visit had been prearranged in order to have a *full* day of this academic's time. (Incidentally, I was charged for a full day of consulting!) On the tour, the graduate, although knowing my affiliation, described work to me that was being undertaken on a competitor's research project.

Employing *any* consultant may present concerns for confidentiality.

Consultants are usually very tight-lipped about their clients and the nature of the projects they are working on. They have to be or they would not be in the consulting business for very long. However, breaches of confidence can and do occur. The presence of consultants in their clients' organizations is frequently an occasion to be commented upon by staff as they interface with suppliers and customers. Not infrequently these exposures may arise in the organizations of the clients themselves.

SUMMARY

A general summary of the advantages and disadvantages for clients who may want to employ consultants is presented in Tables 3.1 and 3.2, respectively. These have been divided further into external and internal advantages and disadvantages. External advantages and disadvantages have their greatest impact outside a client's organization. These occur primarily in the marketplace, in the immediate community, or within the client's targeted audiences. They are "in the field."

Advantages and disadvantages that have their primary affect within a client's organization are, of course, internal. These involve the organization, the systems making up its structure, and their internal workings and interfacings. Included here are changes in authority or changes in channels of communication or responsibilities. There can be physical changes involving a plant and its processing lines or its support

TABLE 3.2
Some Disadvantages to Using Consultants

External Disadvantages	Internal Disadvantages
• Company growth undermined by extensive reliance on consultants	• Deterrent to staff's learning by experience and responding to challenges
• Possible loss of respect for management in business community	• Loss of opportunity to evaluate staff's abilities to face challenges
• Potential risk of loss of confidentiality	• Tacit admission of management's inability to cope with issues
	• Irritant to staff and disruption of daily work
	• Disruption of orderly budgetary planning by repeated use of consultants

systems, the modernization of processes, a merging of manufacturing facilities, or the adoption of ISO control standards.

A point made frequently in this chapter has been the double-edged nature of benefits. This ambivalence can be seen in a comparison of Tables 3.1 and 3.2. Advantages and disadvantages can have both internal and external repercussions.

ADVANTAGES AND DISADVANTAGES
BY CONSULTANT CLASSIFICATION

Any evaluation of advantages and disadvantages will be colored by the type of consultants the clients have employed. Consultants from the various classifications can present their clients with problems, liabilities, and benefits. Some of these difficulties or benefits are unique to the nature of the projects and the class of consultants undertaking the project. Discussing separately the advantages or disadvantages of employing a consultant representing each classification may provide a more complete overview of their advantages and disadvantages.

WEIGHING THE BENEFITS AND LIABILITIES OF "THE AMATEURS"

Clients must recognize that amateurs, though skilled and knowledgable, may lack a variety and depth of experience, and may be inflexible in their outlook. They may be unavailable at critical times — certainly academics have heavy commitments on their time — and be unrealistic in their approach to business and marketing issues. Consequently, amateurs might be an unsuitable choice.

There are several explanations for this disadvantage that amateur consultants can incur. The retirees have skills that have been honed elsewhere in other organizations. Their experience has been gained usually after long years of service with another employer. They can bring a "we did it this way" approach, the trappings of their old working lives and environments. As consultants, they enter a new work environment with their clients where the resources and the *modus operandi* that they were accustomed to no longer applies. They had the resources in their previous work environment to enable them to perform well. These same resources may not be available to their new clients. Any recommendations they make may be inappropriate or unwelcome for their client's circumstances. There is a delightful sign on the office door of a professor at a North Carolina university: "I don't give a damn how you did it up North." This says it all.

Retirees and executives-between-jobs frequently come from larger companies where they were accustomed to abundant resources and sophisticated technology. Such skills and experiences as these amateurs can bring to their clients can prove indigestible if the recipient cannot understand or apply the technology. For example:

> A senior marketing executive, an early retiree from a large multinational food company, was consulted for a marketing assignment for a small, regional food manufacturer. The executive swept in with requests for market information from sources that this small company could not afford to subscribe to. He started to request research on product categories from market research companies whose subscription costs far exceeded this company's marketing budget. He argued that he simply could not do his job unless he had the tools. In addition, he expected the information to be dug out for him and placed on his desk. Formerly, the small company had relied on its marketing director-cum-salesman, who visited stores to talk to managers and relied on his salesmen and distributors for market information.

Amateurs, suddenly cut from large corporations and now adrift in the marketplace, may find the constraints in a small operation daunting. They may lack the flexibility necessary to cope with "flying by the seats of their pants."

Academics too, can be impractical in the eyes of industry. They frequently lack practical manufacturing, marketing, or managerial experience. Their approach to, and solutions for, industrial problems can be naive or even irresponsible. For example:

> A professor was asked to design a water recycling and conservation system for an old food processing plant where water usage was too high and the local water rates were going up astronomically. Also, the local sewage treatment plant was unhappy with the amount of food waste it was required to treat. Conservation was the order of the day. The water recovery system designed was textbook perfect, but totally inapplicable to the plant in question. It could best have been applied had the plant been razed and rebuilt around the design the professor offered.

Little or no consideration was made for the need to work within the restrictions imposed by the existing plant.

Academics present an interesting duality as consultants. They are, at once, highly knowledgeable in very specific and frequently narrowly defined fields, as are some retirees and executives-between-jobs, but, at the same time, they can frequently be dreadfully naive about regulations in the business world. Again, another example demonstrates this issue:

> Stability problems with a processed meat product were encountered. All attempts to preserve the product by lowering the water activity played havoc with both the texture and flavor of the product. An academic, well published in the field of water activity,

was consulted. He suggested that glycerol be added to lower the water activity! When it was pointed out that this was illegal, he merely shrugged his shoulders, saying: "Nobody could prove you were adding it."

Both this anecdote and the preceding one illustrate the insularity and impracticality that can occur between industry and academics. The latter anecdote points up the need not only for an awareness of food legislation, which has only recently begun to be taught in food science departments, but also for courses in ethics. Nevertheless, academics are beginning to have to grapple and to cooperate with the business world in their search for more funding to offset the loss of funding from government sources.

There are academics who are highly inarticulate. To hear and read them, one is forced to believe they think in the passive voice and confuse scientific bafflegab with erudition (so do some professional consultants). There are other academics, however, who can explain the most complex problems lucidly without scientific jargon.

In the heady atmosphere of academic research, investigation and rechecking, theorizing and debate are accepted, indeed, encouraged. Consequently, there are some academics who do not appreciate that the client wants the problem resolved expeditiously, and preferably today. These few cannot see the forest because of the trees, and straightforward problems become complex mazes. They are in a world of academia and scholarship. Yet other academics can move brilliantly and incisively to the nub of a problem and provide the assistance needed. Clients are advised to develop contacts with prospective academics and investigate them and their research carefully before hiring them as consultants.

The newly-formed OTTs (offices of technology transfer) are dispelling this academic insularity by providing better communication of industry's needs to academics and, at the same time, giving industry an idea of academia's position. A recent survey (Morand, 1995) studying the gap between industry and academia found some stumbling blocks to cooperative programs. Industry leaders, mainly CEOs of large companies, cited the universities for their lack of understanding of the time pressures industry faces. Another barrier to cooperative programs cited by these company presidents was university policies respecting intellectual property and patentability.

Any clients who intend to use academics as outside resources must be prepared for unusual (unusual for industry, that is) snafus to easy communication. The 1990s have seen a profound transition from a previously aloof attitude on the part of academics and universities to one of greater interaction with industry.

Industry, too, must come to understand the position of academics. Academics consult as a sideline to their regular occupation as teachers. They are constrained by other priorities that their teaching obligations bring. Lecturing, personal research, supervision of graduate students, the need to travel to deliver scientific papers, grant applications, departmental meetings, and sabbaticals can make academics very elusive if frequent contacts on a regular basis are required.

Communication with academics can be difficult. This can be disconcerting to clients requiring expert advice in an emergency if academics cannot always be reached easily on short notice. Kenward (1992) has described communication problems with academics and their seeming indifference to deadlines or to urgency. As Kenward points out, "profit is the name of the game," and academics have to realize these facts of business life. If academics want industry's money, they must be prepared to meet industry's requirements.

Collaborative efforts with academic staff can be difficult. One personal example that occurred when I headed a technical services department in industry, highlights this:

> Critical analytical data were not forthcoming as promised from a university laboratory. A telephone call to that professor's laboratory asking his whereabouts was answered by one of his students with, "He plays tennis every Friday afternoon when the weather is nice." It was Friday afternoon. The weather was nice. He was playing tennis.

To this anecdote can be added the story of the professor who disappeared on a sabbatical leave in mid-project without any notice to me. Even the departmental secretary did not know how to find him! All work on this project had to cease until he returned. This latter occurrence cannot be an entirely unusual or infrequent one, as Kenward (1992) also noted an example of it in the U.K. Nor is it typical of any one university. My personal experiences with academics have involved universities at several locations in both the U.S. and Canada.

In defense of academics, however, it must be stressed that the foregoing incidents do not reflect all academics nor all university attitudes. It does provide a cautionary warning note to clients, however — *caveat emptor*. An attitude of buyer beware is very important for clients when researching the amateurs as consultants. Amateurs frequently do not, or cannot, provide referrals. They may not even, in some instances, be able or willing to mention the names of the clients they consult for. Some are moonlighting unbeknownst to their current employers. Investigation of references is, therefore, incomplete, and clients have no good knowledge of what they are buying. This is a distinct disadvantage for potential clients.

WEIGHING THE ADVANTAGES AND DISADVANTAGES OF "THE PROFESSIONALS"

Professionals can also be guilty of the same sins as some of the amateurs. Therefore, any clients requiring the services of consultants must accept that they should hunt as extensively as their needs permit and thoroughly investigate any consultants before contracting for any work. "Buyer beware" is the key advice, and clients must investigate consultants even if they are professionals.

Professionals have references attesting to their work experience that can be investigated by clients before they are engaged. Clients can contact other clients that their potential consultants have served. These contacts can alert new clients to possible difficulties that could be encountered with any particular consultant. Problems encountered by others can be discussed and avoided. By investigating thoroughly prior to any commitment, clients improve their chances for a trouble-free relationship with the consultant and for maximizing the anticipated benefits.

Furthermore, clients can find professionals more readily than they can find amateurs. Professionals can be found in any number of directories (see later for a more complete discussion of finding consultants). Professionals have consulting as their core business. They pride themselves on flexibility and their ability to respond to a client's needs quickly. This flexibility and greater availability is a distinct advantage over academics, for example, who may be constrained by teaching and research responsibilities.

However, there are constraints to the availability of professional consultants. They must devote a good portion of their time to promotion (seminars, courses, conferences, and trade exhibitions) where they are establishing contacts for future assignments. They also cannot neglect self-improvement, lest they no longer be on the leading edge of the specialties or technologies they espouse. Academics, on the other hand, are on this leading edge of technology and are best positioned to transfer this technology to their industrial clients. The foot prosthesis (see Chapter 1) developed by Medicus Ltée is such an example of this technology exchange (Bagnall 1996).

The need for professionals to promote themselves, to make contacts, and to develop new skills may limit their flexibility just as teaching pressures limit academics. This can represent a disadvantage that clients should be aware of. Consultants may farm out assignments to colleagues in their organizations. Clients then do not always get the advertised goods. This can be especially true of big-name consultants. Clients can find themselves with a substitute, a franchisee, so to speak.

Professionals have been exposed to a wide variety of activities with clients. As a result, there is a better understanding of the needs of industry. In addition, they have more experience in the fundamentals of consulting which is, in its basics, an exercise in technology or skills transfer.

Professional consultants can become identified with particular dogmas, hobby horses, pet theories, or fads. Some examples of these idiosyncracies may be;

- Some novel management technique based loosely on management theory but modified by the consultant.
- Simplified procedures for reducing the number of trials required in new-product development adapted from statistics.
- Unusual applications of control systems in areas such as QC or R&D.
- Novel organizational structures.
- Novel, even bizarre, training procedures.
- Questionable interpretations of consumer behavior.

If consultants are obsessed with their own particular theories, they can push these to the disadvantage of their clients. These consultants are no longer providing analytical objectivity. Clients will find their organizations being forced to fit the theories espoused by these consultants, rather than having these theories adapted to their own exigencies. The danger can frequently be foreseen when these consultants present some packaged versions of their dogma to their clients. These packaged theories are the consultants' versions of paint-by-numbers artistry.

A consultant's wealth of experience or skills must be examined carefully for what it actually is. Clients must examine closely whether techniques or technologies their consultants are trying to promote will fit their organizations. They should not look to see how their organizations will fit the dogmas of their consultants.

Contract Research Companies

There are advantages to investigating large research companies and institutes, including cooperative research programs with universities, for contract research needs. Some of the areas they are best suited for researching are:

- In new process or product development projects where substantial basic research is required.
- In exploratory research into innovative manufacturing processes and other esoteric subjects the client wishes to investigate as the basis for future ventures.
- In unique and sophisticated chemical and physical analyses the company does not perform routinely.

Many types of research, for example computer programming needs, are best given to outside specialists who are expert in programming, or studies on consumer tastes and habits should be presented to experts in the gathering and statistical interpretation of such market data.

Some of the general advantages of farming out research to contract research companies are outlined in Table 3.3. Clients should see and understand the double-edged nature of advantages as outlined in this table. While contract research companies are well equipped to take novel, flexible approaches to projects, their findings must be applicable to the resources and philosophies of their clients. Advantages are lost if the approach taken by these large research companies is not consistent with the capabilities and resources of their clients. That is, these large research companies, with their more sophisticated resources, must be able to transfer their technology to their more unsophisticated clients.

For collaborative efforts to work well with these R&D facilities, clients must be prepared to devote considerable time to monitoring any progress that is made so they can determine whether results will be acceptable to their organizations.

On the negative side, clients will find that their own staff will not learn nor gain the training and experience this project would have brought had they undertaken the project themselves.

Weighing the advantages and disadvantages of using consultants is highly personal to the clients faced with the decision. Elements to be considered will depend on the stage of growth of the clients, on the experience and skills within their organizations, on the nature of the work clients wish to put into the hands of consultants, on the resources the clients possess, and on the type of consultant they have approached. Only clients can properly evaluate the benefits that may result from working with consultants. This evaluation can be properly done only after a thorough analysis of all possibilities and their short- and long-term ramifications.

TABLE 3.3
Advantages of Subcontracting to Research and Development Laboratories

Rapid response time
  • Laboratories have an extensive array of specialized equipment, specialists, and trained support staff
    to enable versatile and novel pilot plant operations
Flexibility
  • Can approach a problem from many directions simultaneously and single out the most effective
    approach
Resources
  • Equipment, time
  • Renting people cheaper than the client can hire experienced staff for in-house development
  • Support staff
Proven record
  • Experience in a broad spectrum of esoteric research and ability to apply these other experiences to
    the problems of clients
Confidentiality
  • Responsible staff aware of dangers of leaking information

Which type of consultant the client will get the most from depends also upon the nature of the problem, the client's type of organization, and such other factors. Even then, it is still *buyer beware.*

4 Activities, Questions, and Decisions for the Client

Fast
> *Cheap*
>> *Excellent*
>>> *Pick any two.*

Words Noted on a Sign in a Service Provider's Office

INTRODUCTION

This chapter will look at the activities clients should undertake for themselves prior to seeking consults. These are internal self-examinations and evaluations that should be carried out to enable clients to define what issues they need to resolve. Clients must evaluate such issues as thoroughly as they can, then articulate what their needs are. Finally, they need to determine the urgency they face, although this is usually apparent. Whether clients are in the throes of a crisis or not, this introspection ought still to be carried out. Clients must still clearly define what they want or expect from their consultants. (In crises, the time for this analysis is obviously short.)

Once clients clarify their expectations, they can truly estimate how much the supposed benefits will be worth to them. Then they can determine how much they are willing to spend for that project. Clients must describe clearly for themselves what they hope the outcome of the project will be. What will a successful outcome bring to fruition for them? Clients cannot, or should not, call in consultants and then tell those consultants that something is wrong somewhere. "Find it! Fix it!" This dangerous move puts the control of their organizations into the hands of their consultants. This has the potential to become a managerial disaster.

When clients claim not to know what their problems are, there can be two meanings. One meaning is healthy if they mean they do not know what the solution is. For example, products could be wearing out faster than anticipated, but the client does not know why. If, however, clients mean that they cannot define the problems they are facing and call upon the consultant to define what is wrong, there can be serious consequences. Consultants are outsiders who initially have no intimate knowledge of the cultures, organizational structures, or business activities of their clients. Clients have, in effect, abrogated their obligation to manage to strangers. The interpretation and management of the situations facing clients have been transferred to an unknown entity. Clients would never condone behavior in regular business activities where they are no longer in control of their situations.

A major theme that will run through this book is that clients must always maintain control of the issues their consultants are assisting them with. At the very least, clients must remain aware of everything that is happening in this client/consultant relationship. They must know what their consultants are doing on their behalf. This intervention (not interference) must be carried out frequently enough so that if anything goes amiss in the relationship, clients will be aware firsthand and be able to limit any damage. Consultants are tools to be used by clients for their benefit in much the same manner that these clients use any other resource in their business activities.

This brings me to the second piece of advice that will be found throughout this book: consultants may be good for the problems their clients confront but not necessarily good for their businesses. Only clients know how to conduct their own businesses. If they do not, clients will not be successful in business for very long. Consultants cannot help their clients if the clients do not know what their businesses are.

The next chapter discusses finding consultants, but clients must understand the needs for which the expertise of consultants is required and what tasks might be expected of the consultants before they can find a suitable one. Clients cannot find consultants for their needs, let alone select the most suitable or ideal consultant from the pack, without such knowledge.

THE PREPARATION

Preparations should be directed solely to the task of being ready for the possibility that consultants will be needed. To do this, clients must ask themselves the obvious question: why do they need, or think they need, to resort to consultants to assist them with some difficulties? There must have been some indication that something was amiss, such as falling sales, complaints from customers or other target audiences, climbing overhead, falling productivity, and so on. There are signs to be read, and clients must learn to read them as accurately as they can if they expect to be competitive. First, the signs must be collated from all sources. After digesting what all the signs might mean, clients can then define their needs.

DEFINING THE NEED

Before consultants can be approached for discussions, clients must have set out very clear ideas of why they need consultants. They must be very articulate about what they want. To be prepared for this, they must first define what they believe the signs they have collated mean.

IN TIMES OF CRISIS

Crises and consultants seem frequently to go hand in hand. Indeed, an employee of a client once referred to me and my kind rather unkindly as "vultures out after a hanging." Truly, consultants do appear to show up after crises. A more accurate, and gentle, description might be that generally we are called by clients in a state of agitation after some crisis has occurred.

In times of crisis, the signs are clear for clients to see. There has been a sudden profusion of customer complaints or injuries. There has been the appearance of public health authorities on the client's premises. There has been a disastrous loss of market share, with both distributors and shop owners clamoring for pick-ups of returned goods. There have been displays of poor staff morale accompanied by absenteeism and overt acts of vandalism or wanton neglect. Suspicions of financial irregularities have become positive indications that fraud has occurred. The need for assistance has been clearly defined, and the time for collation has passed.

In crises, there are two distinct aspects of the issues facing clients to be articulated. First, the problem has been defined. Its repercussions must be responded to. Crises are frequently very public affairs. Consultants can assist clients to contain the damage these incidents represent to the public and to themselves, and be resourceful in maintaining the goodwill of the public toward their clients.

The second aspect is a clear definition of the causes of the problem and its solution. Clients need to solve the problem that caused the crisis. This activity, after the critical part of the emergency has abated, will require an intensive period of investigation to explain what went wrong and rectify it.

IN TIMES OF COMPARATIVE PEACE AND TRANQUILLITY

A need to respond to crises is not the only reason to resort to outside resources for assistance. There may simply be a desire to explore a particular export market as a potential for growth, or an extension to an existing manufacturing plant may be required. One of the more novel, and simplest, assignments I ever undertook was requested by a multinational food company with extensive fish product interests. I was to attend a technical conference and prepare a report of any novel developments in added-value fish products. I dared to ask, "Didn't they send several of their own staff to this meeting?" "Oh yes," was the answer, "but they always come back saying there was nothing new." My client wanted a fresh look at developments in this market. They thought, perhaps, that their own staff had become somewhat jaded about these newer developments.

Where no urgent issues compel haste, the needs clients may have can be researched in depth within their organizations, with their own management and staff. These topics can be reviewed with responsible members of the client's personnel and done so in relative peace and calm. Such topics are: long-range needs for investigative research into new processes, new equipment, and new products, staff training programs, the introduction of new organizational and managerial systems, possible mergers and acquisitions, or market and customer surveys.

Who Should Be Involved in the Review?

Clients ought to discuss pertinent issues with all levels of their management and other staff who may have contributions to make. Staff who are intimately involved with a particular issue in question should be canvassed for their contributions to this issue. The subject matter of the issues dictates who should be invited to participate. There should be no reticence about who ought to be canvassed in the initial stages of these discussions. Communication is essential. Let me provide a small example of a contretemps involving a lack of communication that I encountered:

> During a visit to a pickle packing operation, a capping machine went down. The plant engineer roughly shouldered aside the machine operator and tinkered with the machine, but to no avail. Absolutely no words passed between them. The capping machine company's technical representative was flown in that day. The problem was solved within minutes of the representative's arrival, but only after more than half a day's production time had been lost. When I joshed the capper operator about what he had broken, he pointed out what had been wrong. I asked why he had not told the engineer what was wrong. His answer was simple: "The M-----r F----r didn't ask me."

How much production time, goodwill, and expense could have been saved with better communication! The problem could have been resolved so much more expeditiously. If equipment is not performing up to standard, certainly the operator of that piece of malfunctioning equipment can contribute significantly to discussions of technical and quality problems. A plant floor operator stands beside the equipment day in and day out hearing it and seeing it. That operator can contribute. This instance of lack of communication cost this packer dearly in lost production.

A similar example of a more substantial, but less disturbing, nature drives this point home:

> While a student working summers in a soap factory, I was assigned a thankless job by the plant engineers. This was done primarily, I now believe, to keep me out of their hair. I was to study a manually controlled process and provide data to the engineers for automatically controlling the reaction. The operator, who had been there since the dawn of time and to my naive and uncomplicated mind was an old fogey, nevertheless could control the reaction to within very tight tolerances. The engineers had so far been unable to do so automatically. I collected pages of data, ammeter readings on pump motors, viscosity data, refractive indices of the liquid, and lots more bumf which mostly duplicated what had been done before. The old operator told me he simply listened to the machinery. It told him when the reaction was complete, and then he opened the valves.

The engineers merely thought him a great old story-telling codger. Perhaps they, too, should have listened: sound may have been the answer.

The nature of the task will dictate how wide preliminary inquiries will be. Minor problems on the plant floor need go no further than the plant manager or plant engineer, who can then call in the technical service representative of the machinery company whose equipment is at fault. The levels of management concerned are simple: the machine operator, the plant manager, and the quality control department. All can contribute something to the issues — for example, some description or some understanding that may provide clarification of the problem before the matter requires a consultant.

For issues that embrace a client's entire organization, the entire organization should be consulted. This is, for obvious reasons, an impossibly impractical task. It is practical for only the smallest of organizations. Nevertheless, initially the net should be cast broadly to gather all salient opinions and observations from all who can contribute. The first cast should include a cross section of staff from all levels of the client's organization, from the plant floor and service counters up to top management, who may be concerned with the particular issues being examined.

Tact and shrewdness must be used by clients in gathering information in such circumstances. Clients should be aware of the dangers of asking senior managers, for example, whether there are personnel problems in their departments. In all likelihood those managers will deny the existence of problems because reporting them may reflect on their managerial skills; or they will be evasive or defensive in order to guard their turf; or they will be eager (or vindictive) to have people they cannot get along with removed.

What Topics Should Be Discussed?

The issues that ought to be discussed by clients within their organizations are listed in question form in Table 4.1. These are presented both in a general form, and as more specific and directed questions for consideration by clients. The questions are applicable either to long-range investigative projects, or to general noncritical issues. The questions also apply to issues that are not currently problems but nevertheless portend possible short- or long-range consequences if they are not investigated early. For either projects or investigation of issues, resolution of these questions follows paths that are very similar.

A decision tree derived from an elaboration of the questions presented in Table 4.1 is depicted in Figure 4.1. This demonstrates the steps clients ought to take before coming to any decisions about using consultants. These consist of a series of go/no go decisions in response to a series of questions.

FIRST INDICATIONS: GATHERING AND READING THE SIGNS

Clients must know their businesses. With this knowledge will come awareness of the signs, especially the *changes* in these signs, that impinge on their business activities. The collation, reading, and interpretation of these signs lead to plans that answer the needs. After such an evaluation, clients may find there is no need for any outside resources.

An analogy can be made here. Clients believing they might have problems are much like persons who believe they are not well. They have symptoms: signs such as headache, rashes, nausea, and so on. Initially sick persons self-diagnose, believing that rest, lots of fluids, time, and the proverbial two aspirins should cure all. They frequently get better without seeing a doctor. Organizations initially do much the same. They self-diagnose. Inquiries are made in the various departments. Any departments in their organizations which the client feels are not operating efficiently are given what might be called routine assistance. They self-medicate. Like the sick, they may get better without resorting to consultants. The sick are forced, should the symptoms persist, to refer their diagnoses to doctors, that is, consultants. Clients, should the problems persist within their organizations, must review their needs again

---

TABLE 4.1

Questions to Be Answered Prior to Discussions with Consultants

The Issues	The Questions
Something is wrong in a general, nonspecific sense	• What is it? • Where is it? • How might it be remedied?
Employee malaise	• How do salaries, pension plans, medical benefits compare with other organizations? • Is management the problem? • Is the work environment a factor? • Is worker safety an issue?
Sales performance unsatisfactory	• Is the problem regional? • Are marketing strategies, advertising and promotional materials incorrect? • Are the activities of competitors factors? • Has the product outgrown its innovative edge? Are better products on the market?
Market expansion	• Should market expansion be considered at this time? • Are export markets a good idea? What is needed to explore these?
Product or service malfunction	• Has quality suffered? • What feedback from customers has been received? • Is a redesign of the product or service advised?
Business-related issues	• Should a merger or buy-out of a competitor be considered? • Is refinancing needed? • Is a restructuring of the company necessary? • Should greater implementation of computerization of office systems be carried out?
Manufacturing issues	• Why have production overheads increased? • Is plant equipment outmoded? • Should relocation be considered?

---

with all levels of management and staff where the problems persist *if time permits*. Then they can resort to a consultant after all the facts have been garnered and discussed.

Issues that may present challenges to organizations do not appear suddenly. There usually are some prior indications. It ought to have been apparent that something was afoot within the organization. Developments in technology should have been known generally to the technologists within the organization. Problems in the markets would first have been known to the sales and marketing personnel. These symptoms and others of a similar nature are the early warning signs that something is amiss or likely to go amiss.

The major outstanding exceptions to these early warnings are random acts of vandalism or terrorism. There is no forewarning for these. The only foreknowledge of these events is their occurrence in someone else's organization. Solely on the basis of monkey-see-monkey-do, adequate preventive action can be implemented. The present profusion of tamper-proof or tamper-evident packaging for foods and pharmaceuticals is an example.

There are many internal symptoms that should alert clients that something is amiss. For manufacturers of consumer goods, they can range widely:

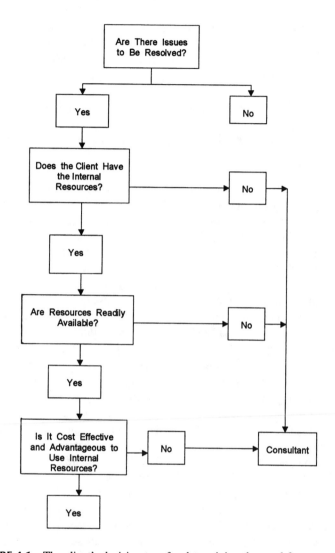

FIGURE 4.1 The client's decision tree for determining the need for a consultant.

- Complaints from customers by telephone, mail, or e-mail.
- Comments or complaints from distributors or agents about product quality or poor deliveries.
- Observations by sales staff about retailers' adverse comments gathered from customers.
- Low morale of staff indicated by high absenteeism and evidence of sabotage or petty vandalism.
- Increased incidence of injuries to staff.
- Cost overruns or inefficiencies in operations.
- Labor costs beginning to rise but production falling.
- Sales volume falling but costs of selling rising.

- Energy, travel, and communication costs out of proportion to budgeted projections.
- Technology that is lagging behind the competition with respect to new products and new processes. The client is unable to take advantage of new advances in technology.
- A burgeoning bureaucracy without a corresponding improvement in communication, efficiency of management, and innovative or creative spirit. There is indecision on the part of management with a perceptible lack of a clear direction.

These and many other indications are all causes for concern.

Signs show up in the marketplace, with the competition, and with customers. For example, a steady increase in sales from a particular region superficially looks like a good, healthy sign. However, if that increase in sales is accompanied by a loss of market share from 85% to 65%, others may see this as a symptom of something seriously wrong. Obviously, competing products are eating into rapidly growing markets.

Losing sight of how, when, and where customers use their products is dangerous to manufacturers. They must learn more about their customers' habits and their competition. Such knowledge is needed to fit better products to changing consumer habits. Clients begin first by collating all the observations they can gather from reliable sources. This means bringing together people to share their observations. Their comments may reveal more and more weaknesses that clients had not expected. When these are all collected and observed together, patterns may emerge that point to major concerns, and this can help clients articulate their needs. An example of this might be the correspondence of poor sales figures to increases in the numbers of specific customer complaints and to dates when processing line changes were instituted. In conjunction with the quality control department's documentation of its historical data, these observations may point directly to the source of a loss of sales. All the collected observations need to be examined together.

Now, with this collated information, clients can bring together those within their organizations whose activities may have a bearing on the symptoms, no matter how far-fetched that relationship might be. A catalogue of these observations and relationships can be made and suggestions put forward on the causes and means to rectify the problems. With reference to Figure 4.1, the clients have started to determine whether there are problems that need to be addressed.

WHAT DO THE SIGNS INDICATE?

The symptoms have been noted and discussed by the client's inner group of responsible staff. But what do they mean? This is the next issue facing clients — to interpret their meaning. This is a difficult task, and it may be here that clients with limited resources might not be able to "see the forest for the trees." They might not be able to articulate the significance of the signs. When there are observations indicating something is wrong and if clients cannot digest these observations and articulate them, then a danger arises. When clients cannot narrow the observations to focus on the causes, these clients are in danger of turning over their businesses to a stranger. They are, in effect, saying to consultants, "Help, tell me what's wrong." Such clients are on very shaky ground in leaving too much responsibility in the hands of consultants.

The need for help may have several causes, but the main one is the lack of diagnostic skills within their organizations. There can be a real inability to explain what the symptoms indicate. Diagnosis is beyond the capabilities of some clients. This inability to see "the forest" may be sufficient reason to call in outside resources. But clients must realize that this is dangerous. Clients, knowing their businesses, must exert themselves to articulate their needs as indicated by their observations. Even if their definition of the problems is faulty or only partially correct, this exercise must be undertaken for no other reason than to have ideas to exchange with consultants.

On the other hand, this exercise may be a formality only. Clients may be well aware of what they want to do but need a third party, their consultants, to make the official diagnosis. Here is the darker side of consulting, the political side, where clients wish to use consultants as tools to support, enhance, verify, or carry out what they want to accomplish. The diagnosis coming from nonorganization individuals can be accepted more positively.

It is, however, hoped that the distillation of comments from the first questions (Table 4.1) can be used to formulate clearly the issues clients face or to describe clearly the objectives they need or want to pursue. Neither the issues nor the goals need be written in stone at this stage. What is needed is some degree of clarification of the issues. These statements may be greatly altered after both the consultants and their clients review them at a later stage. The discussion group in these later activities may now embrace a narrower and more select audience. Again, it will be the nature of the task that dictates who the participants will be.

EVALUATION

There must be some effort by clients to gauge the benefits that would be derived if a consultant were to be called in to assist them. They have a duty not only to evaluate but to investigate and question what possible values can be assigned assistance provided by the consultant. Evaluation, the next task for clients, will attempt to put a dollar figure on what a successful resolution of the issues by consultants would bring. Specific dollar values can be applied only with difficulty. Both tangible and intangible benefits will accrue from any exercise. No dollar value can be placed on such intangible benefits as:

- Improved benefit plans for employees.
- A safer, more pleasant workplace.
- A better product with quality, durability, and safety designed into it.
- Increased employee morale, with a more effective management system.
- Better consumer relations.
- A more highly trained, motivated, and hence more efficient workforce.

These return intangible benefits for which a dollar sign can be assigned with difficulty and only indirectly with such methods as:

- A lowered rate of absenteeism compared to a similar period in the past.
- Fewer employee work days lost to injuries compared to previous data.
- Greater productivity after improvements instituted by the consultant.
- A steady reduction of customer complaints.

All indicate improvements but the improvements cannot be seen immediately. Comparisons of before and after data can only be done after implementation. One cannot predict meaningfully beforehand what any proposed recommendations based on the consultant's work might do for these statistics if they are implemented.

How does the company benefit if the project's goals are met? A favorite question put to doctoral candidates defending their theses in the food science department at one university by one particular professor was always the same, "Will we make better doughnuts now than before because of your work?" It certainly shook the unprepared candidates. Clients should be asking themselves a similar question. Once they have researched and defined their need for calling consultants and have reached the level of questioning tabulated in Table 4.1, they need to ask what the expected impact of resolving the issues facing them is. How much is it to be valued?

Besides weighing the intangible benefits, clients must estimate the more obvious tangible benefits against the disadvantages that might ensue from their decision to resort to the use of consultants. Again, they must ask themselves figuratively whether they will make "better doughnuts" if they proceed to use consultants. Clients need to visualize what impact the completion of this project and its results (whether they can be successfully applied or not) will have on their organizations. The risk/benefit ratio resulting from these considerations provides clients with stronger positions when the discussion of fees and expenses eventually comes up. One obvious disadvantage is the unbudgeted costs represented by hiring consultants. Later when the proposals from consultants have been received and reviewed, the costs of the projects, the consultants' fees and costs, can be balanced against the risk/benefit ratio the clients have estimated. Then assessments can be made regarding the value of any next steps.

HOW TO RESOLVE THE NEEDS?

At this stage, the cataloguing, reviewing, and discussion of all the observations have in all likelihood revealed some avenues to explore. If not, they must elaborate possible solutions that could be applied to these concerns. By no means does this suggest that clients should struggle to resolve their own problems. Rather it is simply the plain statement that clients must review all the possible avenues of resolution open to them.

The need for this exercise is simple also. How else can clients determine whether they need consultants unless they have examined what their options are? In preliminary discussions with consultants, how else can clients discuss and evaluate suggestions from consultants if they have not already weighed alternatives? This exercise prepares clients to exchange ideas with consultants and challenge their suggestions. In addition, it also prepares clients to appreciate what different impacts the possible avenues suggested by their consultants might have on their cultures. Clients must have very clear ideas of what their options are, what the impacts of these might be on their organizations, and what their cost/benefit ratios are. This awareness, plus their evaluations (see previous section), strengthens their abilities to determine their best courses of action.

If the issues are not clearly defined, or if evaluations of the benefits to be derived from resolution have not been made, nor the possible solutions reviewed, clients risk inviting strangers, the consultants, to define the issues for them and propose their own solutions. These strangers are uninformed and ignorant of their clients' ethos. This ignorance can cause such outsiders to opt for solutions that may not properly reflect the situations nor the goals their clients wish to reach. Clients, figuratively, are giving their consultants blank checks.

TO HANDLE THE ISSUE IN-HOUSE OR EX-HOUSE

Answers to the questions in Table 4.1 and Figure 4.1 provide possible solutions for clients. They see whether it is necessary to seek outside resources or work with their own. They must consider what impact undertaking the task in-house might have on their available resources. If these in-house resources are already beleaguered or lack the necessary depth of training or experience, then there may be no choice but to consider consultants to complement these in-house resources.

In crises, clients have no alternative but to go to consultants who have the expertise to manage the many issues that can arise. In sensitive situations, for example financial irregularities, professional accountants, even forensic accountants, from outside their organizations are required. The police may have to be involved. The nature of the emergencies and at what level within the organization they exist will determine the range of outside assistance required.

The impact that employment of consultants may have on staff can influence clients in their decision whether to farm the work out or not. Employees may be resentful of, and even frightened by, the action of farming out work. Unions, for example, may have strong views on this tactic. They may be inclined to see it as the foot-in-the-door leading to management adopting a policy of outsourcing. Employees frequently supply the inspiration for a project, for example a new product or a process innovation. If the employer decides to undertake this project by farming it out to a consultant, employees may resent not having the opportunity to bring their idea to fruition. Individual initiative can be thwarted.

Without any question, projects requiring skills and technology alien to any found within the organization will be performed best with outside expertise. Likewise, where projects involve building a new plant, investigating foreign markets, or researching advanced technology, farming out the activity is efficient and effective. But these projects too, can engender internal opposition where staff are not involved in planning. Trouble can be averted if the client allows staff to contribute.

The projects that deal with intangibles — training programs, re-engineering, and implementation of the current flavor-of-the-month management theories — do require outside resources. However, these activities can often arouse antagonism and suspicion among staff. Clients should think carefully about any conjectured benefits.

SUMMARY

To repeat, the worst situation clients can realize is to call in consultants with no clear idea of what they want. Clients must be in control of discussions with their consultants. That requires that they have a good idea of what they want resolved, some idea of the benefits to be derived from doing this, and whether it can be accomplished internally or not. Focusing on the issues, their resolution, and on what impact they will have on their businesses must be seen initially through the collective eyes of the client, not those of the consultant. The issues must not be presented to the client by the consultant.

The issues may be refocused later with the consultant's guidance and advice but with the complete understanding and agreement of the client. This refocusing will come later when clients have selected their consultants and discussed their needs as they see them in depth. When the consultants have grasped the issues, they will present proposals for their clients describing their understanding of the issues and how they propose to resolve them. Further discussions should follow to clarify or modify the proposals or even to reinstruct the consultants on what the clients see as their needs. Then a final proposal can be presented.

A DIGRESSION

For clients, the next logical step would be to find a suitable consultant, if indeed that is the route the clients believe they should take. This search will be detailed in depth in the next chapter.

Table 4.1, Figures 4.1, and 4.2 suggest that this entire process is a series of logical steps. It isn't: it does not proceed serially. Clients are usually aware of who the consultants are by reputation, by referral, or by a personal visit from some consultant long before. It is just a convenience to present this as a series. Figure 4.2 presents the process with more detail than was attempted previously in Figure 4.1 and it introduces some new concepts.

Certain signs from within a client's organization or external to it cause this client to feel there is a need for some action. What action is immaterial at this time. The observations are then subjected to an internal review of individuals within the client's organization who are those most affected by the signs. Readers should recognize that there may be several such reviews involving observations on different issues within the organization going on at any time.

Collators are introduced in Figure 4.2 as central to this review process. Collators gather all the data, observations from staff, conclusions reached, etc., and write the minutes and any reports ensuing from these panels. A collator will chair the review panel. The chair may be the president of the company or the head of the department most concerned with the topic of the panel. He or she is the point person, the spokesperson, the person through whom all observations are funneled. Later, this collator may be the individual who will play a significant role as the client's facil-

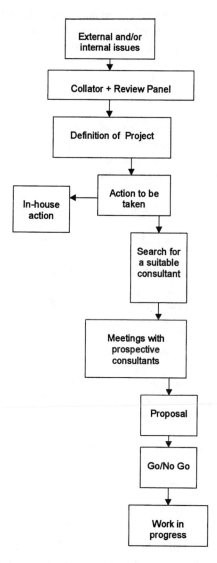

FIGURE 4.2   An overview of the steps required before clients start work with consultants.

itator. Facilitators act as communication links to consultants. They assist consultants as they operate within the client's organization and they keep their employers, the clients, fully informed of the work of the consultants and its impact on their organizations.

In the upper portion of Figure 4.2. observations and information pertinent to issues are collated for an internal panel of responsible concerned reviewers. Their deliberations are passed on to a smaller and more select review panel. This panel clarifies its needs and prepares a statement of the issues it believes the organization faces. A decision is then made by this select panel on what future action to take — that is, to resolve the issues in-house or not. The hunt for suitable consultants to short-list can now begin in earnest. The clients believe they know what they want. Once review panels have sifted the candidates and their references, collators can contact the most suitable ones for more discussions and interviews.

The World Bank provides guidelines for the selection of consultants (Anon., 1981) for both its borrowers and for its own use. Briefly their guidelines, seven in all, are:

1. Develop and prepare a full description of the project.
2. Prepare a budget or a cost estimate of the project.
3. Prepare a short list of consultants.
4. Decide on a selection procedure to be used based on the proposals and the short list.
5. Invite consultants on the short list to submit proposals based on steps (1) and (2).
6. Evaluate the proposals and select a consultant for further negotiations, i.e., contract negotiations.
7. Negotiate the contract with the consultant.

Item (1) is nothing more than the collation of observations of issues facing clients and a clear articulation of these described in this chapter. The second guideline also parallels that described in this text. That is, clients should determine the worth/cost (risk/benefit) of the projects in order to judge any proposals that will be received. Items (3) and (4) obviously require completion of the first two items. Clients cannot prepare a short list of consultants until they know what skills are required or what is to be done. When this is known, consultants with the necessary skills can be put on a short list. The criteria for selection will be based on what is needed, the experience and skills possessed by the consultants, the mechanics of the proposals (when it can start, the finish date, the consultant's participation, costs, etc.), and the client/consultant interaction. The last three items, all involving negotiating, are best discussed in the next section.

NEXT STEPS

Now, having elaborated all the foregoing, let me also say that rarely have the issues that I have been asked by a client to address been the actual problem. They have been a true recitation of what the clients *believed* to be their problem. That overt need, no matter how clearly the situation has been presented to me, has been a manifestation, the tip of the iceberg, of some other related issue. The actual problem lay elsewhere within the company, as did its solution.

This misreading of the issues by clients is understandable in many circumstances. Clients, for example, in activities which are nontechnologically based cannot be expected to clearly define their needs if these are technically based. Likewise, rarely do technology-driven companies fully understand nontechnological issues such as the consumer market they are endeavoring to grapple with. Many scientists, medical doctors included, with innovative products seem not to understand why the world does not beat a path to their doors. Nevertheless, despite these possible weaknesses, it is imperative that clients *demonstrate* control by defining the issues as they see them.

THE VISIT

A client has now decided it needs a consultant. On the basis of the nature of the issues that client has found several possible ones suitable for the task. The references and qualifications of these consultants have been verified, and they have been asked to visit. This introductory meeting should include all senior managerial staff whose activities might be affected by the consultant's anticipated activities.

The objectives of this meeting serve several purposes:

- The consultant, the client, and those within the client's organization who will be interfacing most with the consultant will have an opportunity to meet. Getting to know one another is important. The building of confidence can begin.
- The needs of the client can be introduced and discussed at length. The consultant begins to understand the concerns of the client.
- The consultant can see the client's environment and develop an awareness of all the influences bearing on the client's position.

Are preliminary visits always necessary? The nature of the issues will determine whether they are or not. For major projects, especially those requiring a large amount of client/consultant interaction, preliminary visits are a good idea. In them, client and consultant can exchange opinions, and this familiarization enables the consultant to understand the best approach to helping the client.

The client, during this visit, should do most of the talking. The client (perhaps the collator, the point person) is, or should be, in charge of this meeting — certainly not the consultant. Clients have chosen these invited consultants on the basis of their skills. Clients have already reviewed these credentials. These meetings are not the time for clients to listen to a spiel. Indeed, clients should beware those consultants who control this initial meeting and present a "hard sell." Consultants need only introduce themselves, describing briefly their skills and accomplishments, and then shut up. They are there to listen, learn, take notes, and ask questions pertinent to the issue under review.

The dialogue between the two parties must be open and frank. For this exchange to be productive, clients need to have a clear statement of the issues they want to put to the consultants. Consultants need this input from their client in order to formulate a course of action, later to become the project proposal, that best serves their client's needs.

THE PROPOSAL: THE CONSULTANT'S RESPONSE

Consultants will then depart to prepare their proposals. A proposal is a statement describing a program of work the consultant will undertake to accomplish the client's goals as interpreted by the consultant. It will be based on information the consultant has gleaned from all exchanges with the client, plus all the information from research the consultant has done to learn more about the client, the client's activities, and the issues challenging the client. The proposal will also include such contractual details as the start and finish dates for the project (its timeframe), its expected cost (expenses plus fees), details respecting ownership of patents, and any other legal implications, and how the client or the client's staff may be involved (Will their assistance be required? Will there be work disruptions?).

A seesaw activity now commences. The client will take this proposal for review (see Figure 4.2). The need is to decide whether what is proposed is the most propitious action. There will be to-ing and fro-ing between the consultant and the client as each seeks information, clarification, and explanation. It is incumbent upon clients that they be perfectly clear in their understanding of the proposal. This document describes the consultant's interpretations of what the client wants resolved or attained. There is a sign posted by my wife on our refrigerator door which states the situation clearly:

> I know that you believe you understand what you think I said, but I am not sure you realize that what you heard is not what I meant.

Client beware.

Many clients are disappointed when they first examine the proposal. There may not be too much detail of *how* the consultant will carry out the assignment, especially if the project is a nonspecific or nonstandard project. The *what* is there. That is, if the activity is standard, e.g., a survey of the buying habits of teenagers in Boston, Chicago, and Seattle, the mechanics of the survey may well be detailed. But if the project is nonstandard, e.g., the development of a shelf-stable food product stabilized by hurdle technology, the detail may be lacking.

This detail based on the skill and experience of the consultant is what the client is paying for. It is the intellectual property of the consultant. If clients want this detail, consultants will charge a fee for the preparation of any proposals containing comprehensive information based on their expertise describing how they will carry out their activities. This fee is deductible from the total cost when and if the proposal is accepted by the client.

Most consultants know only too well the dangers of giving too freely of their expertise in proposals. They have seen their proposals rejected only to learn later their prospective clients have proceeded on their own with the methods so carefully detailed by them. I can remember with some amusement a potential client who wanted a shelf-stable thermally processed chocolate pudding. I told him I had formulations which could be designed to his flavor and textural requirements. "But," he countered, "how do I know you can do it if you do not show me a basic formulation. I will only waste money."

The client should now take the consultant's proposal through an internal review process again. There will be questions arising from the consultant's interpretation of the client's needs. Details provided by the consultant may be different from those the client had originally expected. Their impact must be discussed. There will be a need, perhaps, to confer again with the consultant to discuss any revisions, additions, or questions about the proposal. Sometimes the client will want to confer with a lawyer if patents, royalties, joint agreements, or copyrights are involved in the contractual arrangements of the proposal. An example of an issue that may arise in negotiations is the following, which occurred between a client I represented and a consulting laboratory:

> My client wanted to explore the possibilities of extracting plant material to develop a liquid flavorant. Negotiations with a research institute with the necessary pilot equipment to apply the technique were begun. My client would provide all the raw material and bear all the fees and costs of the laboratory's staff who would be involved. In addition, the equipment would be set up on my client's premises where raw material was plentiful. The work would require the assistance of some of my client's staff, including chemists. The consulting laboratory insisted on ownership of the process but agreed to license this at favorable terms to my client. My client demurred.

COSTS AND THE CONSULTANT

The consultant's proposal will include the subject of fees and costs. This is one of the major concerns that can be a sticking point for many clients reviewing proposals from consultants. Gamesmanship abounds in these discussions surrounding the topic of fees and costs. Clients should either be ready to play the game or be aware, tolerant, and patient when the game is being played and they are willing or unwilling participants. It was precisely for this reason of being able to play the game that clients were enjoined to get a clear idea of how they might benefit and how much they valued the anticipated benefits.

Fees represent part of the marketing strategy of all consultants. Fee structures reflect the objectives they have respecting particular clients or business goals. A consultant may be fishing for a client who might attract other clients. As an inducement, the consultant may use lower fees as a bait to attract this particularly powerful or influential client. The presence of that client in the consultant's portfolio will then be a magnet for drawing in other clients. Frequently when it is known that successful big companies are clients of a consultant, other potential clients assume that consultant is, or ought to be, good. This assumption has it foundation solely on the basis that a big client uses this consultant. Smaller clients may be attracted to the ideas that they employ the same consultant that a multinational corporation does. This attracts other clients. It is a very strong advertising ruse. The practice is similar to hiring a particular consultant because he is fashionable in the consultancy trade. Hiring fashionable consultants is widespread and is one of the nastier by-products, of networking.

A lower fee structure may be used in certain growth industries to win clients and so establish a foothold and a reputation in them. This is not a dissimilar tactic to that discussed above. The consultant finds a major pathway to other clients by referrals through the potential for networking in the environment of these new growth industries.

Some projects offer the unspoken promise of continuing work, perhaps on a retainer basis. Consultants apply a lower fee structure since there is, or very likely will be, more work. A higher fee for a short-term project may be sacrificed for a lower fee over a promise of long-term work.

Therefore, clients must remember that the fee structures of consultants are highly flexible and involve a certain amount of gamesmanship. Oddly enough, some clients are attracted to consultants who charge high fees in the belief that if they charge such high fees, they must be good. This reminds me of those people who, at dinner, need to look at the prices on the wine list before they can tell if they are drinking a good bottle of wine. They equate quality with price.

Clients also need to know the tactics that are used in any discussions concerning fees. The consultant's tactics regarding money are ones of elimination. That is, if the proposal comes in with a cost figure, any discussion with the consultant about lowering costs will be disassembling in nature. As the client shows resistance to the costs, the consultant will point out that a lower fee is possible but something in the project will have to go, have to be eliminated. The sign prefacing this chapter:

> *Fast*
> *Cheap*
> *Excellent*
> *Pick any two*

illustrates this perfectly. If cheapness is sought — hardly how the consultant will phrase it, but how it will broadly be hinted at — then quality will suffer. That is, the consultant will be unable to do as "good," or as "complete," or as "meaningful," or as "relevant" a study as the client's organization deserves. The reader should note carefully the appeal to the client's vanity here.

Therefore, client beware. Fee structures vary widely from consultant to consultant. They vary according to the marketing policy of that particular consultant at that particular time. Within any consulting organization the fees may vary widely and wildly from client to client. It will depend entirely on the marketing policies of the consultant, who the clients are, and the nature of the tasks. The least of these is the nature of the tasks.

Consultants rarely will discuss fees in any initial meetings with their clients. They prefer to get to know their clients better and have a more complete understanding of the issues facing them. Clients should accept this as fair play. Clients must also realize that they and their organizations are not negotiating with a used car salesperson. Used car dealers are very likely to start high and negotiate downward knowing when their customer has been hooked. Consultants are not hagglers. They will resist cutting fees: instead they will cut services.

There is another lesson for clients to learn. Using prices established by consultants and presented in their proposals as a yardstick for judging these consultants is very unwise. The best are not the most expensive nor are the cheaper ones poorly qualified. The most important factors in evaluation are the competence and experience of the consultant. This is closely followed by the quality of the consultant's proposal and then by whether the client is comfortable and confident with the consultant. Fees and associated costs, while they are important for budgets, must not overrule quality factors in the selection process. Determining the efficient and proper resolution of the circumstances the client is beset by and using the best resources must predominate in the client's evaluation.

Time-Based Fee Structures

All consultants base their fees on some calculation which, directly or indirectly, factors in the amount of time they spend on a client's project. They will use a basic time-based fee ($ per unit of time) multiplied by an importance factor (derived from the worth of the benefits to the client) modified by some factor based on marketing strategy plus recognition of the technical difficulty involved with the task. Its calculation can be very complicated. Fees based directly on time will be considered in this section.

The timer starts the moment consultants pick up paper and pen or pound a computer keyboard for their clients or communicate with their clients. They base their fees on an hourly rate or on a daily rate. The latter is a much more common practice. For large construction projects, some may even use man-month rates. Consultants are reluctant to state these *per diem* rates to potential clients. These *per diems* do not exist *per se*. They exist for many consultants for calculation purposes only, but clients do ask for them.

Most calculation-purposes-only *per diem* fees range from $350 and up with virtually the sky as the upper limit. They vary not only for the marketing reasons mentioned earlier, but also by the nature of the consultant's area of expertise or activity. For example, the fees of technical consultants generally cluster around the $700 to $1,200 *per diem* range, with expenses extra. But should that same consultant be wanted as an expert witness in court or before government committees, he or she can command over $2,000 a day plus expenses.

Marketing, management, and legal consultants are all expensive and may ask fees of $400 per hour and up. J. Fraser, head of KPMG (Klynveld Peat Marwick Goerdeler), a multinational consulting firm, quoted charges for their consultants as $150 to $450 per hour (Anon. 1997). Clients must recognize that the nature of the task and the reputation of the consultant will be factors in the fee structure consultants will apply. This must be taken into consideration when choices between equally competent and equally qualified consultants are to be made.

There are all sorts of variations in the time-based rate where these are published. Some consultants charge for their travel time, usually at half their daily rate. Others charge on a falling scale rate: the rate for the first day may be $1,000, that for the second day $850, and $750 for all subsequent days.

There are some dangers with time-based rates which clients need to recognize. They favor the inefficient consultant especially when hourly or daily rates are used. The inefficiencies of the consultant are visited upon their clients in the form of greater costs. The longer projects take, the more money goes into the consultant's coffers. This is a danger in projects where clients have not established an upper limit based on costs or time. Personally, where a task takes longer than I had anticipated or is more difficult than I had foreseen, I stop the clock, so to speak, and charge what I had originally expected the job to take — one wins some and loses some.

Another danger for clients, if there is no braking mechanism to costs, is that time-based fee structures encourage greater intervention by consultants. It leads to a bad rapport between clients and consultants. The consultant tells the client, "Trust me, this is what's best for you." After all, the more consultants intervene, the greater will be their fee.

The incentive for both quality of work and efficiency is badly served under a fee for services based solely on time. For this reason, clients must communicate closely with their consultants to monitor their activities. Failing this, clients should impose an upper limit on costs.

Perceived Values (The Importance Factor)

Many consultants prefer not to, indeed, will not, quote a *per diem* rate and do not, in fact, have such a rate except as an internal and private figure for calculation purposes as noted earlier. The reason for not having or not quoting a daily fee rate is very simple. *Per diem* fees are limiting. They are based on time, the consultant's time, of which there is a limited amount. Time becomes a commodity, a scarce one, and there is only so much of it available. But unlike commodities in limited supply which go sky high in price with demand, *per diem* fees cannot soar to high levels. By fixing a figure for this limited commodity, consultants limit their earning capacity. The mathematics are clear:

- There are 365 days in a year
- Less $52 \times 2 = 104$ weekend days = 261 days remaining
- Less 10 statutory holidays (the usual number) = 251 days
- Less 3 weeks of vacation = 236 days.

This time must be utilized by the consultant for:

- Developing new contacts and clients (no charge can be made).
- Self-improvement and research to hone skills (again no charge can be made).
- Such miscellaneous time used for travel time, sick leave, and administrative purposes required in the management of their offices and staff.

A not unusual assignment of time for these non-income-producing activities would be 20% to 40%. The grand total of days remaining to earn money can range, therefore, from approximately 150 to 200 days. The consultant's expenses (support staff, office rental, medical and dental insurance, pensions, taxes, communication costs, etc.) continue all year around.

The constraining effect of quoting time-based fees becomes apparent if clients examine what consultants might be expected to want. For example, a competent consultant might want:

- A salary commensurate with his or her training, education, and experience and at least equal to what might be earned in industry. This will be equal to that of the vice president of a medium to large company.
- Medical and dental plans covering himself and his family as well as a good pension plan.
- Paid vacation equivalent to those of equivalent rank in industry, i.e., up to 5 weeks or more.
- A company car plus a travel and expense account. Further perks may be membership in a good country club and in other trade and professional associations for networking purposes.

If these expectations are used as a basis for calculations, it is impossible for the consultant to use a time-based fee for calculation purposes of much less than $600 to $800 per diem.

There is yet another reason, perhaps the most important one, for a reluctance to quote a daily rate. By doing so, consultants give the appearance that they are selling time. This is not what consultants are selling: consultants sell value. Consider the following anecdote related to me by a fellow consultant:

A freighter arrived in Montreal harbor with a damaged propeller that prevented it from departing on schedule. A very specialized piece of equipment was required to make the repairs. Demurrage charges of several hundreds of dollars a day began to mount. My colleague heard of their need and knew where such a piece of equipment existed. He informed them. The problem was rectified. When asked by the ship's owners what he wanted for his services, my colleague was nonplussed and said "a couple of hundred dollars" (based on the time he had used to track down the equipment). This time it was the ship's owner's turn to be nonplussed at such a small sum.

Here one can see the vast difference between a service based on time, a couple of hundred dollars, and one based on a perceived value which well could have returned several-fold the time-based fee. Costing and fees in the opinions of many consultants ought to have been based on the savings the ship's owners recovered by my colleague's intervention.

Time, it must be repeated, is a limited resource. The consultant, who is so naive as to quote a project based on a *per diem* is then stuck between a rock and a hard place with the number of days the project will take. The consultant sold days not value. The true value of the service, as in my colleague's story above, is in the improvement or resolution of a client's problem. The value is not in the time it took him to resolve that problem.

This fosters the consultant's typical answer to the client's question, "How much will this cost?" The answer will be the following standard one or a variation of it:

"I can best give you a reliable estimate when I and my staff have discussed this further and we have had an opportunity to consider the many ways in which we can help you."

Frankly, this is consultantese for:

> "We have to figure out what the value of this is to you, how much difficulty and
> time will be involved and what you will bear."

But the client should note the gamesmanship that was played here in this response.
There are key words like "reliable estimate" — whatever that means — and the
holding open of the door with the "many ways" help can be given that clients should
recognize. The answer does allow the consultant room to maneuver by asking for
time to think about things. Cynically put, the "many ways" means the consultant
does not know how help can be given, nor where help can be obtained, nor how
long it will take. Less cynically said, clients must remember that in first-time
meetings consultants are ignorant of all the issues their potential clients face. They
need time to digest all they have learned in these initial meetings.

There is another reason consultants are reluctant to base a project's cost on a
simple relationship such as: days the project will take × daily rate = fees. Clients
have a second target in addition to the *per diem* to carp at. This is the length of time
the project will take. If the daily rate is inflexible, clients will turn their attention to
the time the project will take and challenge this. For these reasons, many consultants
base their project proposal fees on the perceived value of the services that will be
rendered to the client plus costs and do not attempt to break down the professional
fee any further. That is, after assessing the statement of the client's problem, the
consultant counters with a proposal that evaluates the worth of the successful completion of the project to the client.

The consultant's use of perceived value as a marketing tool is the reason, in the
first section of this chapter, that it was stressed that the client should attempt some
appreciation in monetary value of the benefits that will accrue from the resolution
of the issues faced. It is important to estimate this value figure not so much as a
bargaining tool but at best as a yardstick for comparison in negotiations with the
consultant. The client may rest assured that the consultant has been doing this
figuring.

Fixed or Flat Fees

There are certain tasks, repetitive tasks, for which some consultants will charge a
fixed or flat fee. For example, lawyers or accountants or other experts may charge
a fixed fee for particular services or activities that are requested of them, such as
expert witnessing (Matson, 1994). Personnel recruiters base their fees on a percentage of the annual salary of the new recruit they brought to their clients. Acquisition
specialists charge a finder's fee based on the cost of the acquisition. There are
accepted formulas for calculating these finder's fees. New product development
agencies may charge a royalty fee (rare), or some similar fee based on the new
product's volume for a certain period of time (not as rare), or a flat fee per product
(most common). Flat fees of between $1,000 to $2,000 for the development of
recipes are common. Many clients prefer this type of billing because knowing what
they will be charged does provide some security. It is predictable.

For some activities, a consultant will charge a fee based on a percentage of the benefits the services provided the client. These benefits may be increased sales, decreased waste, or reduced costs. The consultant will review the client's present costs for a particular operation to obtain some baseline figure. If, after the consultant has provided services, the cost for this operation has been reduced or turned into a profit center, the consultant will be awarded a remuneration based on the annual savings.

All the above might be considered variations of a flat fee system, i.e., the consultant charges a set amount or an amount based on a recognized formula for doing some repetitive or standard bit of work such as advising on and preparing a small company's year-end report or tax returns, name searches, patent applications and searches, mergers or acquisitions, etc. Flat fees are reserved for routine tasks and are usually not applied to complex tasks that consultants might be asked to perform.

A client is wise to recognize that there is a danger in flat fee costing systems similar to that found in time-based fee systems. Flat fee systems may not provide an incentive for quality work but only for routine work on the part of the consultant. Quantity is the key word in flat fee systems, and quantity does not always go hand-in-hand with quality or careful and caring work. Where work is repetitive or routine, consultants frequently pass the task off to an assistant in their organizations.

Also there is a danger that a consultant will use some plug-the-right-numbers-in software program or use routine methodology to perform the work. These may not always be suitable methodologies to provide solutions for the work the client wants done. By using such packaged routines, consultants or a technician on their staff may overlook an important detail that would have been significant to that client.

Where the possibility of financial reward is removed, the quality of consulting work very likely will fall. Routine methods invariably produce routine results.

There is another *caveat* for the client reviewing flat (or base) fees. That is, clients need to explore carefully what the fee includes or does not include. This situation is no different from what a car owner experiences when going to a garage for a tune-up — just what is included in the tune-up? *Caveat emptor.*

Research Associations

The consulting fees for members of research associations are their annual subscription for membership. A company joins by paying an annual fee based on some criterion such as the member's production volume, production value, or the added value of products manufactured or of services they provide. The company declares its area of major interest, and the major portion of its membership fees goes for research in that area after the deduction of a portion for overhead.

Another technique for setting costs for projects used by many large consulting companies and particularly by research institutes where clients do not become members is based on the time spent on the project by particular ranks of technologists assigned to work on it. These organizations cost a project by indicating to the client that X% of a senior scientist's time at so many dollars a day will be used, Y% of a junior scientist's time at a smaller *per diem,* and so on down the ranks of all the employees who will be used on the project. But as was pointed out earlier, time is a limited resource. A consultant supervising several projects cannot "sell" more than 100% of his time.

This technique is largely a means of justifying the cost projection in the proposal. Its importance in attempting to justify costs to clients is questionable. Indeed, it is an exercise in inanity. First, no client can verify that those people designated in the proposal were used for the percentages of time stated. Second, the consulting company cannot accurately foretell the amount of time a senior or junior scientist will use on a project. No client should be impressed by such accounting practices to justify a cost figure.

Hidden Costs

Hidden costs should be identified in any project and recognized as such by clients in the same detail with which they would inquire what is included in a car tune-up. If plant trials are required, then normal plant production may be interrupted. Expensive raw materials or parts could possibly be irretrievably lost in the factory trials should these trials prove unsuccessful. A well-documented proposal should clearly define the extent to which the client's resources, equipment, and personnel will be committed. These items can be a formidable cost factor.

Costs incurred by consultants are usually charged extra as they occur. Common examples of these are hotel and travel expenses, subcontracting costs (to other consultants), specialized laboratory costs, and costs for product pick-ups in different markets. Some consultants include such costs within the total project costs. That is, these are not separated out, but it is advisable that clients inquire whether the total costs do include *all* the expenses, including travel-related expenses.

Costs by Consultant Classification

Normally there is no difference in the *per diems* or fee structures of amateur or professional consultants. However, an unexpected cost item for many contracting out research to academics is overhead that can be charged to research monies. These costs can greatly reduce the amount available for actual research. This overhead reflects indirect research costs broadly described as secretarial assistance, travel to deliver research papers, library and photocopying use, publication costs, heating, light, laboratory supplies and so on.

For every dollar given to a university for research, forty to eighty cents may go for such overhead. McCormick (1996) stated these overhead costs usually range around 40% (for Canadian universities), but they can vary widely from university to university. Overhead as high as 80% were quoted to me by a professor at a midwestern university if his clients dictated to him the specific nature of the research they wanted to have undertaken. On the other hand, a no-strings-attached research grant to this professor with only the stipulation that it be used for research on meats (his field of interest) would incur much lower overhead fees. Overhead fees rose as the grantor became more specific in the requirements in the research topic. Overhead costs can substantially reduce the amount of money actually available for research at universities.

One professor, head of a food science department at a West Coast American university, confessed his department tried for 66% overhead, but he did admit that overhead costs were "highly negotiable." This has been my personal experience. Clients must plan carefully to maximize the research value that can be obtained with their funds whether they negotiate with universities, private consultants, or consulting firms, research institutes or associations.

He who pays the piper may call the tune.

Old English Proverb

RETAINERSHIPS

Many companies have retainerships with consultants, sometimes with several at the same time. Retainerships are fee-for-services relationships. The consultant is available, so to speak, to that company on very short notice. Such open-ended relationships do get out of control unless there is an upper limit placed on the costs (or time) that might accrue. Obviously, it would be in the consultant's personal interest to be available, indeed to intervene, in a company's activities as frequently as possible. Therefore, an upper limit should be imposed. It has been repeated before and must be clearly understood that the use of consultants, experts, and specialists by a company is *good for one's problems* and not necessarily *good for one's business.* Retainerships should be based on a specific activity asked of the consultant that has a stated cost and very clearly stated objectives.

NEGOTIATING FEES

In summary, negotiating the costs in a consultant's proposal can be likened to a "game of chicken." Each move by the client in the game will be challenged. The consultant will counter with "what do you want left out of the proposal?" This is the disassembly part of the gamesmanship mentioned earlier. The client will then counter with some suggestions for omissions. The consultant will point out how the project will be weakened if these are left out or how the client's hopes for a successful conclusion may be jeopardized. And so the game of chicken will go on until "someone blinks."

The well-prepared client will be better able to negotiate "the best deal," i.e., a project that answers the client's needs at an acceptable and reasonable cost, only if that client recognizes that negotiations are, in essence, a game. Knowing the rules of this game is the first step in being prepared for these discussions.

FURTHER QUESTIONS CLIENTS SHOULD ASK

Who will do the work? Clients usually negotiate with their prospective consultants directly. With large consultancies, negotiations may take place through representatives of these firms.

Clients are attracted by big-name consultants who advertise themselves prominently in trade journals and business magazines and are continually being interviewed on radio and television. Clients seek these for consultation fully expecting these big names will be intimately involved in any work that they contract. They are frequently disappointed to find that after the proposal has been agreed upon Mr. Big Name is nowhere to be seen during the execution of the project. Instead it has been assigned to someone else. Clients find they are involved with a licensee or an assistant.

Large consulting firms are under the same constraints regarding the economy as any of the other companies they serve. They too, have downsized. They too, need consultants, and they too frequently subcontract (outsource) projects to other consultants. I enjoy the following anecdote:

> An added-value poultry meat processor approached me as well as several other consulting firms to bid on a project they wanted. I lost to a large consulting firm. I knew the meat processor well enough to ask why I missed out on this project. His answer was simple. He was more confident that one of the "big firms" could handle it better. Little did he know, nor did I tell him, that the "big firm" subcontracted part of the project to me. I was one of several others who actually carried out the study. We had been outsourced by the big firm.

A client, if particularly attracted to a big-name consultant and that person's credentials, should establish early in the proceedings how involved that person will be. If that person will not be involved, then that client needs to find out who on the consultant's staff will be most intimately involved and what their credentials are. Finding the "right" consultant is a very personal matter. The best relationships for a successful project are established with mutual confidence between client and consultant. Clients must develop this relationship, and this can only be accomplished by determining clearly with whom they are working.

Who owns what as a result of any discoveries that are made? The ownership of any intellectual property must be clearly spelled out in the proposal and any subsequent agreements arising from the project. Surprises need to be avoided. A company may work closely with a consultant during the development stages of a project, contributing money, labor, and some expertise and find that at the end of the exercise the consultant is the owner of the art.

SUMMARY

Before agreeing to a proposal for work by a consultant, clients should discuss the project with all within their organizations who have a contribution to make to the project. Second, clients should produce from these dialogues clear statements of their needs and present these as succinctly and cogently as possible to prospective consultants. Third, when consultants have returned with their proposals, clients must read and understand these clearly; then they should discuss them with the senior management who will be affected by the undertaking, and equipped with the suggestions of their staff, discuss all the questions again with the consultants. When all is clearly understood and such understandings and explanations as are required are written into the agreement, clients then may sign the agreement for work to proceed (Figure 4.2).

Does the process have to be so formal? No, and to be honest it rarely is. Each situation and each client will require a slightly different *modus operandi*. The size of the organizations, the nature of their needs, and the urgency they require to resolve these will all influence how they prepare. Nevertheless, the general principles outlined here and depicted in Figures 4.1 and 4.2 should be followed by all clients if they wish to receive maximum benefits from the exercise.

5 Finding and Selecting the Consultant for One's Needs

"By their fruits ye shall know them."

Matthew 7:20

If it walks like a duck, looks like a duck and talks like a duck, it is a duck.

Anonymous

INTRODUCTION

Finding consultants is certainly not difficult in today's world. They are everywhere. When they sense that a client wants them, then that client usually will have to fend off consultants touting every new technique or other gimmickry that is guaranteed to improve the client's efficiency in management systems, new product development, worker training, research organization, quality control systems, marketing, production, and so on.

The trick for clients is to find not just any consultant, but the right consultant at the right time who can satisfy their needs. A client's search for this "right" consultant depends largely on the answers to three closely related questions:

- What is the nature of the problems, issues, or opportunities the client is encountering?
- What resources within or without the organization does the client need to resolve these?
- What urgency is there to have these addressed and resolved successfully?

These questions are a distillation of the preceding chapter. They are repeated here to emphasize that a proper search for a consultant cannot begin unless clients have answered these questions.

ISSUES FOR CLIENTS TO CONSIDER

Sometimes the answers to the above questions are apparent, indeed glaringly so. Crises with public health consequences do not require deep analyses of their nature, rarely can they be handled solely with in-house resources and they are urgent. Why they happened presents a different problem that can be analyzed later. The immediate concern is for safeguarding the public.

A malfunction of a poorly designed key component in a piece of equipment, resulting either in numerous customer complaints or loss of customer confidence, clearly defines the areas in which assistance may be required. Intel Corporation's problem with its Pentium chip in 1994 is an example of such a design flaw. There was no danger to the public except as an inconvenience to those doing some obscure mathematical calculations, but the damage to image and the annoyance of customers forced hasty remedial action.

The critical nature of the issues obviously determines how much time clients have to diagnose their circumstances, define their needs, and find the best resources. Time to select suitable consultants is constrained when clients are forced to move hastily in a crisis.

In a hypothetical crisis the needs are as follows:

- Numerous customer complaints show the problem to be a design flaw in a product. The problem has nuisance value to the public. It does have the potential to cause the loss of customers and to present the manufacturer in a bad light.
- The resource requirements are several fold:
  - First, the public must be informed of the nature of the hazard. If the hazard is serious, the government must be informed. In addition, a well-crafted announcement that is informative and not alarmist must be made to the public.
  - Second, a returns system is required to recover product from the public's control in the retail and distribution channels and to collect product already in the public's hands. Included here is the need to either provide a refund, a replacement, or ask customers to return the product to selected locations to have the problem rectified.
  - Third, the client requires a public relations resource to protect the company's image and institute damage control.
  - Finally, the cause of the product breakdown needs to be investigated and changes instituted to prevent its recurrence.

In a crisis, the various needs require consultants with different expertise despite the connective thread — a product malfunction — running through them. The skills needed will be in public relations, answering legal questions regarding responsibilities, advice in technical and analytical matters, and product redesign.

Crises require a rapid assessment of the skills required in a consultant. (Clients may rest assured that consultants will appear quickly after the announcement of a crisis.) Nevertheless, some assessment must be done. It is equally important that the consultant be investigated in noncritical situations. Here, more time can be taken for a full analysis of the client's circumstances. Knowing what the issues are — doing the homework outlined in the previous chapter — narrows down the field of those consultants who might have to be contacted for help, i.e., which skills or which type of expertise is needed. Then and only then, does the client know whether consultants are needed, which consulting skills to look for, and what urgency there is to resolve the predicament. This preplanning is, in fact, an essential part of the

TABLE 5.1
Sources for Finding the Consultant or Consulting Services of Choice

Source	Amateurs[1]	Professionals
Trade directories	Unlikely	Very likely
Professional associations	Likely	Very likely
Conferences and exhibitions	Unlikely	Possibly
Seminars and training courses	Possibly	Very likely
Word-of-mouth	Likely	Very likely
Advertisements	Unlikely	Very likely

[1] Consortia and research institutes comprising largely academics will be exceptions. These will promote their skills in much the same manner as professionals.

selection process. It will narrow the search for a consultant. Unfortunately, many clients neglect it.

HOW CONSULTANTS MAKE THEIR PRESENCE KNOWN

Clients need only browse through any trade or business magazine, any financial newspaper, or magazines devoted to specialized topics (e.g., *Quality Control, Chemistry and Industry*), or glance at any conference's list of attendees to find consultants. They write articles for magazines. They are the subjects of journalist's articles for magazines. They are advertisers. They are speakers at conferences.

If the client belongs to any professional association, to any fraternal or social clubs, or to any community or charitable organizations, that client cannot fail to rub shoulders with a fellow member who is a consultant or works with a consulting firm. Consultants join such groups and actively participate in their functions. They do *pro bono* work in the community groups. This activity allows them to meet other professionals, executives, politicians, and "movers and shakers." They are not shy about making their presence known. It is in these activities that they make contacts and look for prospective clients. Consultants network.

GENERAL SOURCES

In Table 5.1 there is a breakdown of the many sources where those seeking consultants can begin their search for a consultant. These sources have been broken out by consultant classification as defined earlier. Some general comments about these sources and the consultants who may use them to broadcast their skills will assist clients in their search.

Amateurs, as a group, usually do not advertise in trade journals and business newspapers, but this is not a hard and fast rule. Amateurs are more likely to consult as private individuals and not as an incorporated company. Their advertising will be more subtle. For instance, they may be active participants in seminars, conferences, and they may teach short courses on very specific topics. It is here that clients get to meet them and coincidentally learn that these people also consult. Advertising, other than the seminar or conference advertising, is largely word-of-mouth. Some are loosely affiliated with professional consulting companies. Moonlighters, a category of amateur who are gainfully employed by day and who work evenings and weekends (and sometimes on their companies' time), do not advertise.

Academics like other amateurs do not advertise their skills either. Their services, however, are advertised collectively and indirectly through research associations or institutes within their universities. Their primary means of advertising is through the papers they and their students publish in research journals or present at conferences.

There is a popular tendency for academics to make public the findings of their research activities or theories at press conferences. This trend may be abetted by their universities' OTTs. The announcements at the press conferences ultimately appear in the science columns of the daily newspapers as well as in financial and business papers. Here clients can obtain access to them. All amateurs will use their memberships in various associations to broaden their base of contacts and make their availability for consulting known as their counterparts, the professionals, do.

Professionals can exercise all the avenues listed in Table 5.1 to become known in the industries they wish to serve. Indeed, many consultants actively seek out potential clients by arranging visits with prospects to whom they make presentations in which they promote, rather slickly, their skills or the advantages the client will enjoy by employing them. These visits usually allow consultants a good opportunity to meet several of their potential client's staff.

CONFERENCES, SEMINARS AND TEACHING

The bread-and-butter of consultants is teaching and participating in seminars and conferences (Rush, 1982). Among their activities are the following:

- They present papers at conferences that demonstrate the virtues of some technique or skill they have developed for shortening the time for new product development, for measuring and researching consumer buying habits, and for improving the results so obtained or for whatever. These are frequently anecdotal papers.
- They teach short training courses on subjects of their own devising which can best be described, many of them, as infomercials. They sell the books, tapes, and videos that go with these. (These latter have the added value of being a piece of take-home-to-the-company advertising which reinforces the original message).
- They write articles for trade magazines, newspapers, and scientific journals.

These activities keep their names before targeted audiences. Seminars, conferences, and training courses are directed to very specific topics. The audience is, therefore, one that is interested in that particular topic. They are target audiences.

The consultants are able to narrowcast their skills to an audience attracted by the specialized topics. By participating as speakers, as discussion leaders, or chairpersons at these events, consultants obtain maximum exposure, by name at least, to a narrowly targeted audience.

How common is this avenue for finding consultants? Clients need only review the lists of speakers at these affairs to see an extensive array of individuals who are representatives of consulting firms. For example, a brochure announcing a Canadian seminar on sanitation and pest control listed 16 speakers or panelists. Seven of the 16 are plainly described as consultants in the industry. The other participants were two academics, three government representatives, two speakers from suppliers of sanitary products, and two speakers from suppliers of sanitation equipment. In all, just under 50% of the participants were consultants, and four more, the technical sales people, could also be described as consultants. It is very likely the two academics also performed consulting services.

Another brochure described a conference on food processing to be held in the U.S. Thirty-six percent of the speakers or panelists were consultants or representatives of consulting firms. A further 10% were representatives of consortia comprising universities, industry, and sometimes government; and 16% were academics. The remainder, 38%, were from industry, government, or trade associations. This makes an astonishing total of 62% of the speakers who were consultants or served in a consulting capacity. Those industrial companies presenting papers may very well have been technical service people. Definitely conferences and seminars are locations where one can encounter consultants.

Some universities use consultants in their teaching programs. This serves several purposes. First, it provides students with instructors with practical experience in industry and this enhances the students' education. Second, it spares the teaching load of the academic staff, and finally it does relieve some of the economic constraints felt by universities in hiring staff. Many consultants, both amateurs and professionals, teach courses in universities as external or part-time lecturers in undergraduate and graduate courses and also in adult skills-improvement courses. These latter courses include such topics as new product development, experimental design in new product development or in quality control (or any of its offspring such as quality assurance, product integrity, or total quality management), statistical techniques for process control, ISO 9000 accreditation, management theory, export market development, and so on. Many such courses are designed for companies wishing to upgrade staff or for junior staff wanting to gain academic credits. Attendees will certainly meet consultants and begin their libraries of contacts.

It is not unusual for a university course to be made up entirely of guest lecturers who are industry leaders and can include consultants. While students of such courses are hardly in a position to hire consultants, they do obtain awareness of consultants whom they may need in the future.

Connor and Davidson (1990) emphasized the need for consultants to participate in conferences, civic meetings, and seminars. In addition to the potential clients who make up both the general and specialized audiences at these affairs, participation also brings recognition to consultants, and frequently it can lead to being mentioned in newspapers or on television newscasts and often to personal interviews.

Weiss (1992) strongly endorsed the participation of consultants in the activities of trade associations as well as at conferences as speakers, chairpersons, and organizers. Contacts made in these associations provide consultants with broad exposure to possible clients.

Go Where the Consultants Are

Clients are advised to develop lists of consultants with a variety of skills by exploring all the avenues tabulated and particularly by going where consultants are to be found. Here they will find a wide selection of candidates to choose from.

Consultants are found where they are trying to broadcast their wares; teaching, seminars, and conferences (Rush, 1982). Attendance at conferences and seminars devoted to specific topics that might benefit their organizations lets clients develop contacts with consultants. They can also assess their communicative skills.

At Trade Shows: As Exhibitors or Browsers

Trade shows are built around a central theme, e.g., computer hardware and software, automobiles and automotive parts, pulp and paper-making machinery, construction materials, food machinery, and so on. They attract targeted audiences by bringing suppliers of specific products and related services together with attendees who have some interest in the products or services. Sometimes the attendees' interests are peripheral, a just-looking interest to see what is available. On the other hand, their interests may be very dedicated; the attendees want to see one very specific service or piece of equipment. Such affairs concentrate audiences with very specific interests together in one place. Consultants with skills in these topics specifically or in peripheral areas of interest flock to these shows to work the crowds, that is, to find potential clients.

Many consultants (but not all) take advantage of these topical trade exhibitions to make their presence known by manning exhibit booths where they display their services. Here they can personally hand out their trade literature to visitors passing by their displays. They can even waylay attendees to sit down and discuss with them how their skills and expertise could be used profitably by the attendees. They obtain the business cards of those expressing an interest for a later follow-up.

There are consultants who do not believe being an exhibitor at a trade show is profitable. Weiss (1992), for one, considers that the costs for exhibiting do not justify the contacts that are obtained. This has been my personal observation. There is a problem with this promotional approach as many consultants see it, according to Weiss. As an exhibitor, the more narrowly focused consultant receives a broad array of contacts. Many of these are from attendees with little or no interest in the product or service being exhibited. Out of politeness they take the literature being offered and docilely allow their identity cards to be imprinted so they may receive even more literature. These no-interest contacts are too costly for consultants to follow up. Such a promotional activity is too much like a shotgun approach to seeking clients. Consequently, there are some consultants who shun exhibiting at such trade shows and exhibitions. Nevertheless, it cannot be denied that exhibiting at shows does keep a consultant's name before the attending public. As one colleague who is very keen on exhibiting put it, "At least they know I'm still alive." Clients ought not to neglect trade shows as one of many opportunities to meet consultants.

The browsers, those non-exhibiting consultants, attend exhibitions as venues to meet old clients and to make new contacts. By not being tied to an exhibit booth, they are more flexible to target their specific clients by prearranging a meeting somewhere other than on the exhibit floor. They choose to meet in an atmosphere more conducive to conversation by arranging to meet the targeted client for breakfast, lunch, or dinner, or over drinks to discuss one-on-one how the potential client's needs could be served.

These meetings are not, however, good opportunities to get anything more than an introduction, because of the hectic nature of exhibitions. Certainly slightly better opportunities for meetings with consultants are afforded over social events at the trade show luncheons and dinners. However, neither meetings at the booth nor contacts over luncheons offer good occasions to discuss business. There is neither the time nor the privacy. These introductory meetings are only that — introductory.

DIRECTORIES

Trade directories provide listings of consultants and consulting and research laboratories and institutes. These can be found in a visit to any public library with a reference section. Professional associations in which consultants may be members have directories in which consultants may be classified as such. Governments may also provide directory listings of consultants. For example, the Centre de recherche et de développement sur les aliments, a division of Agriculture and Agrifood Canada, publishes a list of food consultants for Quebec. Special interest groups, such as the Institute of Food Technologists (IFT), Institute for Thermal Processing Specialists (ITPS), the Institute for Food Science and Technology (U.K.)(IFST), and the Canadian Institute of Food Science and Technology (CIFST), have membership lists and some, for example IFT and IFST, list consultants under this heading.

Trade associations maintain lists of consultants and will provide these upon request. Referrals by the associations should not be construed as recommendations. Associations are quick to explain that although they provide a list, their referral does not in any way imply an endorsement of those listed. Trade directories can be very useful tools for searching for consultants. In them, clients can find consultants classified according to their specialties and their geographic location. This information can simplify a client's search. The Web is a more novel way to find consultants. Many consulting firms have Web pages with a Web master who can be contacted for further information.

Directories help clients find names of consultants, what they specialize in, and where they are located. However, they provide no information on the reliability or level of competence of the consultants. This information can be gained only through an investigation of references and personal interviews.

ADVERTISEMENTS

Clients may find consultants through advertisements in business and financial news-papers. These announcements usually describe a course or seminar the consultant is conducting. Consultants also advertise in specialized journals or trade magazines devoted to their particular areas of expertise. However, it is not a common practice for consultants to place advertisements. The approach is too hit-and-miss, too unfo-cused. In this respect, it is similar to the problems consultants face by exhibiting at trade shows. It provides the consultant with too broad a spectrum of contacts for follow-up.

The results from my own efforts at placing advertisements are somewhat comical but typical of the response received by many consultants. I received an offer to supervise the design and construction of a large food plant in India. In payment I would receive part of the production from the plant that I could sell to recover my fee. This was, I thought, somewhat better than another response to my advertisement. The assignment was to supervise the design and construction of a food plant in Brazil. I would be paid from the proceeds of a sale of a shipload of lumber which would be sold in Japan for me where I would have to go to collect my money. Most follow-ups to inquiries obtained through advertisements have brought me:

- Numerous requests to design restaurants or devise menu schedules for schools, penal institutes, etc. Areas in which I have no expertise.
- Requests from frustrated amateur and professional cooks for recipes or answers to cooking questions.
- Countless *curricula vitae* from people seeking jobs.
- Requests from company librarians and other consulting firms for copies of my credentials, my trade literature, lists of my past and present clients and my financial statements. These would be filed and cross-referenced!!!!

Needless to say, I stopped advertising early in my career and concentrated on attracting clients through networking, the topic of the next section.

Clients would do well to look beyond advertisements in trade and business magazines. Not all consultants advertise routinely or regularly in these vehicles and any lists prepared from advertisements would be woefully narrow in scope. No avenues should be ignored, of course, but clients are wise not to use these as their sole source for finding consultants.

NETWORKING

Activity in professional associations and fraternal associations provides clients with opportunities to meet with consultants over dinner and during coffee breaks during meetings. Where clients and consultants are both active in a professional or fraternal association, clients have excellent opportunities to see the organizational and per-sonal capabilities of consultants through committee work for the association.

Clients or their representatives attending these affairs can gather a wealth of literature and business cards with which to develop a small library of names of consultants. Thus there are within any organization either a formally collected library of descriptive literature published by consultants in the client's information center or informally collected libraries held by individuals within the organization. These collections can be valuable sources of names of consultants who have the skills the client may need.

This constitutes networking. Consultants also network in order to meet as many potential clients as they can. They network to meet those who can introduce them to new potential clients. They too join social and athletic clubs, trade organizations, and charitable and fraternal groups. It is inevitable that potential client and consultant meet. Networking is two-edged this way: clients meet and get met by consultants. Only the rare individual has not been introduced to, or worked on committees with, a member who is a consultant. The almost traditional exchange of business cards upon introductions is a form of networking.

By far, the most common and sure way for clients to find consultants is to inquire for referrals or comments about consultants through business colleagues. This, too, is networking. It is most conveniently done within the environments of those clubs or organizations in which they are members. A client looking for a consultant or wishing to learn more about certain consultants can inquire of other members. These members may discuss in a positive or negative fashion their own experiences with these consultants; they may comment on the excellent results — word-of-mouth advertising — received from a particular consultant. Those who hear this and may be in the market for a consultant have a reliable reference.

Weiss (1992), Connor and Davidson (1990), and Tuller (1992) all stress the value that referrals from satisfied clients have been to their own consultancies. Bradshaw (1987) estimated that 80 to 90% of a consultant's business will come from referrals. Obviously, referrals are a route to be investigated thoroughly by clients in their search for competent and capable consultants. The best route to obtaining referrals for clients is by networking in organizations, getting comments from those who have had first-hand experience with the consultants.

Allowing their staff to take time to network by being members of, and active in, organizations can be valuable for clients, not only for finding consultants but also for keeping their organizations aware of developments in many fields. Clients can widen their contacts with useful and possibly influential people by encouraging their staff to join and be active in various social clubs, professional associations, and other service organizations. This is one very useful function of the client's membership in the country club — networking, exchanging views, gathering information, and hearing comments from others. This exchange is not always just to find consultants. Participation in the activities of organizations provides members with a firsthand knowledge of the skills, expertise, and experience of others who might be valuable resources in nonconsulting roles in the future.

If the hunt is for a reliable consultant, networking as a tool provides two advantages:

- It provides a means of finding the names of consultants or the sources of those names. In the environment of these organizations, clients can see and know firsthand how the consultant works with others.

• Second, within this networking environment, clients can sift the opinions and comments from others who might have had closer associations with the consultant.

Every avenue to find the best consultant with the skills and compatibility a client needs should be explored. Compatibility as a factor in selection is nearly as important as the skills and experience a consultant may bring. The consultant may have to work intimately with the client's staff. Networking in the contexts depicted above can provide a means to evaluate that compatibility. Some confirmation that the key members of the client's organization who will be most closely involved with the consultant will feel comfortable is possibly important to the success of the project. Temporarily the consultant will become a member of the client's staff, needing, like any team member, the confidence of the other members.

Networking can provide valuable references which can be useful in emergency situations. Clients must realize, however, that these are secondhand references. Where time permits, personal interviews with consultants are essential and preferred.

PREPARING THE SHORT LIST

Using all the possible sources at their disposal, clients can make a list of a number of likely consultants who could service the issues confronting their organizations. These lists should initially be broad, including even consultants who may seem to be on the periphery of their concerns. The selection of candidates can be narrowed down later. Clients may investigate several consultants before they are comfortable with their choice.

Clients have many factors to balance in their investigations:

• The training and depth of expertise the consultant has.
• The years of experience in the particular field the client desires assistance in.
• Other skills and resources to complement the main interest.
• Communication skills and compatibility.

There are other criteria to be reviewed, for example, availability of the consultant for the task, outcome of investigating the consultant's references and, of course, costs. Clients should prepare a list of specific questions for consultants. Included on this list should be:

• What particular expertise do the consultants have in the topics in which the client is interested?
• How many years of experience does the consulting firm have. How many years of experience has the consultant who will be assigned to your project?
• What examples of previous work are available and easily accessed as testimonies to the consultant's skills or abilities?
• Are there references from other clients that can be investigated by the client on a first-person basis?

- Will the consultant be able to perform under the time, environmental, and urgency constraints the client foresees?
- Who will actually perform the work and what portions of the work may be subcontracted? If some portions of the work are subcontracted, will it be inspected by the original contracting consultant and will this consultant be responsible for it?
- If the project is negotiated because of, and through, one consultant, i.e., the big-name consultant, but will be assigned to someone else in that consultant's organization, what will be the input from the big-name consultant to the project? Who is the consultant assigned to the project? What qualifications, references, and experience does the assignee have? During the peak periods of the project will the big-name consultant and the assignee be readily available?
- What costs might be anticipated for the project?

A question to be put to those who referred the consultant or who provided references would probe what feelings of mutual confidence and respect the consultant inspired among those most closely involved during the undertaking. The client will find that the answers to these general questions are a great assistance in narrowing the field to a manageable few.

One consideration respecting fees should be addressed. Clients were previously cautioned not to base judgments solely on fees and costs. They have to value expertise and experience more than fees and costs. A demurrer must be made to this caution. When clients choose a big-name consultant on the basis of this person's skills and credentials and find that in consequence they are paying big-name fees for work undertaken in whole or in part by a lesser-skilled underling in the consultant's organization, they may want to rethink their choice. They must determine what the involvement of the experienced consultant for whom they opted will be. That person's expertise is what they are paying for.

Years of work in a particular area is a very important clue as to how experienced consultants are. Clients do not want to discover that their consultants are less versed in a particular topic than they or members of their own staff are. Degrees, certificates, and licenses are all avenues of investigation into a consultant's background. Dubious credentials should be investigated or challenged.

Besides these general questions, clients will have others that reflect more directly their specific requirements. The answers will all play some part in the final choice of a consultant.

Where the client's needs are for something tangible, questions should not be necessary. Clients can evaluate "bricks-and-mortar" things. Where a new factory is needed, clients can inspect and evaluate other engineering and architectural projects their prospective consultants have done.

The difficulty in evaluating consultants arises when the projects under consideration are less tangible and dwell on the side of consulting referred to as the "soft side." These projects lack anything tangible that can be inspected, measured, or operated. Here, with soft projects, clients will do well to ask for references and probe previous clients carefully to determine how satisfied they were.

Other checks on consultants can be made through the Better Business Bureau and other industry associations of which the client may be a member or have access to. These sources can be used to investigate whether there have been any complaints lodged against the consultant.

Employment of a consultant is plainly and simply one of "buyer beware." The client is in control of the selection process and that control should be exercised. The important warning for the client is to check and recheck as time permits.

THE CONSULTANT'S SIDE OF FINDING CLIENTS

There is some merit at this point to examining how consultants obtained their clients. This reversal of looking at the hunt from the prey's point of view, so to speak, was touched briefly earlier in this chapter. By investigating the ways consultants have found their clients, clients will see more clearly what the successful routes to finding consultants are.

Weiss (1992) found that most clients found consultants in one of the following ways:

- Referrals.   A referral is a recommendation from a satisfied client passed on in a networking situation. Weiss refers to this as passive marketing, largely because it is out of the consultant's hands. The consultant cannot exercise any control over this process except to leave every client pleased with the work done.
- Repute.   Weiss distinguishs this from referrals. Here the consultant's name is passed on by a third party who may not be familiar with the consultant's work but is aware of his reputation from information supplied by someone else.
- Professional affiliations.   These can be found in Buyer's Guides, trade directories, or listings supplied by organizations or governmental agencies.
- Databases.   These are libraries of potential consultants kept by companies on a "just-in-case" basis.
- Advertising.   Weiss does not consider advertising a very successful route for making one's presence known as a consultant. My views on this have been expressed earlier. Advertising as an approach, besides being expensive, is much too broad and gathers in too many unfruitful contacts that are costly to follow up.
- Personal contact.   This is a more haphazard approach depending as it does on an introduction, usually through some third party.

(It must be understood, if it is not already, that Weiss has written a book for consultants to be used by consultants to improve their businesses.)

In my experience, most clients have found me through referrals or by repute. Work I did with a turnkey construction company led to several referrals from their clients. The stimulus for many of these was a need to resolve a crisis. A listing prepared by the Canadian government which I was unaware of brought a client.

Another contacted me because I had written a book about new product development. A consultant never knows where the results of work done will lead.

LOOKING FOR A CONSULTANT IN AN EMERGENCY

Many of my clients started our association with a crisis of some nature that required outside assistance. These were not earthshaking crises involving issues of public health but they did concern problems of processing or product failures encountered in the expansion of markets, in the development of novel products, or in inefficient operation of their research and development or quality control groups. The initial contact was the result of some crisis and the means of contact was through a referral route.

My colleagues in the consulting field with whom I network have had similar experiences. It has usually been some critical event that brought client and consultant together. The mechanism bringing the two together was most frequently a referral. It should not be assumed that referrals are the only routes to consultants in a time of emergency. It is, however, advantageous to phone an associate or a contact who has had a similar emergency for advice and referrals to those with experience in resolving the dilemma faced.

This merely emphasizes the point made by others (Bradshaw, 1987; Connor and Davidson, 1990; Weiss, 1992; and Tuller, 1992) that this route, through referrals, is a favored and frequent way to obtain contacts with consultants. It is particularly useful in emergencies because it short circuits the route described here for less hectic times. If the sources are reliable, clients can contact consultants without further time-consuming research to assist them.

Clients facing emergencies should ask around among colleagues in the business community. Inquiries can be directed to:

- Other companies or individuals who perhaps have faced a similar problem. Many company presidents belong to elite associations of senior executives, e.g., Young Presidents Club. Within these circles much valuable information can be exchanged with other executives who have encountered similar problems.
- Ingredient suppliers, equipment suppliers, or trade associations who may be able to provide names of consultants or who may be able to assist through their own technical service departments.
- Departments or schools in universities dedicated to the field in which the need for assistance is apparent. These are good sources of expert witnesses.
- Government departments that may be able to provide assistance depending on the nature of the problem. These are excellent sources of assistance in international matters where embassies and consular offices in foreign countries are knowledgeable about reliable local resources.

All these can be sources of good referrals, evaluations, and recommendations on a quick referral basis. Clients should not overlook the local Better Business Bureau, which frequently has counterparts in both domestic and foreign cities, for a quick check on whether there have been any complaints lodged against a particular consultant.

There are other resources — the client's own. A catalogue of consultants may have been started in many cases long before a crisis has become a major problem. Most clients have developed databases of consultants that can very useful in emergencies. These libraries of information allow the quick preparation of a short list.

The major difference between hunting for a consultant at the client's leisure and finding one in the midst of a crisis is time. The principles of looking remain the same. During crises, clients do not always have time to follow-up references thoroughly but must rely on the esteem that consultants are held in by others who may have used their services. Nor do consultants and clients have much opportunity except in the exigencies of the crisis to determine whether theirs will be the best working relationship. Nevertheless, it is imperative that clients attempt some quick checks and still ask pertinent questions of their consultants.

To choose the right consultant even in time of crisis, clients must be clear on what their problems are. What do they want to accomplish through the use of a consultant? If this is not clearly established, clients run the risk of putting the responsibility of crisis management into the hands of a stranger, the consultant, perhaps the wrong consultant with an incorrect solution.

Haste, indeed, makes waste, and clients should never select a consultant blindly — even in haste. Clients ought always to be prepared, and one way to be prepared is to be aware of the consulting resources that are available that could serve them should the need ever arise. In an emergency, the need has arisen.

Clients know their businesses. They know the best sources of parts, raw materials and supplies, and other services. Put bluntly, consultants are another commodity clients should have reliable sources of, and they should know their "market value" as they do of any other supply and supplier.

SUMMARY

In most instances, clients have begun a repository of names of consultants either systematically or informally long before the need to employ them has arisen. The client or someone within the client's organization has brushed shoulders at some time with a consultant, and there has been an exchange of business cards. The collection of cards and literature gathered at conferences (reprints and lists of speakers) and at trade shows can provide a rather impressive library of contacts for a client.

These databases can partially serve both the noncritical and critical needs of clients for finding consultants. In addition to these in-house resources, the trade directories, registries, and listings in professional associations will help find consultants. For example, over 300 members of the Institute of Food Technologists (U.S.A.) classify themselves as "consultant" in the 1993–1994 IFT Directory of Affiliations. Their publication, *Food Technology*, annually provides a classified guide to food industry services which lists many consultants and laboratories specializing in food science, food technology, food analyses, and food regulations.

Finding consultants is rarely ever a problem for clients even in emergencies. A much bigger problem for clients is understanding what the needs are for which they have to refer to a consultant. They ought to select the most appropriate consultant, not the cheapest nor the most fashionable and faddish.

6 Working with the Consultant

So much of what we call management consists in making it difficult for people to work.

Peter Drucker

INTRODUCTION

Management, as Peter Drucker, a noted management authority, makes plain, can be the source of difficulties in any organization. Management can also be the source of difficulties when working with consultants. Good managers work efficiently and quietly, competently utilizing the skills of those around them. They provide leadership and give praise and encouragement where it is due. They bring out the best and get the best out of their staff and out of consultants. Unfortunately, there are managers who clutter the working lives of their staff with useless detail, write meaningless directives, and generally muddle through. When faced with problems or with decision-making with which they are not comfortable, they manage by removing themselves from these perplexities. They put layers of lower levels of management between themselves and that which they do not comprehend. In effect, they solve the problem by giving it to someone else. Then they pat themselves on the back for being such good managers. Drucker's observation is a very likely one — management by poor managers can make it very difficult, indeed, for people to work.

Management skills, or the lack of them, can make it difficult for good working relationships to develop between the client's staff and a consultant. As a consequence of the managerial ineptness of their clients, consultants can be hindered in reaching their clients' objectives. Clients must manage their resources and their staff to produce amicable consultant relationships that cause the least interruption of work routines and that keep staff morale high.

In this chapter, the deed has been done. That is, the clients have defined their needs. They have selected the appropriate consultant. Both parties believe they have a clear understanding of the proposal and its content and what is expected of the two sides in this relationship. That belief may not always be well founded. This chapter will first discuss the problems that may arise and then suggest avenues by which clients can minimize these and receive maximum benefits from the exercise.

LOOKING OVER WHAT MAY NOT ALWAYS BE A FOUR-LEAF CLOVER

There now begins an activity by an *outside* resource, the consultant, on behalf of the client. There are many environments in which this relationship can take place:

- First, consultants may work completely isolated physically from their clients. Indeed, they may have no need to interact with their clients until the final results of the completed project are presented, for example audit of products at the store level in several geographic areas or an analysis of particular market segments in foreign markets.
- Second, some interplay between consultant and client is required. The consultant requires data on key business activities, or the physical assistance of production to run manufacturing trials, or the presence of select staff for seminars or training programs in-house. The disruption is usually for short periods of time, perhaps just a day's visit every week or two.
- Finally, considerable input is needed which can be highly intrusive and potentially disruptive to the business activities of clients. Consultants may be on the client's premises daily and perhaps active in day-to-day business. Staff may be absent for extensive training sessions or to provide assistance at some distant location.

Each of these working relationships can bring its own difficulties that clients must organize themselves to minimize.

THE CLIMATE FOR CONFLICT

The problems, or challenges, which this stranger in their environment may bring to clients can be minimized if:

- First, clients recognize that they can occur and be on guard for the appearance of any *contretemps*. Forewarned is forearmed.
- Second, clients keep themselves updated on what their consultants are doing and actively look for potential trouble spots.

The tenet that clients need to always remember is that consultants were called to provide some service for them. Consultants were not empowered to run or disrupt their business activities. Therefore, the activities of consultants require monitoring. No outside resources ought to operate without some awareness by clients of their activities. Consultants are one more resource to be utilized, i.e., managed, wisely. For example, clients would never allow a department or division to operate in isolation from the grand plan of the organization. Communication from all the parts of their organization is essential to good management. What clients do not want are nasty surprises resulting from the activities of their consultants.

Sources of Conflict

Difficulties for clients are magnified when the work of their consultants must be done onsite. The problems that arise can weaken staff morale and hamper the work that consultants must undertake. By closely monitoring activities and being aware of their staff's reactions, clients can anticipate any problems and take necessary action to reduce or eliminate these.

The problems arise from dissimilar facets of the same source, the proposal. They are:

- The project itself. Something goes haywire despite the best planning.
- Problems arising between clients and their consultants, with fault falling on both parties.
- Problems caused by the presence or activities of the consultants among their client's staff.

PROBLEMS ORIGINATING WITH THE PROJECT ITSELF

The poet, Robert Burns, observed in his poem, *To a Mouse,* that "The best-laid schemes o' mice and men gang aft a-gley." To this can certainly be added the plans laid out in proposals. This unpredictability gives full value to that inescapable law of Murphy's that what can go wrong will.

Work described in proposals cannot be assumed to be uninfluenced by other activities that will occur as the work progresses. Circumstances that prompted the project are constantly altered, shaped, and reshaped by both forces internal and external to clients and their organizations. They are molded by everything in the environment surrounding the clients.

Forces Altering Projects

Many forces can alter the substance or direction of projects as work on them progresses:

- Competition to the client in the marketplace moves dramatically and unexpectedly. For example, a competitor introduces a radically new product or a more aggressive marketing program;
- Social forces cause consumers to change, and closely akin to this, social activism occurs regarding issues that the clients face.
- Technology develops which could greatly affect the desirability or superiority of the clients' present products.
- There are changes in legislation which affect how business is conducted or establish new standards to which products must be made, etc.
- The economic circumstances on which a project was based have changed drastically.

These all are reasons to rethink the value of continuing the project. Ignoring them could result in unwanted consequences and expenses.

A new technology can make unnecessary a project that is based on an older, now outdated technology. If, for instance, the newer technology permits a competitor to introduce a line of products with superior qualities, clients will want to redirect their new product research activities. Clients might now wish to rethink the project's direction and value.

The new technology need not be some monumental discovery. A novel application based on old technology can have ripple effects in many other areas where companies have projects under way., e.g., a new packaging material or an electrically conductive paint. For instance, a newly announced electrically conductive paint can replace heating elements like radiators in rooms; it can be used on runways to aid airplanes using infrared detection in landing; it can be used by the military to draw enemy fire to painted decoys and away from vital targets. Thus, a development in one field could influence the course of projects in several other fields.

Consumers can change in their likes and dislikes in the course of a project. Consumers can no longer be accepted as brand-loyal, docile sheep. Today they are more dynamic, better educated, and informed. They age; they are seduced by new fads; and the whims of the marketplace favor one product style and then another. Projects, if based on what proves to be a consumer whim, will require rethinking.

On the other hand, misreading a trend in consumer tastes as a fad can also force the redirection of projects. IBM's persistence with bigness in computers caused it to miss the beginning of the personal computer trend. It forced the company to rethink its marketing strategy but only after a disastrous fall in share value and loss of market share.

Social activism can be a powerful factor affecting clients. Women's groups deplore the demeaning depiction of women in promotions and advertising. The elderly ("grey power" groups) demand products meeting their needs and abilities. Promotional campaigns and product development programs are redirected.

An example is sudden increase in deaths of children and injuries from the misuse of all-terrain vehicles. A similar increase in accidents resulting in deaths from single-person, motorized boats, plus the annoyance value these boats and vehicles have, has led to a public outcry against their use. The public demanded legislation imposing restrictions on their use, and a reduction of their horsepower and of their noise level. Manufacturers are quickly changing marketing strategies and the horsepower of these vehicles, and attempting to polish tarnished images.

New government legislation will change rules in the marketplace and so alter the nature of a project. For example:

- Advertising directed at children is restricted.
- Safety or manufacturing standards for certain products are published, for example, emissions from autos.
- Trade restrictions or embargoes cut the availability of raw materials or parts.
- Approval of some ingredient has been rescinded for food use.

All can spark changes in the programs they touch.

A sudden and spectacular upward spiraling of the cost of an internationally traded commodity, a vegetable oil, caused the collapse of interest in the further development of some new oil-based products that I was involved with. A new line of product development was quickly found, but the project had to be redirected.

Developments external to the client and the consultant may cause both to re-examine their objectives and to abort a particular project. It may be redirected to more socially or publicly acceptable goals. Anything can make original plans "gang aft a-gley."

Developments in the Project

A change in the original project can be precipitated by unexpected observations that are made in the course of the work. For example:

- In a multistage project, one step in the series of necessary activities is found to be too costly. Going from A to C involves a step A to B which produces B, the desired intermediate, in too small a yield.
- The technology to accomplish any one step in a series in a reasonable time is unavailable. Developing the technology is not in the interest or within the capability of the client.
- Early observations in the project may lead to startling or unusual conclusions that require a redirection of the entire project into more exciting avenues.
- Unexpectedly hostile reactions to the conductance of a project demand a reconsideration of its continuance.

Any of these or variations of them result in a project's redirection.

Clients must be aware of all developments and implications for themselves as a project unfolds, since any observation may require its reassessment. As stated earlier, the need for, importance of, and substance or nature of projects change with a variety of pressures within and without the client's environment and as the project develops.

Problems Between the Client and the Consultant

A proposal should have clearly explained to the client all the engagement letters and contracts, costs, reporting procedures, and involvement required on the client's part (for example, the hidden costs) and the responsibilities of the consultant. Nevertheless, problems can and do arise, especially if clients adopt a *laissez-aller* attitude toward consultants and their activities.

There is a strong warning to clients here. By calling in consultants, clients ask strangers to their environment to provide them with a service from which they expect to receive some value. The project is another aspect of the client's business, much like marketing, sales, finance, or operations over which the client exercises control. And just like these activities, the consultant's activities deserve the client's full attention. Clients ought to view consultants and their activities as any other business activity to be managed. This latter point cannot be stressed too much.

It must be made abundantly clear what is meant by managing the consultant or the consultant's activity:

- It means keeping a loose rein on the consultant and all activities related to the consultant.
- It means being aware of what the consultant is doing and monitoring how this activity is affecting staff, customers, suppliers, the environment, and the community — in short, what has been called the ecology of the client.

- It means being aware of the progress, if any, that has been made in the project, the direction the work is taking, and the impact the progress and direction are having throughout the organization and the community.

Control does not mean interference with, or redirection of the consultant's activities. It does not mean second-guessing the consultant.

Control certainly does mean that clients must not forget that they do have projects placed with consultants in progress that require their attention like any other activities in their organizations. Awareness is necessary if clients should find it expedient to intervene *for valid reasons* at some later date in the progress. Awareness can only be accomplished through monitoring.

What are some "valid reasons"? These could be any of the following:

- Costs getting out-of-hand through misapplication or an inappropriate use of funds in the project.
- Staff becoming demoralized or disrupted too much by the intervention of the consultant. They could even be being abused or harassed because of the training methods applied by the consultant.
- Production down because of nonsanctioned interventions by the consultant.
- Bad publicity in the community or among customers resulting from the project's progress or due to new procedures introduced by the consultant which have repercussions outside the client's premises.
- Lack of progress for various reasons, including invalid procedures employed by the consultant.
- Lack of regular and full communication of the progress by the consultant, especially when the activities of the consultant are offsite.

These are just causes for immediate discussions with the consultant and later perhaps for intervention by the client with the consultant.

Some of the items on the list of valid reasons deserve further explanation. Clients are hiring consultants for the specialized expertise these people will bring their organizations. Clients cannot be expected to be knowledgeable about the esoteric technologies or methodologies their consultants may apply. This puts clients at a disadvantage in assessing the work or in evaluating any progress.

This lack of knowledgeability should not prevent clients from questioning the validity of the results obtained, the progress that is being made, the impact on their staff as these technologies are applied, or even the methodologies employed by the consultants. Clients should make consultants explain, and explain in language they, the paying clients, understand.

The second issue is this. In promoting their services, consultants may inject, advertently or inadvertently, some hyperbole into promises of what they can do or what the value of the business philosophies or other technical theories they espouse will bring. Clients would be wise to remember that. This hyperbole should have been stripped away by questioning and challenging those methodologies when the proposal was submitted. It is imperative that methodologies and findings during the progress of the work that clients are confused by or do not agree with be questioned.

It is the responsibility of the client to learn, to gain knowledge, to evaluate, and to understand what is going on.

Knowledge and methodology are the intellectual property of the consultant. Consultants are not gods: they can and do err. The client's prerogative is to decide if the results or activities of the project are applicable or even proper for the organization. Here there can be conflict.

PROBLEMS FROM STAFF/CONSULTANT INTERACTIONS

A variety of difficulties can arise from interactions between the consultant and the client's staff. These are likely to occur whether the activities of the consultant are onsite or offsite. They are frequently derived from any of the following:

- Frequent interruptions of routines and work schedules by the consultant.
- Resentment to the access that consultants have to the client's senior management. Somehow the consultant who is frequently onsite always manages to monopolize the boss's time.
- Confusion, irritation, concern, and insecurity among the client's staff as they are interrogated and challenged by the consultant about their routine activities during the course of the consultant's activities.
- Resentment by some of the client's staff to the very presence of outsiders "on their territory."
- The need for (confiscation of) office space and equipment by the consultant, no matter how temporarily, may dislocate staff and cause them some insecurity.

From these situations, trifling as they seem, very real difficulties can arise which may hamper the progress of the project.

Disruption of Routines

Businesses run on routine, and staff have their own subroutines, their personal ways of doing things. Activities are scheduled to accommodate the needs of the marketplace in an orderly fashion. Production is scheduled to keep pace with the purchasing of parts, raw materials, and ingredients, and the delivery of finished goods to distributors and customers. Management wants to maintain low inventories. Just-in-time delivery policies require tight scheduling of purchasing and production.

The annoyance of a production floor supervisor responsible for a product quota is understandable when his schedule is interrupted by a consultant planning a test production batch. Such trials of new equipment or new procedures are very disruptive. They require dismantling a productive processing line to fiddle with something. Material is used up; overtime may be needed to make up production; and the sales forces are deprived of enough product to sell. Their annoyance falls on the production supervisor, not the consultant.

Where the production personnel are on production bonuses, nonproductive experimental production runs are, indeed, resented. Production targets might not be met;

bonuses might be less than hoped. Consultants can see special production work done sloppily or as rapidly as possible with only cursory attention paid to the special detail the new procedures require. This sloppiness serves neither the clients nor the consultants well. Interruptions irritate staff pressed with getting the client's business and production out on time. Staff, absent to attend training sessions, return to desks piled high with tasks held for their attention. Frustration can prevail. Resentment to the interruptions develops, and with resentment comes a reluctance to cooperate wholeheartedly.

When staff are in seclusion at some training resort or enduring some wilderness experience for a week or two, considerable disruption occurs in the client's affairs. These absences interfere with family life of staff as well.

Time taken from other tasks must be reckoned by clients as one of the hidden costs in the project. They should have clearly in mind before the beginning of the work the hidden costs that are caused by the absence of staff or by the disruption of production.

Resentment to the Consultant's Freedom of Action

Staff need access to their immediate superiors and to the more senior ranks of management. Having an audience with "the boss" or the boss's boss is looked on as a privilege, and to have the boss's ear is prized much like any business perk, such as a parking spot with one's name on it. Not having this access or having it disrupted frequently will annoy those accustomed to this privilege.

When the consultant has ready access to senior management, lower levels of management can be frustrated, jealous, envious, and fearful of the consultant. Lack of access may seem like a petty issue — and it is — but petty issues have a habit of becoming major ones when access to senior management is denied or reduced. There is competition for this access and competitors are rivals.

What staff see is an outsider who pops in and out with no responsibilities for day-to-day work and who is not subject to the (unwritten) mores of the organization. There begins to be a seed of jealousy that that upstart has more of the boss's ear than they do. The consultant becomes a rival for some who want or need the boss's time. If the consultant's activities impinge on the "empires" or "turfs" of some individuals, fear and insecurity can develop. They fear the meetings with the consultant are about them.

Interrogations and Challenges: the Clash

One management consultant starts his training program with: "Whatever you have been doing before is all wrong and I am here to set you right." How does one react? How is the staff supposed to react? This opener may have been, in this consultant's opinion, a dynamic beginning meant to get everyone's attention. It may have made him feel very positive, but it irritated many in the room, including myself. And frightened some. One poor soul came to me afterward asking whether she had been doing everything wrong. Some may even see the consultant's attitude as abusive by accusing them of doing things incorrectly and, by inference, calling their intelligence into question.

As the consultant pokes, prods, and questions people about their activities, asking why certain things are done in particular ways, an element of insecurity may creep into the staff. They are challenged. They feel inadequate if all they can answer is "it's the way we've always done it," or "that's the way I was taught." They feel defensive.

There can be another clash. This time from the so-called management gurus. Kay (1996) reported an incidence of a "process re-engineering program" (a phrase Kay describes as "unorthodox business training"). The training techniques caused some participants to seek psychiatric counseling. Independent psychiatrists reported that the participants had been subjected to "coercive persuasion," otherwise known as brainwashing.

Some management training programs can reach ludicrous extremes. They include wilderness training, which may involve contrived emergency situations in which the trainees must cooperate to "save" someone, or play acting to "let it all hang out," or being required to verbally abuse the colleague sitting next to them and listening to that colleague in turn verbally abuse his companion and so on around the discussion table. Responsible persons in the client's organization should vet all training programs to avoid any unpleasant situations.

Some consultants may take an adversarial role in their attempts to ferret out information. When work habits and established procedures are challenged or "corrected," staff may feel insecure and be demoralized.

"You're on My Turf"

The client's staff will resent "them," the consultants. Isn't this an admission that they couldn't handle the work themselves? That they were less than competent? Certainly some staff do feel this sense of inferiority. The plant manager who told me he would answer all my questions was being very truthful. He answered all my questions. Despite his ready answers, he was, in fact, not very cooperative. Eventually, I found this out to my distress. When I later queried him as to why he had not proffered some essential piece of information when he knew the line of my inquiries, he merely told me: "You didn't ask me that." He then admitted he greatly resented my presence and saw no reason why the company had to air its dirty linen to an outsider.

One consultant requires that his client provide him with an office from which he does all his work. He argues that this allows the client to see that he, the consultant, is actively engaged in business for the client. Office expenses are immediately apparent to the client so there is no hassle over presenting verification for these. Even his travel is carried out through the client's travel agency. His activities have only a minor disruptive effect on the client's office routine, no disruption of the schedules of senior and middle management, and they simplify much of the paperwork involved with his activities. The biggest problem, he claims, is his: he can work with only one client at a time.

I would challenge his interpretation. Moving in with the client puts this consultant squarely on someone else's turf. This risks giving him a high-profile presence which his client's staff are very aware of. They may resent this. They see him able to carry out his activities more freely than they can. They see the access that he has to senior management and the accord he receives from them. Someone probably has been physically displaced to make room for him.

Consultants should keep as low a profile as possible and not give the appearance of being "modern-day alchemists... (who)...dazzle their clients" (Shahin, 1995).

ESTABLISHING A WORKING RELATIONSHIP

Clients must keep abreast of all developments that are taking place as the activities of their consultants progresses. This *sine qua non* holds for any undertaking, from research placed with a university to construction projects to problem-solving to crisis management to management training. There are no exceptions. Good communication between consultants and their clients alerts clients to problems with the project itself, with its progress, or with the behavior of the individual consultants which might need to be addressed at once.

An example where closer control should have been kept by the client occurred in the province of Quebec. The provincial government hired outside resources to develop a promotional brochure describing Montreal as a *bilingual* city to which American businesses could move branch offices with confidence. At the same time, the Quebec minister responsible for language legislation, Louise Beaudoin, was asserting that it was not Quebec's policy that Montreal could, or ever would, be officially bilingual. Someone ought to have worked more closely with the experts developing the brochures to ensure that they conformed to the client's, that is, the Quebec government's, policies. The client certainly should preview any material before it is released to avoid embarrassment and be aware through advance copies of what the message is intended to be.

The first necessity for clients in establishing a productive working relationship with responsible client control is the development of good channels of communication with their consultants. The links should be from a senior, responsible person on the consultant's staff who is intimately involved in the work and a similarly ranked responsible individual within the client's organization.

ESTABLISHING GOOD COMMUNICATION LINKS

Good communication keeps clients aware of what is happening in their organizations, what progress has occurred on the project, and how these developments affect, or will affect, staff, production, their communities, and customers. This can be done in many ways:

- A client can insist on frequent briefings held at regular intervals. If necessary, these briefings can be required daily. Obviously, such frequency of communication is best carried out where the consultant's activities occur on the client's premises and developments from the project occur rapidly.

- Written, faxed or e-mailed reports can be required of the consultant at regular intervals to provide a summary of work to date. Such reports, like face-to-face briefings, do not provide clients with the opinions of the client's staff regarding the progress and developments of the project. The reports are one-sided, the consultant's side.
- Regular inspections of the consultant's activities can provide a means of good communication. Such inspections are absolutely necessary when the project takes place away from the client's premises: for example, the design and construction of a special piece of equipment or a building, or research work contracted at a university. Personal inspections keep clients abreast of developments.

Each of the above has its own drawbacks. Onsite inspections, for example, require that the client's staff be absent from their work. Nevertheless, communication must be maintained.

The most effective channels of communication are kept open by employing a combination of all the above, and the means of regular communication ought to be written into any proposal. Regular inspections of the consultant's activities are recommended by the World Bank for its borrowers to keep themselves informed of the activities of the consultants they hire (Anon. 1981). Onsite inspections (not all of which will necessarily be for construction projects) require that the client's inspector be knowledgeable enough to ask hard questions. In addition to knowledge-ability, this person should be strong and not easily subverted, dominated, or led astray from appointed objectives.

The most effective manner for clients to establish good communication channels is to appoint some knowledgeable and responsible person as a liaison between themselves and their consultant. This individual has the authority to speak for, or readily get authority to speak for, the client in all matters relating to the project. The consultant would report to this person with the frequency established in the proposal or discussed and agreed upon by the client and the consultant. Such a person could be the collator described in the previous chapter. (Reporting, in this context, refers strictly to keeping aware. There is no suggestion that reporting indicates the client wields a supervisory capacity.) Clients would insist that their consultants appoint a similar person to be the contact person for the consultant, speaking with the authority of the consultant. These two people, these two point persons, quite literally should be the only two who are allowed to communicate responsibly to one another concerning the project. Each speaks for his respective side.

THE CLIENT'S SPOKESPERSON

The client's contact person should have the authority and responsibility to make available within the client's organization any documents, technical information, office equipment and other facilities, production time on the plant floor, etc., to enable the project to progress under the direction of the consultant or the consultant's associates. Individuals designated as spokespersons ought to have been thoroughly briefed by their superiors on what the consultants can and cannot do or can and cannot have access to. They know the limits of access their clients have imposed on the consultants.

These contact persons within the client's organization are the consultant's enablers or facilitators. They enable consultants to carry out their assignments. Clients must provide consultants with all the necessary and authorized information and assistance pertinent to the task at hand. If a consultant has questions or special needs, these are directed to one person. Such support comes through these spokespersons and these persons alone.

There is a second function for these persons besides facilitating the efforts of consultants and receiving the reports they make. These spokespersons for the clients act as the client's eyes and ears. They report back to their clients, to a senior responsible manager:

- On the progress of the research project.
- On the impact of the work, both internally on production or externally in the marketplace.
- On its impact in the client's community.
- On the reactions of staff to the implementation of new techniques imposed by the consultants or to the effects of programs on the participants.

These spokespersons are the vehicles for this communication.

The contact person representing the client's interests is not a passive agent, waiting for the consultant to report in. At times, it will be necessary for the spokesperson to dig for information from the consultant's spokesperson and from the client's staff, who are more intimately involved in the activities of the consultant, from the community, and from the client's customers.

THE CONSULTANT'S SPOKESPERSON

It is equally important that clients insist that there be a contact person appointed by their consultants. This individual represents the consultant in all matters. Ideally, this one person who speaks for, and with the authority of, the consultant should be the consultant who was engaged in all negotiations unless the terms of the proposal indicate otherwise. The client's spokesperson needs someone who can answer his or her questions authoritatively and knowledgeably.

The spokesperson for the consultant ought to be easily contactable. My personal experience has been that some consultants, especially big-name ones, can become notoriously unavailable. Where work must be conducted onsite, the spokesperson should be part of the consulting workforce.

This spokesperson would also be responsible for keeping the client's spokesperson informed of what is going on, how the project is progressing, and for interpreting what the preliminary results suggest for clients. All communications to their clients should be funneled through the consultant's contact person and only through this person. The receivers of information will be the corresponding spokesperson for the client. There are, then, two pivotal sources for keeping the communication channels open, the client's spokesperson and the consultant's spokesperson. These two people represent the ends of the channel through which authoritative and meaningful dialogue can pass.

This appointment of the consultant's spokesperson is especially important if the consultant has a team approach to the project, and there are several of the consultant's staff active on the project. The contact person representing the consultant will keep the client's contact person fully informed of developments or difficulties encountered in the project. The consulting firm will make all requests for further client involvement through their contact person.

The need for this close communication is no less important when the project takes place offsite. Indeed, it becomes even more important that clients know what is happening under their aegis offsite, perhaps in some foreign country. The contact person must simply press harder for information if it is not readily forthcoming from his or her counterpart.

Clients should avoid letting sick projects get sicker simply because they are out-of-sight-out-of-mind. Frictional problems associated with onsite work may be gone but communication is still required to ensure that everything and everybody in the offsite project is on-track.

Offsite activities require that clients combine site visits with the regular reports of their consultant's contact spokesperson. Such visits ought to be unannounced if possible. The dangers of announced visits is that frequently the inspector finds only a spit-and-polish image presented.

INFORMING STAFF ABOUT THE CONSULTANT'S ACTIVITIES

When projects require extensive activities by consultants on the client's premises, misunderstandings between the consultants and the staff can arise. The very presence of a stranger, the consultant, can be the start of all sorts of rumors. These, in turn, can be causes for unrest and misunderstanding among the staff, between clients and their customers with whom staff interface, and in the community where the staff live. Such rumors, once started, could potentially hamper the progress of the work and, hence, cause serious errors in the findings, efforts, or understanding of the consultants. Staff may become uncooperative or, like my plant manager, simply noncommunicative, which can, in turn, lead consultants into incorrect observations and conclusions. These errors, in turn, may cause clients to base business strategies on faulty data or misinformation received by consultants.

Clients can circumvent such rumors by taking positive action to prevent them prior to the arrival of their consultants. Clients should clearly announce to all staff whose activities will be affected by the presence of these strangers what the purpose of this exercise is and what cooperation may be required. Department and division heads need to be informed of any intrusions upon their areas of responsibility that might be caused by a consultant's activity. This can be done far enough in advance that, where necessary, work schedules can be changed to minimize the impact of any disruptions.

Limits to the activities or range of inquiries that consultants are permitted ought to be established and discussed with staff prior to the consultants' arrival. Those who will be concerned most directly require instructions on the limitations imposed upon information that can be given out. Staff have a right to know, if they are in doubt, what information can be given and to whom they can go for definitive answers to their questions about releasing sensitive information. This instruction and guidance for staff is a function in which the client's spokesperson can be invaluable. This person's identity must be made known to the staff, and they must be made aware that this person can answer their questions.

Usually limitations to what information can be asked for is defined between the client and the consultant prior to the start of the project. However, these restrictions need to be communicated to the client's staff, who will not have been privy to the details of these discussions or to the proposal contract. Therefore, they need to know to whom they can go for clarification.

Staff with the closest contact with consultants may require more detailed guidelines on to what extent they may provide proprietary information. These employees may feel insecure about the presence of consultants. The client's contact person should take special pains to explain the reasons for a consultant's presence and for their involvement in these activities.

This communication is especially important to those undergoing training by the consultant. Feedback from the trainees is important to the client's spokesperson. The opinions of the participants about how the program is going, whether they are indeed learning something useful, and whether the value of the techniques employed merit application in their organizations provide useful information. Again, staff members require reassurance that the consultants' presence is not a reflection on their job performance.

When clients have oiled the wheels, so to speak, with the appointment of a contact person, an ombudsman, a spokesperson — call this person what you will — and have informed the staff and made them aware of the limits of disclosure, the work of their consultants is more likely to proceed rapidly, with fewer difficulties and misunderstandings. An added benefit for the clients is that the findings of their consultants are more likely to reflect true circumstances within their environment.

PREVENTING PREJUDICED OBSERVATIONS

For whatever the task clients have brought consultants in to accomplish, they most certainly want it accomplished and reported upon in an unprejudiced and unbiased fashion. The consultant's work must be conducted in a *real world* situation, and the end-product of this endeavor must reflect that condition. It must reflect the world as it is. It must not reflect what the consultant thinks the client wants to hear. Nor should it reflect what the client's staff would like the consultant to think is the "real" situation in the marketplace, in the workplace, or wherever.

Therefore, it is important that any information given to consultants should not be whitewashed and should not bias their judgment. Consultants base their conclusions on the interpretation of the data they have received and the observations they have made. It is the task of both spokespersons to assure, as much as is humanly possible, that all information they receive is truthful, accurate, thorough and complete, and represents the real world.

Good data found in the client's records and observations on good work procedures must go with the examples of bad data and observations of sloppy, unsafe work habits. Frankness and openness must prevail if the consultant is to present unbiased findings as investigations progress. This seemingly simple observation can frequently be overlooked. When plants and workplaces are tidied up and compromising work habits and procedures hidden away, consultants can be led to incorrect conclusions about why work-related injuries are high or why QC has failed to detect flawed products.

Biasing the consultant can also work the other way. Too much help, if it can be called such, can be a factor in faulty conclusions. Helping the consultant in the investigation can be carried too far. It is frequently done innocently, but it can also be done very openly. First, clients should not direct the investigations of their consultants with selective information that favors a personal view. (The dark side of consulting, the political use of consultants, may be showing here.) There is not a consultant alive who has not heard a client, often innocently, preface remarks with something like, "I want you to find to what extent that such-and-such is causing us this grief." When assistance becomes direction for the consultant, a fine line for unbiased investigations has been crossed.

A good example of this direction happened to me while on an assignment in Puerto Rico. I had been asked to review the organization of the quality control department, evaluate the suitability of the methods used to assess quality control as these applied to the processing in a food plant, and to determine their conformance to HACCP (hazard analysis critical control point)* principles. There had been an increase in consumer complaints coupled with an increase in production costs. The following occurred:

> I was ushered in to the plant manager's second-floor office which overlooked the ground-floor manufacturing area. He showed me QC data sheets and schematic drawings of the equipment layouts of the many products the plant produced. Each was demonstrated from his glassed-in aerie on high. Everything I needed to know, he adamantly claimed, was on these drawings or described on the processing sheets. I didn't need to get my feet dirty on the plant floor! Much to his consternation I insisted on being on the floor with the work crews. My main finding after a week spent working on the plant floor and analyzing the QC data sheets was that there was little resemblance between what was on his drawings, what he thought happened on his production floor, and what actually took place there. He had little understanding of how the employees on the production floor interpreted the production protocols and how quality was measured. It rapidly became clear why product quality had fallen, productivity had slipped and why the union representative was angry.

---

* HACCP programs involve the analysis of a process in its entirety for those steps or operations which, if they are not controlled, would result in off-quality, defective, or unsafe product and either removing the hazard at that point or controlling it within safe and acceptable limits.

This plant manager's version of what happened in the plant would have produced a biased report and conclusions to management had I used only the data and information he had provided me.

Clients should exercise great care to avoid being overhelpful to the extent that the investigations by their consultants do not bear the imprint of views of some overzealous, even prejudiced, employee. Clients and their staff must avoid crossing that fine line between assistance and telling their consultants what they will find.

The dangers of tainted information can be avoided or minimized if the client's contact person reviews, *not edits*, information received by the consultant. Let it be very clear that this review is not in any manner meant to be an attempt at censorship. The reviewer, the client's contact person, can give greater or lesser credence to information the consultant has received. The consultant can later verify the information personally or make a personal judgment of the validity of this information against the backdrop of all the data that has been garnered.

No Surprises

If the two contact people, the client's liaison and that person assigned by the consultant, communicate frequently and openly, there should be a minimum of difficulties arising from any quarter as the project progresses, and neither will there be any surprises with the results obtained.

The techniques to develop this liaison can be formally written into the proposal. It can be as simple as an informal arrangement with a daily bull session about the day's activities if the consultant is on the client's premises. The nature of the task being undertaken will dictate the frequency and depth of these encounters. My own activities are largely in the applied technical fields and largely related to manufacturing. Each day on the client's premises ends with a discussion of the day's activities with my contact person, usually the plant manager. These discussions are followed up with written reports and a final summary report.

These discussions serve several purposes:

1. They allow all the observations and discussions to be sifted through a knowledgeable individual, in my example, the plant manager. Biases originating with this individual can be evaluated personally by the consultant.
2. They prepare clients for any unusual findings or surprising conclusions that ought to be rectified immediately rather than waiting for a final report.
3. Any fears regarding the consultant's presence are allayed by discussions with plant personnel and the plant manager.

Clients do not deserve, nor should they expect, surprises in the final report of their consultant. No report from a consultant should be designed to have shock value. Unusual results from any activity by the consultant should have been reported as they became apparent. Both the client's and the consultant's spokespersons ought to have reported and discussed atypical or extraordinary observations as these occurred.

By maintaining regular reporting, inspections, and site visits, clients prepare themselves early should initial studies indicate that some necessary remedial action ought to be taken. It must not be left to the discretion of the consultant whether or not to inform the client of unusual and unexpected observations that require the client's immediate attention.

GENTLE COERCION

For work that certain classes of consultants do, gently applied coercion by clients is sometimes necessary. Maintaining the impetus of the work is important to clients, and frequently they must push consultants a little bit. With professional consultants this should not be a problem but it is true, nonetheless, that the squeaky wheel does get attention. With amateurs there may possibly be a serious need to push at times. I can only draw my reader's attention to my tennis-playing academic consultant who was never available on Fridays if the weather was nice. Consultants are human and need the occasional prod to get on with the job.

To confirm progress, contact persons representing the clients should solicit information from those on their staff most intimately involved with the consultants' activities. They can provide a good assessment of the progress of the project and how it is affecting them. Together with the reports supplied by the consultants' spokespersons, clients can get a very good assessment of progress. For again, clients do not want surprises.

THE REPORT — THE PRESENTATION AND ITS CHALLENGE

Clients must insist upon this requirement: when projects have been completed, whatever their nature, clients are entitled to final, all-inclusive reports complete with conclusions from their consultants. This is in addition to all the communication between their respective spokespersons. For example, a simple project, a training course, requires a final report from the consultant/teacher to the client describing what was taught, how it was received by the trainees, and what was (supposed to be) gained, together with an evaluation of how the trainees did. Some measure of what improvements or benefits the client might expect from the attendees ought to be part of the final report. (The client should also review with the staff how they benefited, or did not benefit, from the training.) This reporting is one tool among many by which the client develops criteria to evaluate the consultant and the services received.

Clients cannot let projects finish by just quietly fading away. There must be some summary evaluation by their consultants with some formal, oral presentation of conclusions, accompanied by a written report. Oral presentations are deserved for small projects undertaken for small companies. Here these can be much more informal, a discussion during coffee break or over lunch. Oral presentations allow clients to confront their consultants with challenges and questions and have thorough explanations of the conclusions they are not clear on. However, all projects merit a final written document in addition to the oral report — a condition which clients should insist upon in the proposal. This written document should be received before the oral presentation for review by the client's staff. It can protect both the consultant and client.

The reader will note, according to what has gone before, that there should have been a series of reports given to the client during the course of any project. These would have come to the client:

- Through formal documentation received from the consultant's contact person as contracted in the initial proposal.
- Through discussions or meetings between the contact persons representing both the clients and the consultants during the progress of the project.
- Through reports to the client prepared by the client's contact person based on this person's investigative activities.

These should be in hand well before the consultant's final written report of observations and summation of conclusions are received.

Therefore, there should be no major surprises regarding *the data or the findings* arising from the work. There will be some differences in the final reports, however. These occur as raw data and observations are converted to usable information, and interpretations are developed to explain observations. Subtle inferences, interpretations based on the arcane knowledge of the consultants, and other nuances of meaning that consultants can construe from the data can modify the tenor of the report.

Clients should remember that there is a great difference between the observations and data produced in the course of investigations and the interpretation of data and conclusions that may be drawn from it. Data cannot be translated into useful information and conclusions until the investigation is complete. Background resource material and other support documentation require time to collate. Nevertheless, some translation of data can be generalized sufficiently to provide trends that clients have been briefed on during the consultant's activities. There should be no about-faces or even 90° turns that clients will have to face in these final reports and presentations.

THE PRESENTATION

Often this final report is given to the client in a formal presentation conducted by the consultant with the client's group in attendance. Many such presentations can be "smoke and mirrors" occasions, with more entertainment value than factual content. They are often spectacles demonstrating the skill of the consultant. The value of the work and its conclusions can be spun in many directions by skilled presenters. There will be greater value from the report if clients insist on having an opportunity to read the manuscript and circulate the document among their management prior to any oral presentations.

The reason is simple. Reviewing the project and its results before the final oral presentation allows time for the development of meaningful questions by clients. Significant and challenging inquiries can act as deterrents to any "smoke and mirrors" magic shows that consultants might use on these occasions. Clients can demand explanations of methodologies, data interpretation, and conclusions that they feel are questionable, unreliable, or they are unclear about. The presentation should be an opportunity to discuss the project, its findings, and conclusions with the consultant and to receive clear, concise, and jargon-free answers to questions.

THE CHALLENGE

The findings of the consultant's report need to be questioned, even challenged by clients and members of their organizations. Clients should press their consultants to justify all their results or all activities undertaken and to justify the conclusions that were drawn. There should be no doubts or lack of understanding by any member of the client's team respecting the work, the results, their interpretation, and the conclusions drawn from them. No report should be accepted passively. No report is without some question.

There are many justifications for such a challenge. Challenge as a concept used here deserves some explanation. It is not *necessarily* meant as an outright denial of the capabilities, methodologies, data collation techniques, interpretative skills, etc., of the consultants employed. Rather, this challenge is a simple "show me." It is a challenge to show me, the client, how and why you, the consultant, got from here to there. It is an inquiry, a plea for complete understanding on the part of clients.

A small example suffices to provide a better understanding of the concept of challenge:

> Three different consulting laboratories in widely different geographical regions were used by a food manufacturing company to analyze the polysaccharide component of raw material and products grown and manufactured locally in each of the regions closest to the laboratories. The results were absolutely confounding. There was neither rhyme nor reason to them. In order not to lose a season's work and to establish some understanding, each of the laboratories was sent blind samples which included duplicates prepared from a single well-mixed batch of product and carefully diluted samples to give three levels of concentration. Again there was no similarity to data between the laboratories and poor correlation within the laboratories to either duplicates or to concentrations. Inquiries into each of the laboratories revealed that none used the accepted method of analysis for this component. Each laboratory explained that their method was superior in their opinion to the accepted method.

Had conclusions been based on the results obtained without questioning them, incorrect conclusions about the characteristics of raw materials and products made with them would have been reached.

Clients frequently feel at a disadvantage when challenging consultants who are generally accepted to be experts. No one doubts experts. Certainly one does not doubt experts who use scientifically proven methodologies or scientifically established procedures or principles used by scientists. This appeal to the gods of science is pretty intoxicating. It can be intimidating to clients to challenge the experts using scientific methods. However, I leave readers with a thought which has always reassured me: were there no people with common sense and intelligence before this great appeal to science, before science was invented, or before consultants paraded their skills under the protective cloak of science?

There is an inherent Catch-22 situation that clients face when they must resort to consultants. First, they are forced to seek assistance from people whose knowledge is sometimes so esoteric and abstruse that they cannot understand it fully or comprehend its implications for them. The knowledge imparted or to be imparted is too complex. Second, this inability to comprehend fully causes clients to then place their trust in the skills of the consultants they hire to assist them. They, in effect, unquestioningly project their weaknesses onto this savior, the consultant. This unquestioning trust leads directly to a third dilemma. Clients make themselves vulnerable to receiving unsuitable, even incompatible, advice from their consultants. Application of such advice could have disastrous consequences.

Consultants (gurus, counselors, experts, advisers, specialists, mentors, thinkers, etc.) can make mistakes. They are often wrong in their advice, their conclusions, and their predictions. These errors can prove costly to their clients. Figgie International Inc. sued its consultant, the Boston Consulting Group, whom it accused of "erroneous" market studies and providing "flawed" strategies (Ramsay, 1994; see also Anon., 1995b; 1995c). The suit was settled out of court. Andersen Consulting had to defend a lawsuit by UOP, an Illinois-based engineering company, which claimed the consulting company did not fulfill its promises and responsibilities (Anon., 1995a). A further sign that consulting is becoming more frequently challenged by clients is that consultants are becoming more circumspect in their promises, rethinking their proposals, and looking to insurance companies and lawyers more before they promise (Anon., 1995b). A suboptimal performance, in the client's view, is not good enough.

Pierce (1996) commented on several issues where experts or panel of experts called by governments pronounced on issues which later proved them to be wrong. Chlorofluorocarbons (CFCs) were pronounced safe but later proved to be major destroyers of the ozone layer. Lead in gasoline was pronounced by distinguished scientists to contribute only a minor amount of lead to the human body, whereas it was found to contribute 70% of the blood lead levels in the body.

Dr. Arthur J. Carty, president of the National Research Council Canada, on being given an honorary doctorate by Carleton University, Ottawa, in his address cited the following (Carty, 1997):

- "There is no likelihood man will ever tap the power of the atom." This was spoken by Robert Milliken, the 1923 winner of the Nobel Prize in physics.
- "Heavier-than-air flying machines are impossible." William T. Kelvin, 1st Baron, (1824–1907) predicted this. His name should be familiar as that which was applied to the absolute temperature scale.
- "Where a calculator on the ENIAC computer (one of the original computers) is equipped with 18,000 vacuum tubes and weighs 30 tons, computers in the future may have only 1,000 vacuum tubes and perhaps weigh only 1½ tons." The source was *Popular Mechanics* 1949.
- "I think there is a world market for maybe five computers." IBM president Thomas Watson predicted this in 1943.

- "There is no reason anyone would want a computer in their home." This came in 1977 from DEC (Digital) Chairman Ken Olson.
- And, although the statement is denied, Bill Gates, president and CEO of Microsoft, predicted in 1981 that 640K should be power enough for anybody's computer.

So much for predictions from the experts.

Clients should recognize that consultants and their associates, merely because they have special skills and knowledge, are not experts at running their clients' businesses. Here consultants are amateurs, outsiders; they have had no training in these businesses. They do bring a fresh and novel approach to the issues facing their clients. But clients must ask themselves if the novelty of what consultants bring is the best solution to the issues they face or the best path for their organizations to follow. Nobody but the clients and their management understand the individual ethos of their companies. It is the clients who must then evaluate the report, its conclusions, and recommendations against a more intimate knowledge and understanding of their affairs, their people, the community they interact within, and their short- and long-range business goals. The findings certainly should not be applied by any client without a massive amount of questioning of the results and as complete as possible an understanding of the consequences of doing so.

At the risk of repetition, let me state that the client should remember that it is he who runs the business and not the consultant. The consultant was called only to tackle an issue the client faced.

After the digestion of the report by the client, a comprehensive program of remedial action can be established that is understood by all and carried out by responsible persons on the basis of the findings of the report.

7 Implementing the Advice

Now the first bite has been taken in the apple of progress — and there is a worm within its core.

Desowitz (1983)

I keep six honest serving men
(They taught me all I knew);
Their names are What and Why and When
And How and Where and Who.

Rudyard Kipling in *The Elephant's Child* from *The Just-so Stories*

Man's most valuable trait is a judicious sense of what not to believe.

Euripides

A CAUTIONARY WORD TO CLIENTS

Desowitz's quote provides an likely warning of the problems that all clients who have availed themselves of the services of consultants will face. They will be faced with one of three alternatives:

- They will implement the recommendations of their consultants within their organizations, their communities, or their marketplaces.
- They will have to digest the innovations that *have been put in place* within their organizations, their communities, or their marketplaces by their consultants.
- They will agree after discussions within their organizations to do nothing and file the reports of their consultants.

It is the first two alternatives that clients need to heed.

SETTING THE SCENE

Clients received some service from their consultants which they will implement somehow. This, figuratively, is the Desowitz apple of progress which clients are about to bite into (Desowitz, 1983). Implementation of the results of the consultant's activities or living with the results of that implementation is the worm in the apple. Implementation can be a problem for the client.

Desowitz develops two themes which have, in principle, a parallel to applying the consultant's recommendations, namely:

- First, man, through his intervention in the ecology and environment, has been the originator or perpetuator of the intensification of many infectious diseases that he has tried to defeat.
- Second, control over these diseases usually is found when there is a return to a "time-honored, sensible approach of environmental sanitation": that is, a return to common sense.

Man has disrupted a delicate balance.

The parallel to be developed here is this: consultants have intervened in the businesses (i.e., environments and ecologies) of their clients in some manner. The reactions to, or results of, these interventions may introduce new problems. There may be unwanted side effects. No matter how well meant or soundly based (or so it was thought by the consultants) the recommendations were, a modicum of sanity only returns when the clients use their common sense concerning application of the recommendations. To be fair, not all incidents of the intervention of consultants result in problems such as those described by Desowitz. Many do.

WARNING SIGNS

The interventions cited by Desowitz have been instigated by consultants engaged by international aid agencies, organizations such as the World Bank, or by government aid programs. When aid is provided by consultants to needy countries (the clients), the results can be as devastating as if no aid had been provided. For example, one hears of the introduction of food crops where there is no history of the use of that particular crop in the local peoples' dietary history, or animals are introduced into cultures where the animals cannot thrive in the local environmental conditions. This is the worm in the apple of progress or to quote Shakespeare, "There's the rub." A sound caution to clients is this:

> that the implementation of any recommendations made by consultants must be done in a manner sustainable by their clients and *suitable* to the cultures (ecologies) of the clients where these measures are to be applied if they are to have lasting effect.

Suitable services or recommendations are those whose implementation does not produce greater harm to the ecologies in the long term. The recommendations, activities, services, advice, or whatever that are provided by consultants are not necessarily the correct, or even the most appropriate, products for the clients.

THE NEED FOR COMMON SENSE

Many clients override their own innate common sense, their corporate common sense, when they believe everything spouted by consultants. They are overwhelmed by experts using techniques based on "scientifically based principles." This failure of clients to recognize their own corporate common sense in the face of their awe of consultants can be dangerous for their organizations. An example that illustrates the foregoing is described by Desowitz as an outbreak of "Japanese tractor-induced encephalitis" in Thailand:

> The carrier of the infection is a mosquito which much prefers beef to pork. Historically, the Thai rice farmers plowed their fields with water buffalo and kept pigs for food or marketing. The water buffalo cannot be infected and since they are the preferred food of the mosquito, the vector for transmitting encephalitis was missing. The pig, however, is an amplifying vector in the virus disease. Thus, a nice balance had been maintained. Then tractors were introduced and gradually the number of water buffalo was reduced. The virus-carrying mosquito now was forced to feed on the pig where the virus grew, and secondarily also to feed on man. The result was a serious outbreak of encephalitis when the preferred food, the water buffalo, became scarce.

Desowitz's argument is this: the epidemic could have been avoided since all the disease vectors and other knowledge were available. The analogy is this. A consultant made a recommendation that was implemented. However, application of this "improvement" resulted in another problem. Yet knowledge (common sense) was available that could have anticipated the problem.

Implementation of any actions that are developed and recommended by consultants must be done cautiously and judiciously by clients. Clients are well advised to heed the quotes from Kipling and Euripides. Any application needs to be undertaken with an understanding of the impact that its implementation may have on the (sub-)culture of the client.

Tuller (1992) pointed this out when he described the result of actions of a consultant performed for a client. The client wanted expansion through acquisition. His consultant found an acquisition which was approved but was foreign to his client's area of skills. The marriage was not a success, indeed, proved detrimental to the long-term goals of his client. The client sued for bad advice received. Again, the recurring theme that will be found in this book: consultants may be good for the problems facing clients, but they may not be good for the client's business.

The six handy servants described by Kipling boil down to this: clients must use common sense in implementing the services of their consultants. Like Euripides, clients must maintain a judicious sense of what not to believe. Consultants cannot hope to fully grasp a complete knowledge or understanding of the ecologies of their clients. Clients are the sole judges of the applicability of their consultants' findings.

IMPLEMENTATION

The client will find that implementation of the consultant's advice or services can be either a difficult or a simple undertaking. If implementation is merely a handover of equipment with an improved design, a new product formulation, or a redesigned package for a product, then application of the results within the client's organization may be comparatively simple and without problems. Even so, simple handovers can be fraught with hidden difficulties.

Difficulties arise when consultants have instituted wholesale changes in organizations respecting their direction, their governance, and their communication channels. Here clients must use caution as they assist their staff to adapt to the changes instituted by their consultants. Whether implementation is anticipated to be a simple undertaking or not, it is not an undertaking to be taken lightly.

GENERAL DIFFICULTIES

Some difficulties in implementation that clients can encounter can be a reflection of the possibilities depicted in Figure 7.1. This diagram outlines the general course of outcomes that could lead to either a productive implementation or to a disastrous outcome.

In a nutshell, clients may have correctly assessed the issues confronting them and have articulated these well to their consultants, or these issues could have been wrongly understood and incorrectly communicated. A poor understanding of the situation and an incorrect statement of the issues results in misdirection of the consultants. A disastrous outcome will be the only consequence upon any application of the findings of an inappropriate project.

The causes for poor implementation mount from this point onward (Figure 7.1). They seesaw between faults that can be ascribed solely to clients and those attributed solely to their consultants.

Finally, in Figure 7.1, the realization may come that the services provided or their outcome upon implementation were wrong for the clients. Even if all the correct decisions were made and proper implementation carried out, the decisions may have been the wrong ones for this client. Consultants are neither clairvoyant nor omniscient (see Carty, 1997).

Theoretically, the possible outcomes of any consultative undertaking could be that either correct or incorrect solutions were obtained. A good analogy might be the preamble before pronouncements made by poll takers as they present their results. They are quick to announce, for example, that 70% of the population favor a particular political candidate or government initiative. The pollsters finish this statement with the flourish that this result is correct within a very narrow range of percentage points nine times out of ten. Their statement is not complete. A complete statement ought to be as follows:

> these results are either right or wrong. *If they are correct*, then candidate A, or proposal… is favored etc.

Therefore, the starting point for successful implementation must be a consideration of whether the results are correct or not before any other possibilities of the success, or failure, of implementation are discussed.

If the results are not correct for their clients, then implementation of the results by clients will be impossible or, if implemented, they may have disastrous consequences no matter how well their consultants' work was performed. The reasons why the results may not be correct will be discussed later. Clients should be aware that two concepts of correctness are at play here:

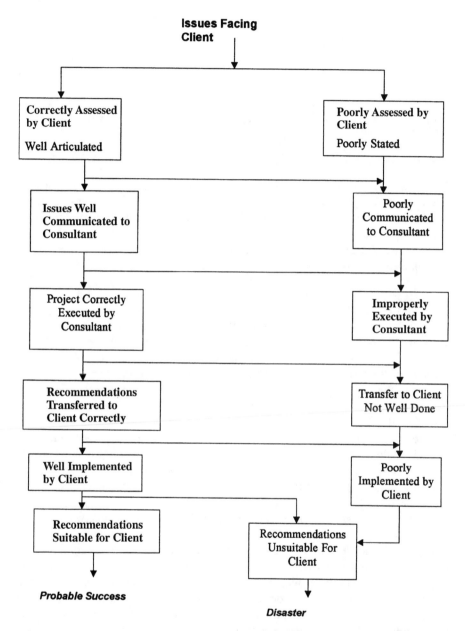

FIGURE 7.1 Possible outcomes that will affect the implementation of the consultant's activity.

- First, there is a consideration of the absolute "correctness" of the results; that is, are they a true (i.e., absolute) representation of the real world?
- Second, the correctness or appropriateness of the results for clients must be considered. That is, are the results germane to the issues facing the clients and correct for them?

The benefits that are anticipated by the successful conclusion of a project and which are suggested by the consultants may not be assured.

Clients ought to consider the possibilities of benefits in terms of probabilities. These are: everything may have been performed correctly or incorrectly by the consultant and these may have been transferred either correctly or incorrectly. What has not been factored into the deliberations is "the rest of the world," or even that part of the world within the client's organization. These play a role in determining correctness.

PROBLEMS IN IMPLEMENTING THE CONSULTANT'S ADVICE

Why is success not assured if everything has been carried out well? The answers are legion and varied. One cannot focus on a single factor as the main reason. It is worthwhile, therefore to review the difficulties that thwart attempts on the part of clients to put the recommendations of consultants into policy and thence into action. As the client proceeds with implementation, an awareness of Murphy's law should be kept clearly in mind: what can go wrong, will go wrong.

TIME

First, all projects have a time factor. Some are lengthy undertakings lasting for two or three years; some may last just for months, while others are merely a few weeks. All projects were proposed at a particular period in time in the past. A consultant carried out the task and reported on it in another, later, period of time. Still later, the client attempted to take action on the basis of the project's results. In that interval from start to implementation, any number of changes could have occurred which invalidate the implementation. For example, the competition could have produced the proverbial "better mousetrap." The ever fickle consumers who were originally targeted could have changed their interests between the start and finish of the project. Most certainly this intended customer aged in this period of time and, at the very least, this targeted audience has been exposed to a myriad of emerging technologies and socictal developments during this interval.

The competition could have launched a counter-offensive against whatever new product, service, or image the client was trying to promote. A simple and typical example tells the story of what could well happen. A pollster is commissioned to gather information about the popularity of a particular leading politician and his party. After formulating the questionnaire and executing the survey, some gaff, some piece of unpopular legislation or some scandal may have occurred involving the politician or his party. By the time collating and interpreting the results and presenting these to the client has passed, the opinions based on the poll may be inaccurate. The poll was correct at one period of time, but any political action taken on the basis of the results at the time they were published are no longer to the point.

THE WRONG STATEMENT

Clients formulated the statements of the issues that they faced. If these statements were inaccurate, it follows that any solutions provided by their consultants and based on these false statements may be incorrect or inappropriate. Implementation can be derailed. In the example cited by Tuller (1992), the client desired expansion with the purchase of a manufacturing facility. This statement was wrong, that is, the client had falsely assessed the goal desired. The consultant dutifully found an acquisition, but in the client's opinion the consultant failed to provide advice that this acquisition was not a good undertaking for the client who had no experience in manufacturing. In the client's opinion, the consultant's investigations had not been thorough enough.

In many instances, the specific problem I have been asked to provide guidance for is really not the causative issue but only a symptom of a different, sometimes bigger, problem elsewhere. The client reported only the symptom to me for corrective action. Figuratively, I have been called to put out a fire. The task should really have been directed to determining the cause of the fire and eliminating it. Thus there is an element of misdirection which can hamper implementation of recommendations.

Appropriate here is a short example that illustrates the dilemma that can arise when symptoms are presented as the problem without the real problem being clearly stated or understood:

> Management at a major pickle processing plant were concerned with a loss of a high-quality rating of their products compared to their competition. Their main concern centered on crushed dill pickles found in gallon jars. Their smashed appearance was a mystery to QC and production alike. The cause soon became apparent. The line supervisor had provided his own solution. He had stationed a worker armed with a rubber mallet who bashed every dill pickle extending above the rim of the gallon jars back down into the jar. The worker had been placed there in answer to QC's previous reprimand for poor seals. This was the overt cause of the mashed pickles. Inquiries determined the real root cause of the contretemps. It was a lack of cooperation and communication between quality control and production. The QC procedure had been a series of insular visits by analysts to critical points in the line. For example, the quality control analyst would emerge from the air-conditioned laboratory, which was far removed from the plant floor, walk to the line, collect the requisite finished product samples from the line in this case after the filler, and return directly to the laboratory. The analyst apparently wore blinkers and failed to notice activities just before the capping machine where the mallet wielder was stationed. It rapidly became apparent that QC considered themselves the "good guys" out to show up production, "the bad guys," doing something stupid. Production and QC finally sat down together to resolve, successfully, their mashed pickle problem. A QC inspector was assigned to an entire line and not just to segments of it.

Mashed dill pickles was the symptom. The cause was a QC department that had not recognized that its main function was to assist production in putting out a quality product. QC spent as little time as they could on the production floor instead of working with production in determining the causes of quality problems and remedying these cooperatively.

Certainly a clear, complete, and full statement of what clients believe the issues to be can ultimately ease the implementation of the consultant's recommendations.

Speaking the Same Language But Using Different Dictionaries

Communication is the process of getting the sender's message across to some target audience. In good communication the message:

- Has been received by the target.
- Is understood by the target.
- Will be responded to favorably by the target or certainly in the manner the sender had hoped for.

Contrariwise, bad communication results from any breakdown in the above as depicted in the following:

- The message was not received by the target.
- The message was received but not understood by the target.
- The targeted audience is incensed by the message; ignores the message completely; or fails to act upon the message. In short, the target does not respond as desired by the sender.

Clients must communicate well with consultants if they want to benefit from their work.

Failure by consultants to communicate effectively to their clients can impede implementation of any action. Do the clients understand the reports and their conclusions as prepared by their consultants? Or do they understand the systems that were put in place, how these should be managed, and their implications for their organizations? Understanding is essential if any technology transfer is to be successfully sustained after the departure of the consultant. To understand requires good communication. There can be failed communication from the consultant back to the client.

Miscommunication could be a result of language. We may speak the same language, but the words used in that language may not have the same meaning for both the client and the consultant. The jargon that can develop in certain disciplines (computerese, managementese, and governmentese, to name a few examples where names have been applied to specific jargon) can be incomprehensible to those not initiated into it.

Does such jargon cause a lack of clarity? Is the report too technical, too obscure, too cryptic? When jargon is combined with technicality, obscurity, or arcana — call it what one wants — it prevents the clients from understanding consultants' recommendations. In its turn, this lack of understanding can be an impediment to the proper application of the consultant's recommendations.

There are many reasons for the use of jargon in reports. Some clients and consultants alike look upon its use as erudition. Ignorantly believing it to be a sign of expertise, clients may be impressed by the jargon spouted at them by consultants. When a computer consultant mentioned in typical computerese that something would be "disintermediated," I gasped. What did he mean? Questioning revealed the meaning was simply that something was to be eliminated. Why didn't he say so?

Another reason for jargon could be fear. One can hide in its obfuscation. Let me illustrate with an anecdote:

> While working in a government laboratory in the very early days of gas chromatography — days when one built one's own equipment as I had — I was asked by the research director of a company whether I thought it would be worth this company's while to invest in the technique. I wrote favorably about the technique, with reference to my own work and other published work. The head of my department, who insisted on approving all out-going mail, intercepted my letter and edited it severely with copious use of government jargonese. I simply could not send such a positive reply! Taken into his office, I was informed that if I should be wrong in my prediction, this would reflect on his department! I dutifully signed his rewrite of my letter but took a copy home to my wife. She could not for the life of her determine whether I thought gas chromatography had a future or not!!

Reports are often written to be ambivalent and obscure. The reason? Perhaps to protect a consultant's own dilemma over an interpretation of the results. Or perhaps some consultants may write in this vague manner in the belief that if one cannot be proven wrong by what is presented in the report, one can be assumed to be right and therefore the work was successful — ambiguity that my superior in the civil service would have loved. After all, successful ventures beget more assignments.

To demonstrate obfuscation beautifully, there is a wonderful exchange to be found in *The Complete YES MINISTER,* written by Jonathan Lynn and Antony Jay and serialized in the BBC television series, *Yes Minister.* In this excerpt, James Hacker, a newly appointed government minister, is being introduced to his Permanent Secretary, Sir Humphrey Appleby, by his private secretary, Bernard Woolley: (Hacker writes in the first person)

> "I believe you've met before," Bernard remarked...
>
> Sir Humphrey said, "Yes, we did cross swords when the Minister gave me a grilling over the Estimates in the Public Accounts Committee last year. He asked me all the questions I hoped nobody would ask."
>
> This is splendid. Sir Humphrey clearly admires me. I tried to brush it off. "Well," I said, "Opposition's about asking awkward questions."
>
> "Yes," said Sir Humphrey, "and government is about not answering them."
>
> I was surprised. "But you answered all my questions, didn't you," I commented.
>
> "I'm glad you thought so, Minister," said Sir Humphrey.

From *The Complete YES MINISTER,*
Published by BBC Books, London, U.K., 1991.

BLINDED BY FASHIONABILITY

Clients often choose consultants because a particular consultant is currently popular as evidenced by frequent write-ups in business magazines or in newspapers or by appearances on television. The theories espoused by this consultant are fashionable. Some clients need to be seen as successful, on the cutting edge, or "with it." This desire can be answered only by getting on the current popular bandwagon. This pandering to faddism can also present an impediment to implementation of a consultant's services.

Selecting a consultant for his fashionability indicates that the client has opted for the Cinderella's-glass-shoe approach to resolving issues. The prince in the Cinderella story searches the kingdom for his vanished Cinderella with only a glass slipper as a clue to her identity. He tries to find her by trying the glass slipper on every maiden in his kingdom. It fits none of them. When he tries the slipper on Cinderella, the slipper fits and he is reunited with his vanished Cinderella. Consultants tour the countryside with their versions of a "glass slipper," i.e., some theory or technique that they have developed that they have promoted heavily and successfully. Everybody wants to try on this slipper, and clients flock to these fashionable consultants. Unfortunately, the "glass slipper" fits very few.

The danger for clients is in the blind and unquestioning application of theories or techniques promoted by such consultants without concern for the impact these might have on their organizations or their activities. They, the "gurus," bend their clients, so to speak, to fit their pet theories. The shoe, figuratively, may be fashionable but if it does not fit, what then? Clients will have difficulty applying the recommendations of these consultants, which are based on something not suitable to their needs.

Such popular consultants are successfully promoted in business papers and trade magazines. They write books, and these are reviewed widely. These management books have produced such a growth industry in book publishing that it has been dubbed management by bestseller. The theory or technique that is espoused by the consultant is not in itself wrong or without benefit, but the principles in it may not be applicable to all clients or in all activities that clients undertake.

An analogous example of this mindless application of packaged procedures has been condemned in the analysis of psychological testing. Statistical software packages are being used more and more frequently to analyze psychological test data. The reason is simple: these packages permit the use of statistical tests which would be tediously impossible to do without a software program and a computer. However, the American Psychological Association wants this practice to stop (Kiernan, 1997). These packaged statistical methods of analysis are being applied inappropriately by research workers who do not understand them. The outcome is that inappropriate, even incorrect, results are being published in research journals. Although this does not describe a client/consultant relationship, it does describe a condemnation of the uncritical application of techniques akin to those proposed by popular consulting faddists.

There are software packages to reduce the number of trials that need to be carried out in developing formulations and make new product development more efficient. Their designs are frequently only loosely based on a rigorous statistical premise. Nevertheless, new product development consultants blindly adhere to these modified experimental designs for producing optimized formulations disregarding the possible shortcomings that might result from using them.

Henry Mintzberg, himself a top-ranked management consultant, was quoted by Leger (1995) as saying, "Faddishness is really killing management because people apply things without thinking." Mintzberg emphasizes that such management techniques (the "things") must be adapted to one's own culture and needs, and they may be useless for some kinds of organizations (see also Hammer 1994).

All recommendations from consultants must be adaptable to the needs and ecologies of their clients. If the actions recommended by consultants are not in keeping with the spirit of the clients, opposition to the imposed recommendations will make their adoption difficult if not impossible. If they are adopted blindly and rigidly by clients, the spirit of their organizations may be broken. Staff may become disillusioned and dissatisfied with the changes. They lose the focus of the previously established ethos of the company. Implementation most certainly will suffer.

Kipling's elephant child, indeed, kept good serving men (see chapter preface) which clients would do well to emulate.

GOVERNANCE WITHIN ORGANIZATIONS

The governance of those microcultures that can be found within any organization can be a serious impediment to implementation of any recommendations for change. In an organization, or in small organizations within larger ones, e.g., departments within subdivisions within divisions and so on, the governance of these microcultures becomes important. These may well be able to subvert any changes to the structure of the organization that are being implemented and that are contrary to their views.

Management is credited with having much more power than it really does. Management in the form of one's immediate boss may be someone hard to like or work for and that person may even appear all-powerful, but there is not as much power there as might be supposed. Imposition of changes from on high are not always diligently followed or adhered to as those imposing the changes might want.

C.P. Snow (1961) in the Godkin lectures, described governance in organizational structures as forms of "closed politics." "Closed politics" for Snow referred to any kind of government "with no appeal to a larger assembly… or (to) what we call loosely social forces." This closely describes the systems of government found in most, if not all, organizations, from multinational companies to small companies to unions to trade associations to political parties to tennis clubs and bridge clubs. There is no meaningful appeal in these bodies to a parliament, to a senate, or to a judicial body for redress of decisions or wrongs. Those making decisions are not responsible to an electorate after any unpopular decision has been made.

Snow described three such systems of closed politics. These were:

- Committee politics
- Hierarchical politics
- Court politics

They cover well the organizational structures that can be found within any organization even though such organizations may vary widely in their activities and purposes.

Committee Politics

Committee politics describe the administration of the least complex organizations. In companies, societies, or organizations run by committee, each member has a say in the affairs of the group and all vote, each vote being equal (but rarely ever is in reality, *vide infra*). This is the government found in the local tennis club or board of elders of the local church. These are usually very simple organizations. This type of governance is formed in worker-organized companies, in companies formed by laid-off workers who bought a discontinued product line, or in family-run businesses. One other example known to me was a company formed as a result of a class project that was carried out cooperatively by the students involved in the project. Upon graduation, they pooled their skills to form a company based on this joint project.

Any who have volunteered for work on a committee heading up any social club, or been appointed to a church board of elders realize the problems, rivalries, jealousies, and frustrations that organizations governed on a "committee politics" type of administration can engender. It is the rare organization that can work smoothly. Equality is most unusual, and acceptance of anything innovative is difficult to move through to full adoption. The most extreme example that I have observed was in a family-run business. All decisions and activities needed full family agreement. There had been an unfortunate falling-out in the family such that signatories to checks (which required two signatures) refused to co-sign if the other signatory had already signed!

Implementation of highly innovative changes can be difficult in organizations with governance of the sort Snow refers to as committee politics.

Hierarchical Politics

Hierarchical politics dominate the administration of large organizations such as a multinational corporation. In these there is a distinct chain of command. Rarely, however, does this chain of command have the power one might suppose, as Snow is quick to point out:

> "To get anything done in any highly articulated organization, you have got to carry people at all sorts of levels. It is their decisions...above all, the absence of their passive resistance which are going to decide whether a strategy goes through in time."

In hierarchical politics, implementation is enhanced if all levels involved can see positive gains with the least fear for their own security or station within the organization as it exists. Therein is the difficulty for implementation of any recommendations that consultants might try to institute or that clients attempt to follow through with. Implementation requires the cooperation or acquiescence of many layers within the organization. If members of these layers do not approve or want the changes suggested, implementation is dead.

Court Politics

Snow called his final example of closed politics "court politics." If one gets to the individual with the most power or the greatest concentration of power, then any recommendations or new strategies that have been put forward have the best opportunities for successful implementation. Herein this type of administration differs from that of hierarchical politics since the titular head of the organization may not be the most influential or powerful individual and may not be involved in acceptance or implementation of the changes.

Frequently "power" is in the hands of those without titular power. For example, power may reside with the most productive scientist, with the best salesperson, or with someone whose personality, wit, creativity, or charisma holds a productive group together and functioning. It may simply be someone who has the boss's ear or controls access to the titular power. This individual need not be the "boss," and rarely is. It could be the secretaries of bosses who effectively screen everything from their bosses and efficiently delegate to others within the organization any tasks not, in their opinions, for their bosses.

Within many organizations, there is such an *éminence grise* who wields power and influence over the organization's affairs but does so not in any official capacity. Without the support of these people, or this person, within their organizations, clients may see the introduction of any innovations suggested by consultants fail miserably in their introduction.

The foregoing describes rather concisely how most organizations function. Within such organizations, to implement the recommendations of consultants effectively, clients, and, indeed, the consultants, must understand the closed politics system, that is, the system of governance, within which both work together. Without this understanding, implementation is lost. As the saying goes, you can lead a horse to water, but you can't make him drink.

SUSTAINABLE ORGANIZATIONS

Hammer (1994) discusses projects undertaken by aid agencies acting through the consultants they employ and which fail to be implemented successfully. She makes a novel comparison of aid projects carried out by consultants in fashion terms. Most aid programs are *prêt à porter* designs. That is, they are much like the programs of consultants who force their pet theories onto clients. Very few designs are *alta moda*. Furthermore, the common designs are rarely designed with normal, everyday women, "real women" as Hammer comments, in mind. So it is with aid projects, which are frequently designed without the clients (Hammer's word) in mind. Her point is this: a designer has produced a design for use by a fictitious client. The result is that the client is "not happy with the fit." A consultant carries out the project work for implementation in a developing country, but the work must be designed for use at the grassroots. Her question is this: "Will the new activity ultimately improve their lives or simply stretch them more thinly?" Her answer is: "The choice of technology and its scale is crucial in a project. And *what may be appropriate technology for one part of the world may not be for another.*" (Hammer's italics) The article makes fascinating reading as is, but if it is reread substituting "consultant" where Hammer uses "aid agency" and "client" for "developing country," a new perspective can be gained for understanding failures of implementation of projects.

The size of the client, whether a country or a company, makes no difference in this discussion. Some companies are, indeed, larger financially than many developing countries. Client/consultant or developing country/aid agency relationships are the same. The only difference may be the magnitude of the projects that are undertaken. Even so, many clients pay millions of dollars to "re-engineering" consultants, and this sum is often as much if not more than some developing countries receive from aid agencies.

The points in Hammer's paper deserve amplification here. Any project must be modeled to the needs of the recipient. This comes down to clients knowing what their needs are, i.e., defining the correct problem or need, and communicating this clearly to the consultants. Conversely, consultants must get down to the basics of the problem, to its grassroots conception as Hammer puts it. Consultants need to understand two elements:

- The problem. This can only be done by making a thorough analysis of all issues and their relation to the client, particularly the client's "closed politics" as Snow (1961) would put it.
- The mechanics of implementation of their completed services and how any benefits derived from these can be made sustainable after they leave.

There are corollary issues. For example, application of any results, recommendations or organizational systems that are put in place must be sustainable with the resources that clients possess or can afford to possess. Furthermore, their adoption must be capable of being incorporated and managed within the managerial structure and capabilities of their clients. Clients must have the leadership and managerial skills to adopt and adapt the innovations to their organizations. This ability to assess their internal skills is essential to clients.

The continued presence of consultants cannot be a necessary requirement for the ongoing success of the application of the recommendations. The initial implementation of any novel interventions by consultants may require the presence of the consultants for the training of staff and fine-tuning the interventions. However, if consultants are an essential part of the implementation process, the seeds of project failure have been sown.

TECHNOLOGY TRANSFER

Barwell (1983) discusses technology transfer and emphasizes the theme that applicability to the client is all-important, as a factor in technology transfer. With the setting, again, for projects in developing economies as was Hammer's above, Barwell's topic is, however, a purely technical one, the design of equipment, and is one in which he was personally involved.

He makes the point strongly that for a technology to be successfully implemented it cannot be separated from "the materials, components, and manufacturing processes and skills available locally," a theme not unlike that in the previous section of manageability of the system. This advice can also be applied, as was Hammer's, with little difficulty to problems of implementation of a consultant's services to a client whether it be a country or a company.

Providing a small manufacturer in a rural area with a highly sophisticated manufacturing process where there is no local skilled labor force nor readily available raw material or where the costs of transportation or production are too high is doing a disservice to that client. As Barwell put it, "A prototype made in a well-equipped workshop staffed by skilled technicians is produced under very different conditions from those applying in a small-scale industry."

Any technical assistance, if it is to be implemented, must be applicable not only to the client's business as discussed above but also to the resources, both human and material, which the client presently possesses or which are readily available to that client at reasonable cost. Cottage craft industries, for one, cannot utilize overly sophisticated solutions. Implementation cannot be accomplished using a sledge hammer to fix a Swiss watch.

SUMMARY

Successful implementation of the recommendations of consultants can be very simple or very difficult. Many elements, from the nature of the governance of the organization of the clients to the very essence of the recommendations themselves, must be digested before clients can adopt or adapt the recommendations of a consultant.

The single most critical question that clients can ask is, "Are these recommendations applicable to the issues we are facing and which we want addressed?" If they are appropriate, then the next question is, "Are they good for our business?" Clients must recognize the vast difference between these two questions. The next question is, "Do we have the skills and material resources to apply them?"

Consultants are not divine oracles. They are suppliers of skills like any other suppliers of resources that clients can use to manage their business affairs. Such resources can be poor or high quality and used well or poorly by clients. Critical judgment must be applied in implementing the recommendations.

Euripides's aphorism can be paraphrased and expanded as follows:

> The most valuable trait of clients is a judicious sense of what not to accept without a critical evaluation of what the outcome might mean in both the short- and long-term future for their organizations.

Clients must acknowledge that there may have been many changes since the projects so desirable some time ago were commissioned. Wages may have risen, and the original figures developed for costing the project two or three years earlier are, perhaps, no longer applicable. The original estimates for labor wages, raw materials, parts, equipment, or ingredients could have changed. Wage stabilization programs may have altered projected labor costs. Price stabilization programs, control of supply through cartels, embargoes, marketing boards, or trade legislation, and politics (trade barriers) affect implementation. Time can invalidate the original estimates of costs. Nothing is stable. Stable equilibrium situations do not exist.

Events only indirectly related to costs can arise during the time span from the initiation to the implementation of the results of a project. These may cause projects although successfully completed to be poorly put into practice. Mahoney (1990), for example, commented that the many product liabilities which have resulted in terrifyingly large judgments have prevented many companies, especially smaller ones, from embarking on new ventures. Liability insurance puts the costs of the introduction of new products out of reach of some companies.

Economic conditions that change in that passage of time can increase the cost of money. Interest rates can rise. This increase can put financing for development costs out of the reach of smaller companies who may not be able to get or afford the credit or venture capital needed to proceed. Mahoney reported that the rate of return for covering financing was, according to the Federal Reserve Bank of New York, 20.3%. In turn, this requires that a development project must return $6 in ten years for every $1 spent.

Implementing the advice of consultants can be beset with many problems if clients are not wary. Clients would be very wise to follow the advice of Kipling and Euripides.

8 Evaluating the Consulting Services Received

Success is relative: It is what we can make of the mess we have made of things.

T. S. Eliot

INTRODUCTION

Clients often question whether their consultants, their *modus operandi*, and their methodologies were appropriate and "worth it." Their list of questions is something like this:

- Could better relations with the consultant have been developed? Could communication have been improved?
- Did we get our money's worth? Or simply, was the right thing done by us?
- Could this project have been handled more propitiously? Would a course of activity other than hiring consultants been more appropriate to our needs?
- Would some other consultant with different skills have been better suited to our needs? And why?
- Was the consultant too disruptive in performing the work? Was the consultant abusive, brusque, or demeaning to staff? Did the way the work was carried out color the results?

If it is not the primary instigator of the project who asks these questions, it will certainly be someone else in the organization who wonders, openly, whether the entire exercise of hiring a consultant was a "good thing."

To answer these questions as openly and honestly as possible clients must evaluate how well the work was carried out. The problem becomes, then, one of determining what the criteria will be on which to judge the quality of performance received and the deportment of the consultant during close interfacing with the staff. For example, if training was accomplished by questionable methods which involve the humiliation or abuse of staff by the consultant's teaching staff, what criteria are used to evaluate the exercise?

The criteria to judge the performance of consultants during the process of development of a new orthopedic device cannot be equated to those used to evaluate consultants carrying out the remaking of a politician's image.

REFLECTIONS ON THE CONSULTANT'S PERFORMANCE

How is this relationship to be measured? Does one judge success or failure of the project among the criteria? Unsuccessful projects, that is, those that did not attain a specific goal, can have merit if their unsuccessfulness established that the client's original goal was unrealistic. They can have merit if they clarify what were unprofitable approaches to the desired goal.

Successful relationships might also be attained in those "unsuccessful" projects, unsuccessful in that they did not attain the goals originally sought, but whose undertaking allowed the client to avoid some calamitous action or gain valuable operating experience. Consultants can salvage projects and turn what might be a disaster into a meaningful result.

Success, as Eliot in the quote prefacing this chapter points out, is relative to what clients make of the mess that was made of things.

CRITERIA FOR EVALUATION

Evaluating the performance received cannot be judged *solely* on the success or failure of the assignment. Nor can evaluation hinge only on the deportment, the behavior of the consultant, in staff contacts. How the consultant carried out the assignment, the quality of the tools that were used, and the thoroughness of the investigation will all color any appraisal.

Bishop (1982) presents a review of techniques that are used in project analysis. These are standards employed by national and international financing agencies for the evaluation of major undertakings. Three broad groups of factors by which projects can be evaluated are described. These are:

- Economic factors
- Technical factors
- Administrative or managerial factors

There is no denying their importance for evaluating the projects that aid agencies must review. However, these same factors, on a smaller scale, can be adapted for use by all clients to evaluate the success of any project.

How the criteria will be weighted for evaluation of the undertaking of projects will differ according to the interests of those whose viewpoints are considered in the judgment. Accountants may weight economic factors most highly. In their eyes, a successful project will be one that accomplished its goal and did not go over budget. If the project was an income-generating one which brought financial benefits to the organization, it was, indeed, successful. These are their performance criteria. There is little human factor involved.

Technologists describe the project as successful if the technology to build a better mousetrap was obtained and ignore the observation that there may be no market for the mousetrap. Technical factors dominate their evaluation of the relationship. Marketing may see a project as successful if it resulted in a marketable product desired by the consuming public. Sales rise, and they are happy. These all reflect selfish viewpoints, the viewpoints of technocrats. They all, in effect, say that if they and their interests were satisfied then the consultant's performance was "successful." They are indifferent to:

- How it was carried out. They only care that it was carried out and was successful by their standards.
- The impact of the consultant's activities within the organization where the activities were carried out.
- The impact in the client's community where the activity may have been performed.
- The repercussions on the client's customers or suppliers or distributors.

Self-satisfaction is their primary criterion.

But there is still something lacking, another criterion, which may not have the same importance for Bishop in evaluating large-scale projects as it does in smaller projects. This criterion is what I would call a performance factor. How the project was carried out and what impact this activity may have had on the client are also factors that deserve consideration. This performance factor weighs heavily especially in those projects where there is an intimate interfacing between client and consultant. The client's organization must have been strengthened not weakened by the effects (rather than the *results*) of the consultant's work for the project to be considered fully successful. The impact that the working relationship had on the client, the client's organization, and the client's community is of prime importance in the evaluation.

ECONOMIC FACTORS

Before a consultant is called in, clients ought to have performed cost/benefit evaluations of their projects. Their assessments of that cost/benefit ratio are now to be put to the acid test. Were the project costs balanced by the project results? If this is how clients put the question to themselves, it is a poor one to ask. It is also a difficult one to answer. The question is simplistic, even naive. It is an accountant's question, which looks only at a bottom line. Can all the fallout from the performances of consultants be measured with a dollar sign?

Evaluations can be complex. The importance of the time element as a factor in the performance of the contract was presented in a previous chapter. Time is also an element influencing economic factors. All projects, their initiation, their carrying-out, and the application of their results have a time span which can be a critical factor in their economic evaluation.

Answers to the accountant's question are a resounding series of No's. Improvements in working conditions, reduction of absenteeism, greater safety in the workplace, labor harmony, noise abatement, or better pollution control leading to improved community relationships are all possible results of the application of the findings of some projects. An accountant would be hard pressed to put a monetary value on these benefits. Indirectly clients might be able to measure reduction in absenteeism, fewer strikes or work stoppages, fewer complaints from the community about pollution, and fewer days lost to injuries. But clients have no criteria by which to measure a more harmonious workplace.

To simply assess whether clients "got their money's worth" (whatever that might mean) is not enough. The only answer that can be given to the question whether clients got their money's worth is a qualitative one that evaluates both tangible and intangible benefits.

The question should be, more properly, one that reflects both quantitative and qualitative elements. For example, is the client's community, the client's company, or some particular microcosm within the client's organization, perhaps a department, where or for whom the work was done, a better and more productive place to work because of the performance, *not the results*, of the consultant? This is the question that begins to approach the dilemma of how to evaluate the consultant's performance of the project more effectively and comprehensively. Purists might cavil at the meaning of "a better place," but if productivity goes up and workers are happy, then the environment must be "a better place" to work.

Not all performances will be so complicated to evaluate. Projects that are carried out with little or no interaction between client and consultant, except through the appointed representatives of each, provide little substance by which to judge performance. A new piece of equipment designed to perform a unique need for a client can be easily assessed for the increased production it brings, the reduction in the amount of off-standard product produced, the reduction of manpower needed per unit produced, and so on. There is little, however, to evaluate the performance or deportment of the consultant save that the job was done as proposed, met all safety design requirements and produced the piece of equipment that performs satisfactorily.

TECHNICAL FACTORS

Where there is a transfer of expertise from consultants to their clients, there will always be problems of how successfully this transfer was made. Technologies that are not implementable or sustainable by clients in their environments have been poorly transferred by consultants. They become technologies that simply cannot be properly applied no matter how good those technologies are. This is most obvious on large-scale agricultural projects where technologies applicable in developed countries are applied with disastrous results in less developed countries and are depicted clearly by Bishop (1982).

Bishop describes the specific situation in which farmers, for example, are presented with a new technology that does not produce the results that experts claim. The reason is simple: the experts obtained their results on demonstration farms. Rarely can farmers using this new technology obtain the same results that were achieved by the agronomists at model experiment stations. First, the farmers do not have the skills that may be required to apply the technology. Second, they may not be able to maintain the technology: if a new piece of equipment is involved in the technology, this equipment can and does break down. If the farmer cannot maintain the equipment necessary to use the technology and repair it in the field, the whole project has become an exercise in futility. Here the consultant may have successfully trained people to use the technology but has failed to see the need to train people sufficiently to maintain the technology provided. The consultant has improperly assessed the resources of the client, in this case, the farmers.

Finally, the conditions prevailing at an experimental station rarely approximate conditions where the technology is to be applied, in the farmer's fields. If activities carried out on the consultants' premises are not field tested in their clients' facilities, circumstances, and environments, then these consultants have not performed properly.

A practical example of this can be found in new food product development. The consultant prepares a recipe suitable for production. Often this work is conducted at the consultant's development laboratories. These facilities may be distant from the client. The result is that the consultant uses raw materials purchased locally or grown locally and, a very important factor in recipe development, local water. When the client tries to work with the recipe, different raw materials are used and a different source of water is used. The result can be, at best, a different flavored product or, at worst, an off-colored and off-flavored product. Raw materials grown with local varieties under local agronomic practices and water with a different mineral composition can make for enormous differences in the flavor, texture, and color of food products.

An understanding by the consultant of the true technical problems and their ramifications for the client's circumstances was missing. In such instances, the performances of consultants must get failing grades because they did not anticipate the full impact. The planning, approach, and strategy of the consultants were faulty. This pronouncement holds whether clients have sought consultants for software programs designed for specific needs in a medical clinic (appointment scheduling, billings, patient's histories, etc.) or for the unique needs of special effects cinematography, or even in the development of new food products.

Discussed earlier (Desowitz, 1983) was how the application of a new technology can lead to other more serious technical problems that consultants ought to have foreseen. Tuller (1992) brought this out with the example of the consultant who completed the task successfully but failed in advising the client on its inappropriateness for his client. If the ramifications of work have not been fully thought through, the performance of the consultant must be faulted.

A crude analogy can be drawn with the situation of a bartender who is asked by his client for another drink. The bartender knows the client has already had too many. If the client drives home, several lives could be at risk. The bartender is obliged to think through all the consequences of his actions. Similarly, consultants cannot perform services for clients without reviewing all the consequences and making some provision for these in their services, which may include advising their clients against some actions they desire. At the least, consultants have an obligation to make their clients aware of the possible consequences of their actions.

The principles embodied in the foregoing are equally applicable to all performances where there is a transfer of technology whether this transfer is the introduction of a new management or accounting system, installing a newly designed piece of equipment or a turnkey operation comprising a whole new processing line and factory. That is:

- Consultants must recognize whether clients have the skills needed to apply the technology in their business activities.
- The new technology must be stand-alone technology. That is, it must not introduce other problems which clients do not have the resources to overcome. If it does bring other problems, the consequences of the (soft or hard) technology should be discussed fully with their clients.
- The new technology must be capable of being maintained by their clients. The work of consultants is incomplete and poorly accomplished if clients cannot maintain the benefits. Again, consultants have an obligation to clients to provide them with both the tools to apply the technology and the tools to maintain the advantages the work provided.
- The new technology must work under the environmental conditions and availability of resources that clients have ready-to-hand. Consultants should ensure that any technologies meet all legislated, public health, and design standards that are applicable to their clients.

The lack of technology, skills, or resources on the part of clients is a shortcoming that consultants ought to have foreseen.

The question for clients is:

- Can the recommendations proposed by the consultant be carried out under the conditions, influences, and circumstances in which the client's organization finds itself?

An answer to this question reflects largely on the ability of consultants to understand their clients' situations fully. That which is transferred from consultants to clients must be utile within the client's capabilities. How well the technology was transferred serves as a useful tool to evaluate the services of the consultant.

ADMINISTRATIVE FACTORS

The argument here is similar to the foregoing. That is, consultants ought to have foreseen...etc. Clients must have the necessary administrative structures in place, or be willing to acquire these superstructures and put them in place, if they are required for the services of their consultants to be successfully applied. Otherwise, the anticipated benefits will not be forthcoming.

Again, the inability of consultants to evaluate the managerial skills of their clients must be condemned in formulating the solutions they did. Reforms or recommendations which are difficult to manage because there is a lack of the necessary managerial skills in the client's organization, will be inappropriately implemented. As such, they become costly and largely wasted projects. If they are managed poorly, the outcome will be a failure to benefit from the results. The consultants put into place something that was beyond the administrative capabilities of their clients to manage. They ought to have recognized this shortcoming.

If the client's management can administer the recommendations proposed, or manage the new business systems put into place, or act upon the advice or services the consultant put into effect, then the services provided can be considered successfully performed by the consultant. If consultants are still required to assist their clients with the management of the reforms long after the project has terminated, those consultants have performed poorly. They have merely feathered their own nests.

PERFORMANCE FACTORS

The consultant's deportment will influence the client's evaluation. The performance factor, the actual carrying out of the work by the consultant, can be examined in several aspects:

- There were conditions and requirements describing how the work was to be performed. Were the terms of the contract fulfilled?
- Where the consultant had to work closely with the client, was the work done unobtrusively with negligible disruption and little generation of antagonism in the client's organization?
- During the progress of the work, was good communication maintained regarding the status of the project? Were results communicated to the client in an understandable fashion?
- Finally, did the consultant not only communicate information on the progress of the project but rigorously explain the methodology, the conclusions found, and their potential impact on the client?

Each aspect is important in evaluating the performance value to the client. The last item demands some effort on the client's part to understand the methodology used. It also demands that the consultant explain and justify in understandable terms how and why the conclusions were arrived at.

The Mechanics

The mechanics of the project represent the elements that are characteristic of any contract or business deal that one might find between a contractor and a contractee, between a buyer and a seller. They can be summed up in the question, "Did the consultant perform all the tasks assigned, within the budget established for the project, and was the work, its reporting, and presentation of conclusions as contracted?" The client contracted with a consultant for a certain project to be conducted under certain terms respecting costs, completion dates, patent rights, fee structure, and so on. All ought to have been done according to the terms negotiated.

John Steinbeck, while traveling in Russia, is quoted (Robbins, 1987), as follows:

> "... we ordered for breakfast, an omelet, toast and coffee and what has just arrived is a tomato salad with onions, a dish of pickles, a big slice of watermelon, and two bottles of cream soda."

Steinbeck's request was obviously not fulfilled. The contractee has not satisfied the contractor's demands. A breakfast of sorts was supplied but not the one that was requested. The contract, i.e., the original order, has not been met. It is hoped that the breakfast hunger of Steinbeck's party was assuaged, but Robbins does not give further details.

No evaluation is implied in the question at the start of this section. It is merely the acknowledgment that a contractual arrangement was carried out that met the terms dictated and agreed to by both parties. Nevertheless, it is not a trivial point, because it will be a factor in whether or not that consultant performed to contract and is contacted again or, more important to the consultant, whether that consultant is recommended by the client to others.

Impact of Consultant's Performance

The impact on the client's staff of the consultant's performance of work need not be belabored here as it has already been discussed in previous chapters. The disruptions that can be caused do represent hidden costs for clients. The need and timing for these interventions should have been cleared in advance with clients.

The important issue to be considered here is how such disruptions were handled by consultants to minimize their annoyance value. Tactful preparations can help considerably in smoothing relationships between clients and consultants. Such may be:

- Forewarning the client's staff well in advance of when their assistance will be required.
- Describing clearly what the nature of their assistance will be and advising them early what special supplies or information will be required.
- Preparing the scheduling of manufacturing trials at slow periods of production and in cooperation with plant management.

The care that consultants show in these preparations for using the time of their client's staff and facilities will ensure that work will be carried out properly with minimum stress.

Good consultants will never be far from the heart of the project as it is taking place. They will discuss the procedures and the results with those most closely involved in the work. They will closely supervise their subordinates. If clients find that their consultants spend most of their onsite visits in the president's office "dazzling their clients with action plans" (Shahin 1995) or are otherwise absent while juniors carry out the work, those clients have cause to look closely at their relationships for what is being done. Clients cannot receive good advice or decisions from absentee consultants and will receive only inadequate advice from the juniors.

Communication

There is a difference between reporting and communicating. Reporting is bare and cold: it states only the facts. Communicating is much more. It involves a two-way understanding of the messages between consultant and client, between the consultant's contact person and the client's facilitator. For communication, both must understand throughout the performance what is going on. They must both "speak the same language," use the same symbols. The language of all interim reports, of all meetings between responsible parties, and of the final reports themselves must be understood by both the clients and the consultants. This is far from a trivial consideration. It is one very important criterion that cannot be dismissed by clients in the evaluation of their consultants.

Clients and consultants must communicate using the same language. This need cannot be emphasized too much. If consultants use symbols (i.e., jargon or "in-words") recognized only by the initiated, then bad or no communication results. These symbols are not translatable by their clients because there is no mutual understanding of them. The inputs and recommendations of the consultants are untranslatable and hence not understood by their clients. (The elements of good communication have been discussed earlier.)

Hammer (1994) strikes out in a biting condemnation at the "insiders' jargon" that consultants often use in communications and project proposals prepared for the United Nations that effectively say much but mean little — much like my letter cited earlier advising a company on the merits of gas chromatography that my superior had altered. Hammer, an anthropologist and FAO (Food and Agriculture Organization) consultant, reproduced four columns of words found in U.N. jargon that had been used in proposals, recommendations, and correspondence. By themselves these words are quite meaningful. To say much and mean little, one chooses a word, any word, from each of the four columns. My own selections from her tabulation produced the following pithy sounding but quite meaningless phrases:

- Centrally integrated cooperative initiative.
- Rationally controlled growth-oriented incentive.
- Totally motivated urban dialogue.
- Dynamically integrated sectoral participation.

But what wonderfully meaningless phrases! They sound so seminal, so pregnant with potential, that the unsuspecting client can be duped into thinking there is something real here, something erudite that the client should not want to miss. But it is all froth.

Is such blather so rare? I recently received a letter from a consultant with the following phrases in it:

- "...progressive human resource infra-structure...."
- "...true shared-leadership culture...."

The foregoing phrases were, I swear, not made up. If clients can spot such jargon in their consultants' proposals or in any of their consultants' speeches before any contract has been signed, those clients would be advised to find other consultants quickly. Such fuzzy communication is a possible (indeed a very likely) symptom of fuzzy thinking. Jargon must not become a substitute for thinking.

"The chief merit of language is clearness, and we know that nothing detracts so much from this as do unfamiliar terms."

Galen, ca A.D. 130–200

How prevalent is this double-speak? Certainly Hammer's paper is not the first reference that can be found. Stackhouse (1991) referred to the confusing language of consultants thus:

"…frustrated clients are still trying to translate what their consultants have told them."

Why has a cartoon strip such as *Dilbert*© become so popular if it has not touched so many people familiar with the confusing lexicon of consultants, management experts, and business people?

When the symbols used in communication are not understood universally, communication between consultant and client is lost. Therefore, clients have only one conclusion: the consultant is incompetent in communication. Technical and scientific reports must be written to communicate with nontechnical people. Project proposals, reports of work done, or action plans written by consultants in such untranslatable symbols that cloud communication are sure signs that the client did not, or will not, get "its money's worth." These bring the consultant's performance into serious doubt.

The introductory chapter to this book was liberally sprinkled with euphemisms for downsizing, such as:

- Managing personnel resources.
- Outplacing.
- Returning to what we do best (the core business).

This was not entirely an effort at levity. There was a purpose. The world of consultants is prone to jargon, and by jargon one knows the consultants who will prove incompetent in communication. Clients are well advised to avoid the consultants who practice jargon and run for another consultant if words such as "world class," "customer-focused," "client-driven," or even "market-oriented" keep popping out of their consultant's mouths or off the written page.

Methodology Used by the Consultant

"The end cannot justify the means, for the simple and obvious reason that the means employed determine the nature of the ends employed."

Aldous Huxley in *Ends and Means*

Too often the client accepts what the consultant produces as "hard" data as if it were Holy Scripture and not to be challenged or questioned. Consultants are not divinely inspired people — this has been pointed out repeatedly in this book — but they are intelligent and versed in very specific areas of expertise. They are mere humans and prone to err. Sometimes the applications of their expert services can be inappropriate, even wrong, for their clients.

Clients need to focus not only on the results obtained by the consultant but also on *how* they were obtained. Was the methodology used to collect the data correct? This is a consideration quite distinctly different from the *impact* of the results on the clients or their organizations. Clients should consider whether the project provided the *correct* information, product, or expertise, or whatever it is that they needed to relieve themselves satisfactorily of. This is the most critical evaluation. Were the objectives of the project *correctly* met? Were true, real-life, absolute results obtained? This is not the same as asking whether the project was *successful*. The question is simply whether what the client asked to be done was, indeed, carried out *properly using the correct analytical tools* by the consultant and whether it *truthfully* represents the "facts" or in absolute terms, the truth.

Sometimes consultants can use the wrong methodologies to collect data from or for their clients. If the methodologies were wrong, the results most assuredly will be wrong also. (Methodologies should have been reviewed before the project began even at the risk of clients having to pay their consultants for a very detailed proposal. The extra cost is worth the insurance.)

Wrong procedures in gathering data may not be the best descriptive phrase here. Inappropriate procedures is a more likely term. These are procedures that could perhaps introduce a bias or error into the results. Poor training procedures (Kay 1996), incorrect chemical analytical procedures, sampling procedures that introduce a bias, poorly conducted surveys, or poorly structured questionnaires (Fuller 1994) can all introduce errors into the results obtained. These inappropriate procedures confound the problems they were created to resolve. Results based on them can only lead to faulty solutions.

Clients have an obligation to verify as best they can that the proper methodologies were used to obtain accurate data and that the conclusions drawn are as true as possible, i.e., the best available. The methodologies, if not readily apparent in the proposal and challenged there, must be challenged (that is, questioned) during the undertaking (another important reason for the client to have spot checks on the progress of work). Clients should carefully analyze all data sent in through interim reports and in their consultants' final reports. Only by intensively questioning their consultants and probing what was done and what the results mean (not how they can be used) can they evaluate the validity of the services they received.

For example: surveys of consumers' opinions are frequently a task set for consultants. These polls may be carried out in a shopping mall, solicited by mail, or conducted by telephone. A key to a good survey is that the respondent should not know what the questioner is after. The reason is simple. Respondents frequently like to "help" the questioner if they know what the questioner is after. This so-called help may bias the respondent's answers and hence influence the results of the survey. Therefore, the format of the questionnaire must cleverly deceive respondents into not knowing what the subject of the survey is about. Respondents then are "blind" and cannot bias the results with "helpful" answers.

Much skill on the part of consultants must go into designing questionnaires. A poorly designed questionnaire with bad questions may lead consultants to provide misleading information to their clients. If this sin is compounded by a poorly conducted survey, the results can be very much in error.

SUMMARY

Any evaluation done by clients of their consultants' activities has several facets to be considered. Each must be rated before clients can truly estimate the value of the relationships and whether they got their money's worth.

All consulting projects are exercises in technology transfer to some degree. That is, the consultant transfers expertise/advice/skills, i.e., technology, to those who for a variety of reasons cannot resolve a present difficulty and require this technology. This transfer must be done to benefit the client. Clients must be able to use and maintain the technology that was transferred.

The underlying principle in all consultancy is that the consultant should assist the client and then "outplace" himself. The recommendations which have been provided to the client should not pose an unmanageable and costly burden on the client. They certainly should not require the continued presence of the consultant to implement them. If they do, then the consultant has not performed competently.

Evaluating consultants is an activity that must be divorced as much as possible from an evaluation of the project itself and its completion. Admittedly the two activities do intermesh. Clients, however, must attempt a separation of these two to be able to properly evaluate the performance and competence of their consultants. A successfully completed project does not mean that there was a good client/consultant relationship.

Factors such as the economic consequences of the activities of the consultant, technical feasibility of the project for the client, administrative superstructure to manage the project and performance of the consultant throughout play large roles in rating the consultant. All are important, but the most critical ones — critical since they relate most closely to the interface between the consultant and the client — are the performance factors. These involve most importantly the ability of the consultant to work nondisruptively with the client, to communicate, and to transfer the project and its results successfully to the client.

9 To Continue to Hire Consultants? Or to Expand In-House Resources?

A man in the wilderness asked me,
How many strawberries grew in the sea.
I answered him, as I thought good,
As many red herrings as swam in the wood.

Iona and Peter Opie
The Puffin Book of Nursery Rhymes

INTRODUCTION

Whether to continue using consultants regularly to complement in-house skills or, its alternative, to expand the resources of the company and so reduce the need for either consultants or outsourcing, will surely arise for clients from time to time. The questioners frequently come from inside the organization: from the expansionists in the organization, or from those who want to keep the organization lean-and-mean. The interests of both are self-serving. The expansionists want to build empires; the others, the minimalists, want to keep overheads low, to see profits and, sometimes, their bonuses grow.

The nonsense riddle in the nursery rhyme above was more easily and aptly answered than either of the questions to be discussed here. Riddles are meant to have an element of nonsense as well as being a brain teaser. One looks for a novel and whimsical answer. But these questions above are not riddles, and one does not expect a nonsense answer. They come up again and again throughout the organization's life cycle.

An attempt at providing answers was begun earlier in Chapters 7 and 8. There, some indirect clues to the answer were provided. Chapter 8 examined tools for the client to evaluate the performance of a consultant; Chapter 7 provided awareness of, and guided the client through, problems of implementation of the consultant's recommendations. These ideas can be used to balance the views on these questions.

REVIEWING SOME OF THE CONSIDERATIONS

The criteria on which to begin to form answers to the above questions and arrive at a decision will be greatly influenced by two major factors:

- First and foremost is a consideration of the client's ambition. What are the client's goals? Where does the client want to be now, a few years from now, or several years from now? These objectives are highly personal to the clients and to their particular needs at any time.
- The second factor is the nature of those tasks that clients find need to be undertaken repeatedly by consultants. What must be frequently shored up? Are these incidences of resorting to outside intervention indicative of weaknesses?

How both factors are viewed and assessed by clients provide clarification to the issues. Any attempt by clients to categorize these under headings such as financial, marketing, management, or employee morale soon founders on the old dilemma: how to equate advantages and disadvantages to which neither a dollar sign nor any parity value can be easily assigned.

The issues will be confounded by two opposing parties. Protagonists of either minimalism or expansionism will both produce convincing arguments to support their views. The minimalists will put forward arguments that would keep the organization's work force structured to maintain only its core functions. Therefore, any need for specialty services would favor the use of consultants.

Indeed, the philosophy of minimalism would be advocated by consultants at every opportunity. It supports their continued intervention. This argument is the essence of all sales and promotional pitches of consultants — "of course, you are better off with me because...." And there would follow a litany of how overheads would be kept lowered, a more specialized service designed to the client's needs would be offered, only bottom line expenses are involved, the need to pay only when services were used, and so on.

Contrariwise, if within the client's staff there is an ambitious "empire builder," this individual's desire to build a power base with more skilled staff may be irresistibly strong. When the demand for expansion comes from highly productive people in the organization, for example a highly inventive developer of new products or a very innovative marketing person, management will be concerned that refusal to grant the expansion may result in the loss of these assets. An expanded resource base within the organization may then be condoned without any recourse to further discussion. Management may feel its hands are tied to do otherwise.

As organizations attempt to pare down to what is seen as their core business, they see justification in farming out (outsourcing) certain tasks which, though important, do not contribute significantly to the company's profitability or its core business. Thus, the minimalists may want to outsource such tasks as security, warehousing and distribution, building maintenance, packaging, legal affairs, financial matters, and many other activities.

The expansionists will counter that such narrowness stifles the ability to respond to change and to be innovative. Creativity will suffer if new blood is not introduced. Staff will not learn or be challenged if crises, or a better phrase, stimulating circumstances, are always farmed out. Flexibility to respond to change demands not leanness but a certain amount of "fat," healthy fat if that is not an oxymoron. There will be a neverending seesaw between these two polarized positions within organizations.

Clients require a dispassionate review of the advantages and disadvantages of both arguments.

CONSIDERATIONS WITHIN THE ORGANIZATION

In any evaluation of these two contrary views, clients must focus on two considerations. They are:

- First, what the productive and profitable elements within the organization are.
- Second, what particular circumstances create the situations that force consideration of resorting to consultants.

By such analysis, weaknesses in the organization can be determined.

Highly productive and efficient departments or divisions within the organization that need frequent support from consultants for their continued strong performances may indicate a weakness and perhaps expansion is justified. Weaknesses, if potentially dangerous to the well-being of the organization, may be improved by additional expert staff. Emergencies, if infrequent and not generated within the organization, may best be left to outside resources. Much depends on the nature of the emergencies. By focusing on these problem areas, clients can make decisions on whether changes are needed in their managerial or structural organizations.

THE STRUCTURE AND PHILOSOPHY OF THE COMPANY

An organization's "closed politics," as Snow (1961) would put it, play a major role in how that organization will evaluate the factors posed above. Organizations administered on the basis of committee politics might opt for the use of consultants to supplement their resource base in times of need. Some family businesses are run by committees best described as either patriarchal or matriarchal.

In addition, many functions or systems within an organization are run by committee. The comparatively recent motivational technique of "circles" comprising staff from different disciplines to study and make improvements in products and processes are essentially systems run by committees. It might even be argued that the newer concepts of the "wall-less office," although meant to foster better communication between people and departments with like functions, is an attempt at organization by committee politics.

Such organizations might want an unbiased, third-party expert opinion when there is, perhaps, an inability to come to a unanimous decision on controversial issues. Outside assistance may very well be a necessity if the resource base within the organization, i.e., the committee, is so narrowly focused that a broader range of expertise is required.

Organizations with a distinct chain of command, i.e., systems with hierarchical politics (Snow, 1961), might consider the use of consultants differently. Such pyramidal organizations, in order to use consultants, require a resolution to do so; that is, they require the acquiescence of all levels between the power to authorize and the need. Expansionists in this chain between the power to authorize and the source of the request may be reluctant to approve using consultants. Passage of any request for outsourcing upward from the need to the granting authority may be obstructed. The message may be "colored," indicating their preference to opt for expansion instead.

Minimalists prefer the use of outsourcing and consultants to any suggestion that the organization should grow. They would encourage communication from the need to the power to authorize that favored consultants.

Then there are those who fear for their security should either minimalist or expansionist policies be adopted. They may be very reluctant to provide acquiescence or enthusiasm for either decision.

In organizations where Snow's court politics predominate, the power within the organization will determine whether there is a need to expand the resource base. This center of influence may be an individual, the *éminence grise* referred to in an earlier chapter, or a dominant department within an organization, or a highly productive division within a multinational corporation. Any decision to expand internal resources or to maintain the present organization and supplement it with consulting services will be greatly influenced by the philosophies of these centers of influence and power.

Medium-sized and large organizations have a combination of these governing politics within them. Small organizations are a curious mix of committee and hierarchical politics. One or the other system of governance dominates. Each structure and each substructure within other structures will present different arguments for or against minimalist or expansionist policies. The governance structure, its closed politics structure, can be a powerful factor in determining whether the organization builds them or prefers to complement its own resources with the use of consultants.

MATURITY AND EXPERIENCE WITHIN THE ORGANIZATION

The maturity, competence, and experience of individuals in the management of the organization and its collective maturity need consideration. The organization's stage of growth is intertwined with other considerations in determining how an organization will weight these factors, then balance them, and come finally to a decision to expand or not.

Young organizations with inexperienced managers may have a greater demand for the services of consultants as external advisers than do older mature organizations. The latter, through their own corporate and collective experiences, have developed a wealth of observation and exposure to draw upon. Young organizations have no such resource base. The consulting requirements of organizations will change as they mature and, with maturity, acquire experience.

Young companies face problems in putting together business and marketing plans that are strong enough to convince their financial backers of their viability. They lack not only experience but they may also lack expertise. For this they require assistance with their forecasting, their projections of cash flows, or inventory controls that call for a greater skill level in, for example, accounting, to guide them.

Scientists, attempting to capitalize on their inventions, frequently lack skills in preparing business plans, but they will also often be devoid of any skills in marketing and promotion. Companies whose main strengths arose primarily because of technological innovation can indeed be very hapless in commercial undertakings.

Initially, young companies may have to choose between hiring, for example, a financial adviser to guide them or building a responsible financial department. They will, however, be faced with the dilemma of determining the value, both quantifiable and qualitative, of which course of action to take and when to take it. That is:

- Is it more beneficial in the early stages of growth to go initially with a consulting accountant to guide them?
- Is it more sensible for the organization to hire an accountant and support staff, develop a more sophisticated financial department as an in-house asset right from the start, and have salary and overhead costs at this stage in its growth?

These are hard decisions for the young entrepreneurial company. They may opt for a middle course, i.e., to hire the consultant now but gradually develop the in-house resource with the assistance of this consultant. Options in other areas of expertise are similar.

Established organizations will have entirely different considerations to ponder. Their already developed financial department, to continue this example, may require, instead, investment counseling as they prepare to issue a public offering of stock or when they require guidance in securing funding for expansion. The need is for a consultant, a specialist in investment counseling but not as an in-house resource.

Older companies may require assistance in areas of reorganization of ailing superstructures, or in developing new markets with old established products, or in diversification. Again, the need is primarily for a skill to be used for a limited period and not for a new department within the organization.

The question will never be *finally and absolutely* decided but will become one whose resolution will change with time according to the particular pressures and circumstances influencing the client. Thus, as time progresses, there is a constant balancing of the pros and cons of using consultants or developing these same resources in-house. What may have been a determinant pushing the decision one way at one time may in other circumstances at some other time be unimportant. The history surrounding previous decisions and their resultant benefits, therefore, cannot help clients in new situations. Each new circumstance will require a new evaluation that will have no relationship to previous evaluations.

PERSONNEL CONSIDERATIONS

Personnel considerations can be determinants in the balancing process between expansionism and minimalism. Resistance to, or resentment of, consultants can occur in any working environment. Staff may feel that they, or their positions, are being evaluated prior to their possible dismissal or the elimination of their jobs. They may feel that they have the skills to undertake the assignment given to the consultant. They would like the opportunity and challenge to tackle these more exotic problems. Employee moral may be dampened by having their skills passed over by the constant use of consultants for challenging tasks. Staff will deduce only that management lacks confidence in them. When clients sense these feelings, avenues other than resorting to clients may be best. At this point, clients might consider minimizing their use of consultants and begin to build internal resources in those areas where consultants are most frequently used.

The switch from the frequent use of consultants to the development of in-house resources may become an imperative. Clients may be forced to do so based on the negative reactions of employees who are inconvenienced, irritated, or demoralized by the activities of the consultants. By developing the skills of employees through training in tasks previously warranting the use of consultants, clients can promote a greater sense of self-confidence among the staff.

Anyone familiar with the Topsy-like growth of management structures soon realizes expansion brings its own problems. For example, to expand a one-person traffic department would require hiring a replacement, an assistant. The original incumbent now might feel that the assistant poses more of a threat as a rival and may put forth a strong case for needing another assistant. If this is granted, the department now will consist of three people who are now rivals one to the other. Each will agitate to expand his or her own area of responsibility, and so growth begets growth and bureaucracies are built up.

CONSIDERATIONS RESPECTING THE NATURE OF THE TASKS

Some activities should not be put in-house. Pleas from expansionists to do so should be ignored. Outside resources may be much more competent to handle these tasks. Such activities are:

- Product audits
- Crisis management
- Training programs
- Security
- Legal matters
- Advertising

These are all activities few companies can cope with expertly in-house. Some tasks are best left to experts. There may be no, or only a marginal, advantage to build up in-house resources for doing these and, indeed, there can be distinct disadvantages if this is done.

AUDITS

There are many types of audits. They can range from financial audits to plant audits to product audits at the store shelf level. In audits, clients want a systematic examination of whatever the auditor or inspector was called in for. In product audits, clients want an examination of their products as the consumer sees them. These surveys are normally conducted at all retail levels where their products are exposed, from the mom-and-pop store level to the megastore level or warehouse store level.

They may wish to survey in areas where they have a promotional campaign to determine its effectiveness. They may survey for comparative purposes in areas where they meet stiff competition or as a simple internal check on their process and quality control systems.

Consulting firms that specialize in conducting audits are much better prepared to collect data and evaluate a client's products methodically and record all the pertinent data, such as price, location in the store, date codes, prices of competitive products, and all the other information that may be required in the audit.

Few sales forces, very few distributors, and only the rare agents in foreign countries are prepared to do this task properly. Their mandated jobs are sales and distribution, and such tasks as audits, thorough audits, take time from their core activities and their incomes. My personal experience with having the sales force perform an audit was not a good one. I had argued unsuccessfully for a product audit by a professional audit company. My client preferred to have the company's sales force perform the task. The result was a study replete with incomplete data respecting facings, pricing data, and competitive product pricing. Even such simple information as what cities the samples had been taken from and from which types of stores they had been collected was missing. There were long delays in receiving products, because the sales force collected samples as they made their regular rounds of their customers in their sales territories. Thus, there was no audit at a particular point in time. Rather, we received an audit that extended over a two- or three-month period, during which the samples trickled in with incomplete information.

Clients' salesforces are not likely to canvass stores thoroughly. First, this is not their job: they are not competent to do this as a customer would. They would do it as a salesperson. Second, they may introduce an element of bias. They may be reluctant to return samples of products if it might suggest they had done a poor job at replenishing or rotating stock or if it might make them look ineffective in their efforts at getting facings as compared to the competition's efforts.

Audits are prime examples of functions best left to consultants specializing in them. They are not activities to be brought in-house.

CRISIS MANAGEMENT

Crises involving matters of public health or safety, terrorist activity such as product tampering, sabotage, threats from outside groups or during strikes are best handled with the assistance of outside resources. Complementing the client's emergency team should be audit consultants, liability lawyers, public relations consultants, technical experts, trade associations, government authorities, and the police, who all may be required to assist. In addition, the services of skilled analytical laboratories may be required to provide unique testing services.

Public safety is paramount in any critical situation. Where safety has been compromised, litigation may result. There is the need to investigate why the crisis occurred, to establish responsibility, and hence liability. The company's brand image must be protected. There may be an attendant loss of goodwill. Customers who received defective parts require compensation. There are a myriad of problems that need resolution by experts in such crises.

Clients should have an emergency response team, but it is asking too much of the level of skills in any organization to handle such serious crises internally. Too much is involved for any organization.

TRAINING PROGRAMS

Training programs are activities that should be undertaken by experts. First, teaching is a skill best left to well-trained professionals and should not be left to nonexperts. (One trusts the outside resources conducting the courses do have professionally trained teachers or communicators.) Teaching, the skill *per se*, has limited value as a tool within most organizations. Second, the subject matter of the training program normally requires an expert in that branch of knowledge. These individuals are not usually resident on the staff of most organizations. Finally, training programs are best conducted away from the client's premises with expert instructors. These conditions allow the attendees to immerse themselves in the topic, network with other attendees, discuss the course material in bull sessions, and be free from the routine distractions of their homebases.

Certification in the various ISO (International Standards Organization) quality programs has become fashionable both because it has a cachet of "goodness, quality, and motherhood" and hence is a sales gimmick, but also because customers are demanding that their suppliers become certified. The particular standard they want their suppliers certified in is usually ISO 9002. Consequently, many clients see value as a marketing ploy in becoming certified. Clients should note carefully that certification is not necessarily adopted to improve the quality of their products but merely their marketability.

Hence, courses and consultants abound for training courses in ISO certification. Such courses should be taught by professionals in centers that have been certified to do so.

SECURITY

Do clients have the control of their security that they wish? Or the security for sensitive projects that they require? In food plants that I have been asked to visit I make it a point to watch start-up as employees arrive for the day shift. If I can reach the manufacturing floor before being challenged, that plant has a serious security problem. Many food plants do have a serious security problem.

Security is much more than merely preventing the entrance of unauthorized people onto the premises. It is also:

- Security for product in transit. So-called high-ticket items, shipments in bond (whiskey and cigarettes to mention only two) are prime targets.
- The losses by employees, which could include the loss of movable equipment, tools, or parts from the manufacturing plants, or even the removal of finished products.
- Assurance of protection against vandalism, sabotage, or attacks within the organization from despondent, disgruntled, or sick employees. This

is a major concern: "going postal" has entered the vocabulary to describe such violence.

- Protection against the loss of intellectual property, as well as special security checks where secret and confidential developments are taking place.

In addition, the security of senior management as they travel to areas where there is political unrest must be assured. Security consultants gather information regarding "safe behavior" for senior executives in troubled areas. These consultants also network in foreign countries and can provide lists of "safe areas."

Sales data, marketing information describing forthcoming promotional strategies, and financial data must be secure from the prying of competitors. Security also involves the protection of workers to ensure that they are not working in a hazardous environment.

Security and the training of employees in secure procedures is not to be delegated to nonprofessionals.

OTHER CONSIDERATIONS

There are considerations that defy classification under either those within the organization or those relating to the nature of the tasks. They are influences affecting neither the philosophies of the minimalists nor the expansionists. They are unique and warrant separate classifications.

GEOGRAPHIC LOCATION

Clients must also consider geography. There are geographic areas of any country that are less desirable areas in which to live. The geographic location of the client can seriously affect the availability of the resources, both physical and human, that are at the client's disposal. For example, in economically depressed areas, unusually high salaries would be needed to attract the skilled personnel required to supplant the expertise provided by consultants. Clients have not only the costs of highly skilled staff to consider but also must be concerned about the availability of facilities for the families of staff. In depressed areas, availability of housing may be a problem, schooling for children may be poor, cultural events may be lacking, and crime may be an issue. Consequently, it may be much more economical and reasonable to employ consultants when specialized skills are required. The overhead, salaries, and fringe benefits that would be necessary to keep and maintain in-house resources may outweigh the costs of employing consultants.

When organizations require the skills of specialists to be on staff, the salaries of these skilled personnel may be so high that clients in low-income areas of the country may be reluctant to incorporate these specialist functions into their organizations at the particular stage of growth they are in. In these cases, companies may be more inclined to favor using consultants on an if-and-when-needed basis.

Availability of Skills

This is a consideration similar to that associated with geographic location. If the needed level of expertise is not available locally, then clients must pay extraordinarily high salaries to obtain personnel with the skills required to come to their geographic locations. The alternative is to be forced to use consultants with the necessary skills to complement their resources. This, in a nutshell, is the point raised in the previous section.

If clients have a pool of labor in the neighborhood with the desired level of skills and these skills are available at a reasonable cost, then clients may choose to build an in-house resource base. But there are competitive pressures. Here is a hypothetical situation:

> A small manufacturing company is in a prosperous area dominated by a noncompetitive industry. This latter could be the oil industry or the car industry. Skilled personnel are readily available but the local salaries of these richer industries puts this manpower out of reach of the small manufacturer unless it pays comparable salaries. A depression comes. For example, oil prices fall or people stop buying cars. The local industries downsize severely. The level of skills available rises. Salary demands drop.

The small manufacturer expands because the necessary technical skills become attractively available. Unfortunately, another crisis occurs, albeit many may not see it as such. Oil prices rise, or the demand for new cars may grow. The small manufacturer loses staff to higher-paying jobs.

Thus, another question can be introduced. Is there a great enough long-term need for the specialist employees sufficient to justify an expansion? To supplant consultants with in-house resources requires that clients have steady work for the new staff or create work for them. This has repercussions in other areas, i.e., the expansion of markets, the development of new products for new markets, etc. Clients must keep the new people busy with tasks that utilize and challenge their skills. Clients cannot have employees with specialized skills sitting about idly waiting for a need for their services to arise.

A catch-22 situation arises. Are the resources this new staff represents readily available should a crisis arise? As readily available as they would be if outside resources had been requested? They may already have a considerable degree of pressure on them because the client has found work for them within the organization. Any increased demands on their time for new projects may result in some time being taken from necessary routine jobs. The questions for clients now become:

- Can these routine business affairs be disrupted to respond to new needs and issues that face the clients?
- How available are these expanded in-house resources when needed?

If the answer is "yes, they are available," then minimalists might argue that these resources were underemployed and the building of in-house resources was ill-advised. If the answer is "no," that is, in-house resources though present are unavailable for untoward situations, the argument has come full circle. The client must resort to availing itself of consulting services. Building in-house resources did not supplant the need for consultants.

ECONOMIES: MINIMALIST VS. EXPANSIONIST ARGUMENTS

Many smaller manufacturing plants keep a corner of their QC laboratories for research and development work or perhaps a corner of the plant engineer's workshop is turned into an experimental workshop. Small companies usually combine many functions in their organizations.

I advised one client to develop an in-house research and development capability that would be separate and distinct from the resources currently used in the quality control department. This, I reasoned, would centralize all my client's R&D efforts and technical information needs into one department free from the pressures found in quality control. The advantages I saw were the development of:

- A cadre of research skills to be used in-house.
- An R&D group able to respond rapidly to production and marketing pressures and to troubleshoot any product crises.
- A more disciplined approach to long range technical needs. Projects presently in the hands of universities and outside research companies could then be brought into the newly formed R&D group.

Admittedly, my recommendation would have created two distinct departments, one for QA and one for R&D with two equal status managers, where before there had been a single department with one manager.

My client saw things very differently:

- A senior executive to direct the technical resources of the two departments that would be created would be required.
- That senior person would demand a secretary, a company car, and other fringe benefits.
- A middle management individual, the R&D manager, would be needed with support staff and equipment.

My services satisfied my client's needs when needed and saved my client money in the long run. I had become a bottom line expense, a cost of doing business with no overhead.

Ip (1996) reported another element for consideration in the building of R&D groups. R&D and certain specialized or capital-intensive methods of manufacturing have become too expensive for some companies to acquire in-house. Consulting-cum-outsourcing is the only logical way of life. Ip even suggested in a burst of hyperbole that the traditional company is *passé* and will not be able to compete in the future. Rather, supply chains, that is, companies who outsource activities to other companies, who in turn outsource activities to yet other companies, and so on, are the future.

Gay (1996) presented a much more cautious view regarding outsourcing. He found that some companies only broke even and others actually lost money relying on outsourcing. While there is a difference of degree between consultants and outsourcing, Gay's observations suggest a cautionary approach.

Certainly, there are financial considerations to be faced by any company preferring to employ consultants or by the company believing the correct path is the development of internal resources. Consultants do not come cheaply. Kay (1996) reported, for instance, that one company spent $24 million on a consultant company for a re-engineering project.

Equally, however, the costs of developing internal resources can be expensive. Salaries for the skilled staff, their need for specialized equipment and other resources and their housing within the organization can be costly.

SUMMARY

Should the organization use outside resources for those extraordinary needs that can arise, sometimes with frightening regularity, or should it develop in-house resources to respond to these same needs? There is no easy answer, and there are many considerations.

There are costs to consider. The yearly expenditures for consultants can be equated to the projected costs of establishing a permanent in-house resource. In most cases, clients will find that costs associated with consultants are the cheaper figure from this bare-bones equation. If the need for these same resources is more and more frequently encountered, then it may behoove clients to develop in-house resources, but both policies bring advantages and disadvantages that cannot be measured in monetary value. Minimalism, for instance, may stifle creativity and innovation and the ability to respond effectively to change. Controlled expansion to allow some flexibility within the organization gives staff a chance to meet some of the challenges requiring consultants. Staff learn from these opportunities. However, growth, if uncontrolled, can be an expensive indulgence. To invest in specialists requires that these people be kept busy, and clients must only make investments in staff when there is a continuing need for specialists.

Provision of advice in esoteric topics in technology, advice from specialists in all the consequences following crises, review and editing of technical brochures for accuracy and accordance to prevailing legislation, inspection of manufacturing facilities and product audits, customer surveys, and training programs are all tasks for experts which should not be undertaken in-house. They are also tasks on which it is hard to place dollar values.

There are both short- and long-term advantages and disadvantages to keeping consultants on retainers. Such relationships allow consultants to become familiar with the staff of their clients and to gain their confidence. In such situations the staff do not feel threatened by their presence, but retainerships do encourage frequent intervention by consultants.

Reasons to continue with consultants and other outside resources or to discontinue this practice and develop in-house resources will be highly personal. The causes that require consultants are singular ones representing different issues clients face.

Each occasion must be evaluated individually and independently by clients asking themselves whether the need to refer to consultants frequently suggests that there are weaknesses within their organizations. If these occasions are frequent and always for the same reasons, then surely these represent a fragility within the organization. This must be addressed.

Consultants can provide a reservoir of expertise and cutting-edge technology that allows a company to channel its activities productively and efficiently. Experience may be a good teacher, but this experience can be both costly and slow to acquire in-house. Sound use of consultants may help a company to avoid these problems and leapfrog into new ventures. The smart company learns by the experience and knowledge provided by the consultants. Or as one anonymous writer put it,

> *"Learn from the mistakes of others — you can never live long enough to make them all yourself."*

10   Reducing the Need
for Consultants

*Only when he has ceased to need things can a man truly be his own master and so
really exist.*

Anwar al-Sadat

INTRODUCTION

In the preceding chapter, the dilemma of whether clients should hire the requisite
staff to replace their frequent need to call upon consultants or whether they should
continue the repeated use of consultants and delay the hiring of permanent employees
was examined. It is not an easy question to resolve, and there is no easy answer to
this problem that is satisfactory to all clients. To paraphrase an old saying: "What's
sauce for the goose may not be sauce for the gander."

Clients are highly individualistic. The environments they operate in are different.
The circumstances that arise in these different environments are also different, and
each client will respond differently. Their individual needs will be dissimilar, and
what is suitable for one client may not be suitable for another.

Nevertheless, all clients can reduce their reliance on consultants *if there is a
desire on the part of management to develop within the organization the philosophy
of self-reliance, innovation, and scholarship.* Clients can become self-reliant, reduce
a dependency on outside resources, and still maintain a progressive and dynamic
outlook. By building stronger and more self-reliant organizations, clients will gain
maturity and have greater self-control. They will develop those analytical and deductive skills and experience — those possessed by the consultant that they have come
to rely upon — to become more competitive organizations. Other side-benefits will
be the development of greater competency and confidence within organizations as
staff gain the skills to manage without recourse to consultants. Pride of accomplish-
ment will grow and morale will improve — if greater self-reliance is undertaken
properly. Obviously, even the costs for consulting, which can be substantial, will be
reduced. But this is a minor issue compared to the other benefits.

NURTURING SELF-RELIANCE

Table 2.2 classified the tasks that consultants are most likely to be asked to assist
their clients with. These could also have been classified as follows:

- Income-generating projects (market expansion, new product development,
  energy and waste conservation programs, investment opportunities, etc.).

- Administrative projects (re-engineering, applications of innovative management technologies, computer and communication systems, legal and financial matters, etc.).
- Physical projects (construction and design of new plant or equipment, etc.).
- Knowledge-based projects (advisory services in specialized technologies including crisis management, basic research, investigative studies such as surveys and product audits, training programs, etc.).

Any reduction in the need for these tasks will, of course, minimize the need for consultants. That is common sense.

However, not all the needs or causes for the tasks can be reduced. Upgrading employee skills is, for instance, a continuing activity that should not be eliminated. Wanton vandalism of products in the marketplace will crop up periodically, causing crises which must be managed with outside resources. Nor is it wise for clients to avoid the use of consultants in ventures requiring technologies in which the clients have little knowledge or experience. Consultants help them avoid wasteful mistakes and long learning curves.

Nevertheless, the development of self-reliance can be accomplished within organizations but only if management is willing to make the effort. If the will to do so is there, then the need becomes one of enabling the internal systems of these organizations to be developed sufficiently to defend against, or take advantage of, the unexpected. *Ergo*, organizations become "better places," an unquantifiable but distinct advantage. Clients, through having developed more self-contained, self-possessed, and competent organizations, will have built greater awareness and innovation within their organizations.

The danger for clients comes if, by reducing the need for outside assistance or simply denying themselves access to outside assistance for whatever reason, they may turn a blind eye to this change going on around them. Blindness to change brings unforeseen short- and long-term disadvantages. Becoming self-reliant brings with it the ability to be aware and rational. It does not confer insularity within the organization.

WHAT CAUSES THE NEED FOR OUTSIDE INTERVENTION?

If the above question were answered honestly, most managers with the responsibility for using consultants would have to answer that "change" was the cause. Something in the course of their daily business life has changed, sometimes dramatically and suddenly. But just as often, change comes slowly and relentlessly. Management had not foreseen the change or, if they had, they chose to ignore or play down its effect on their affairs. Now, they feel helpless. Their own internal resources are inadequate to handle what was once some minor change but which has grown into a very apparent big change.

Change is, however, to be expected. It is a natural event. It is constancy which is unusual, unnatural, and atypical. There will always be, for instance, someone who will find a way to build a better mousetrap or provide a better service that will cause

TABLE 10.1

A General Examination of How Certain Factors Initiate Effects Which Force Organizations to Alter Their Activities

Cause	Possible Effect
Advances in technology	• Faster, better, cheaper, or more efficient process • Improved product or service • Innovative product
Legislative enactments or government intervention	• Imposition of trade restrictions through both tariff and nontariff trade barriers • Removal of trade barriers allowing foreign competition • Change in fiscal policies regarding taxation, sales taxes, interest rates • Prohibition of certain trade practices, e.g., advertising to children banned
Consumer activism	• Aggressive consumer reaction, e.g., to irradiated foods • Consumer boycotts of products or services, e.g., of sweatshop tactics • Bad publicity due to promotions or advertising, e.g., sexism, chauvinism, racism
Labor problems	• Nonavailability of skilled labor • Labor unrest • Union activism to force a closed shop
Environmental causes	• Complaints from local authorities respecting noxious odors • Water and sewage rates rising precipitously • Waste disposal too costly
Marketplace forces	• New competitor • Old competitors with new products or services and more aggressive promotion of these • Introduction of new retailing practices, e.g., micromarketing vs. macromarketing techniques
Administrative changes	• Organizational changes leading to staff disenchantment • Communication channels disrupted

change for competing products. Since change is to be expected, then change is a process to be managed wisely by clients.

In Table 10.1 some causes that can evoke unexpected changes have been tabulated along with some of the changes engendered by these causes. As one can see, there are a few basic causes:

- Advances in technology allow a better product to be made or something to be made more efficiently. A good example would be the announcement by IBM in 1997 of their ability to make chips using copper instead of aluminum. Intel, the leading chip maker, now has some catching up to do.

- Governments at whatever level can enact legislation that has profound effects on the business communities locally, nationally, and internationally.
- Developments in the marketplace respecting either the competition or retail marketing practices can alter how customers see the client's products.
- Consumers and their capricious attitudes will force changes in products and services to meet their changing demands.
- Changes in management practices, in how businesses are run and organized, can be developed.

The changes that these developments can produce are only briefly sketched out in this table. It would serve no purpose to elucidate on them further nor to produce a more complete list of the effects. It suffices for clients to know that any of the developments cited could have far-reaching ramifications.

Much value can be obtained, not by analyzing the causes, but by examining their genesis. If the subtle harbingers presaging change could be recognized, then this awareness of the coming change should alert clients to take some evasive or defensive action.

An even better outcome of this forewarning is the possibility that clients might be able to take *advantage* of the coming disruption. Early awareness of the causes of sudden change can provide time to develop a comprehensive strategy, enabling clients to circumvent the need to employ consultants. Thus, clients might get ahead of their competition and gain market share from them or in some manner gain economic advantage. Change, or the elements contributing to change, can be prevented, circumvented, or even harnessed if clients take certain necessary precautions. A crude analogy might be made in order to clarify this point. An individual suffering a heart attack requires emergency treatment. However, had the victim paid attention to certain warning signs such as overweight, poor diet, high blood pressure, excessive smoking and alcohol consumption, and had taken preventive action through eating a prudent diet, adopting a moderate exercise program, plus applying stress reduction techniques and losing weight, the need for the emergency intervention may have been avoided. Even if such precautions had not prevented the heart attack, they would have reduced the odds of a heart attack or reduced the severity of one.

Why do clients not see the subtle beginnings of trends that are happening around them? There are three conditions or signs, much like those in the above analogy of overweight, high blood pressure, and poor diet, that clients ignore. These are themselves leading causes for most problems that consultants are called in to resolve (Table 10.2). These are:

- Shortsightedness in business planning. Clients adopt the attitude that it cannot happen to them because they are too small, too big, or not mainstream enough.
- Unawareness of activities incident upon their own business activities, in their communities, or in the marketplace.
- Inflexibility, causing an inability to respond rapidly to change, whether through unpreparedness, through rigidity in management thinking, or being too lean-and-mean without sufficient available resources.

TABLE 10.2
A Generalization of the Genesis of Causes for Companies to Employ Consultants

Initial Cause	Ultimate Result
Shortsightedness	• Lack of direction, with no goals to inspire staff
	• Inattention to long-term trends
Unawareness	• Ignorance of their business
	• Inattention to developments in their immediate or more distant markets
Unresponsiveness	• Inability to respond effectively and efficiently
	• No depth of skills to implement remedial action
	• Intransigency coupled with inflexibility

Attention to the signs within their organizations and basing preventive action on them should help clients develop self-reliance to harness the changes. Thereby they reduce those situations for which consultants are required.

SHORTSIGHTEDNESS

Many clients, particularly those with small organizations, frequently feel that their smallness will somehow shield them from competitive pressures in the marketplace. They believe they are too small to attract their competitors' attention. They may even go so far as to believe the government will overlook them in their little peccadilloes because, in their mind, the government is after the "big guys." To them also, newer technology is not for the likes of them. These are all shortsighted mindsets. Change will affect them, and unless they take a more aggressive and foresighted view regarding their futures, they may not have one. Shortsighted management become in time the ideal clients that consultants feed on.

Lack of Direction

When clients place more emphasis on the short-term needs of their organizations and neglect their long-term needs, several critical events occur:

- They will fail to provide focused directions to their organizations.
- Without planning, they will not be able to prepare themselves for the many steps necessary to attain their goals.
- They will not be able to anticipate obstacles that require surmounting next week, next month, or next year.
- Goals and purposes will be lost as these organizations try to cope with events breaking around them or, worse still, that have broken around them that they ought to have foreseen.

These changes, whether in the marketplace or in the business community, cannot be analyzed intelligently and acted upon rationally if clients are only concerned about today's problems. Any knee-jerk reaction that clients may give to change can be damaging.

Attention to day-to-day activities must be part of a bigger plan. It must be a part, a studied part, of a longer-range strategic plan. Where the clients' *only* focus is on the end of their day or week or month, those clients are not prepared for the unexpected, and they are poorly prepared to cope with the expected.

Clients must be ready to ask themselves many questions. Where are they going? Where do they want to go? What do they want to accomplish, and what do they want to do better? They ought not merely to ask whether they will get today's orders out on time. This introspection is the first step in planning their strategies for longer periods of time. Planning business strategies is the key. For example, if a client plans to take a certain course of action, what corollary problems might there be respecting suppliers, competitors' reactions, customers, government, or other publics, such as seniors, religious groups, and social activists? These elements can present problems that clients can anticipate and prepare solutions for. Some crude modeling of possible outcomes as a result of certain actions can be studied. A series of what-if situations must be looked at critically.

Once direction and destination in the long term are known, then clients are positioned to be aware of what intermediate steps must be planned for and taken. An examination of the intermediate steps forces clients into finer and finer studies of trends in their environment and of possible external impediments to their direction. They can seek solutions to these and be prepared when these foreseen barriers to their progress confront them. These analyses will reduce the chances of unexpected surprises.

INFLEXIBILITY

Is an inability to look ahead an acknowledgment that clients need more staff? No. Rather it is an acknowledgment that a lean-and-mean philosophy does have a downside if it produces inflexibility as a by-product that renders the client unable to take the time to look ahead. Flexibility is necessary to allow clients an opportunity for forward thinking and planning. There comes a time even in minimalist organizations when someone should have the flexibility to sit with his feet up on the desk and think. Clients should not view flexibility as laxity if it gives staff the opportunity to expand the horizons of the company.

Flexibility within organizations would serve to allow staff to be aware of their immediate business world. They would have a moment to study all those internal and external activities that influence their abilities for effective management and for applying new technologies. The opportunity to meet to discuss with their colleagues the events in the market place would create the atmosphere for creative approaches to issues. It would empower staff to keep aware of the advances and changes around them.

FOSTERING AWARENESS

Man's peripheral vision is a valuable asset, especially for driving. It allows awareness of movements at the outer edge of the field of vision, movements that may signal danger. People with tunnel vision have their field of vision restricted. They are like blinkered horses which see only directly ahead, oblivious to sights to their sides that may distract them. Unfortunately, it is this awareness of something approaching from the sides that may save a life. Some clients operate their businesses as if they had tunnel vision, were blinkered, unaware of any activity within their environment that is not directly under their noses. They are only vaguely aware of changes or trends that may ultimately affect them.

Nothing in the business environment, including in the marketplace, is static. Consumers, those users of services and products, are a volatile, even fickle factor in the marketplace and within the business community in general. Added to that volatility, are competitors bent on wooing these consumers with better, cheaper, larger, or somehow improved products and services. The result can be a very chaotic, far from static, situation. Managing such charged arenas in an aura of unawareness of the forces influencing the marketplace will put clients in an untenable position.

BENCHMARKING

To gain awareness, clients must understand the who, why, how, and where of their products, their services, and most importantly their clientele. That is, clients with whatever products and services to present to their clientele must understand their clientele sufficiently well to know:

- Who their targeted market clientele is.
- Why their products are chosen over their competition's products.
- How their products are used by their customers and which of the properties of these products are most desirable and which need to be improved.
- Where, and even when, their products are used to make these products more versatile.

The needs of customers must constantly be assessed to develop products and services that best suit the applications customers have for them.

The astute reader will readily recognize, if the reader is up on new management techniques, that the above is the essence of "benchmarking," a new management technique for continuous quality improvement. Camp (1989) provides the following definition for benchmarking, citing D. T. Kearns, Xerox Corporation as the source:

"Benchmarking is the continuous process of measuring products, services, and practices against the toughest competitors or those companies recognized as industry leaders."

The recurrent theme in benchmarking is to continuously strive to improve all aspects of one's organization against competitors, to copy, if necessary, what they are doing better in order to improve. This is a theme not inconsistent with the ISO 9000 concept to continually improve service to, and products for, clients.

Developing awareness can be accomplished following the general principles laid down by Camp (1989) respecting benchmarking or espoused in the above definition. Simply put, clients should take the time to look about in the marketplace and in the business community at what is happening with their and their competitors' products and customers. One anonymous commentator suggested that if a company is conducting business the same way it did five years ago, it is probably in trouble at the present time.

Camp (1989) listed four basic steps in benchmarking:

- That management should be thoroughly familiar with their companies, their operations, and their strengths and weaknesses — this is the introspection.
- That management should thoroughly know who their competition is and be aware of their position in the marketplace. The strengths and weaknesses of the competition ought to be minutely examined.
- That armed with this knowledge, management must capitalize on it to strengthen their position.
- Then they must move decisively to gain superiority.

The first three steps posed by Camp: self analysis, an environmental analysis encompassing the competition, and utilization of this knowledge, amount to the essence of awareness that every company should have. Readers can call it benchmarking if they wish. It is awareness of the ecosystem around them. Clients need this knowledge to move their organizations forward.

Clients cannot be unaware of either their own weaknesses or their own strengths. For if they are ignorant of these, they can neither reinforce the one nor take advantage of the other. Ignorance of their strengths or weaknesses can lead to gross miscalculations in production projections, in forecasting markets, even in determining what their consumers want, for example. Any misjudgments in the marketplace may alienate customers and will be pounced upon by the competition.

If clients lack awareness, they will also lack an effective feedback mechanism that provides information in technology, on pertinent developments in legislation, about the dynamics of the marketplace, the consumers in their markets, and on the activities of their competition.

CREATING LEGISLATIVE AWARENESS

Developments in legislation that create standards for products, restrict certain marketing practices, alter rules and regulations in the work environment, establish environmental control standards, or ban certain food ingredients are rarely the surprise that many feel they appear to be. Rumors and rumors of rumors circulate well before any piece of legislation comes into force. Governments frequently leak information from the ubiquitous unnamed sources or via the White Paper mysteriously found under some journalist's door to test the waters. However, keeping more reliable channels of communication into the "corridors of power" is a wise move on the part of any client to prevent a sudden surprise enactment of the legislature.

While attending a Food and Drug Law Institute meeting I sat, by chance, beside a fellow attendee, and we had an opportunity to talk. When we met again at a *Codex Alimentarius* meeting in Ottawa, we had the opportunity to dine together. He was employed by a major international food company and his job was simplicity itself. He traveled to all meetings anywhere in the world where there were any discussions on food legislation. At these he made contacts into these corridors of power with government representatives from the various countries attending. I learned more about past, present, and pending food legislation around the world than I ever dreamed possible over a pleasant meal and a good bottle of wine. Admittedly, not all clients can afford the luxury of such liberality respecting the narrow field of food legislation by having a "floating legislative ambassador." But keeping abreast of legislative developments is not impossible.

Rules and regulations which affect business and the marketplace arise from several sources. On the international level there are agreements between nations that affect the trade, prices, and standards of products passing between countries. Such are the General Agreement on Trade and Tariffs, North American Free Trade Agreement, International Standards Organization, and so on. The next level of legislation would be at a country's federal level. Here the country passes an act, the primary enactment, and attached to this are the regulations, the secondary enactments. These, in effect, constitute the law of the land. The next two levels are regional, the provincial or state level, followed by the municipal or county level. These regulate regional trade. Finally, there is the quasigovernmental level — a level producing regulations that have the support or effect of law. Here are the marketing boards, Crown corporations, self-regulating professional and trade associations. All can have some influence in the promulgation of legislation and regulations.

Trade or professional associations keep their membership aware of pending legislative activities in both international and national levels. Frequently these associations act in advisory capacities to their government's representatives on these international bodies. Clients should encourage their staff, especially the managerial levels, to be active in associations pertinent to the activities of their organizations. Such networking keeps clients aware of legislative developments that may have some impact on their operations. Even fraternal organizations that are frequented by local politicians at the municipal or state level can be venues in which trends in legislation can be discovered or discussed.

AWARENESS THROUGH NETWORKING

The value of networking in finding and evaluating consultants has already been discussed at length in an earlier chapter. Its value is apparent in the foregoing section. Networking will develop awareness by exposing the networker to the stimulus of others in related fields. When networking is directed to specific interest areas that are critical to clients, such as legislation, technology, or consumerism, then the networkers bring back to their organizations an awareness of technical and legislative developments in these areas.

Activity in the particular professional or trade organizations devoted to the specialties of the client broadens the knowledge of the networker. It need not be limited to such organizations but can also profitably include social, fraternal, and philanthropic organizations. Much can be learned over a quiet drink with knowledgeable persons. My roving legislative ambassador was a perfect example of an individual active in networking.

Attendance at exhibitions, conferences, and trade shows also brings about awareness of what developments are taking place. Discussions with speakers, conversations with the presenters at poster sessions, and discussions with exhibitors strengthen the general awareness of attendees. They return with information on the trends occurring in fields important to their organizations. The additional benefit is the opportunity to network and broaden their sources of information.

AWARENESS THROUGH TRAINING

Upgrading the skills of staff can have many beneficial returns. First, the staff return better trained and with a sense of having been rewarded. They are more competent in their jobs, and their training makes them potential candidates for future managerial roles.

Second, these people also have had an opportunity to meet with others from similar backgrounds. In the environment of the classroom and the social functions accompanying the training sessions, they could discuss mutual problems and their solutions. They have bull sessions with the experts who taught the courses. They have been introduced to the values of networking.

Finally, they have been exposed to, and made aware of, recent advances in the particular fields of endeavor their courses were devoted to. This will help them see the trends coming in the future in these fields.

AWARENESS GAINED FROM THE CONSUMER

Establishing clear lines of communication to their targeted audiences, the customers, is most important to clients. Good communication allows clients to get to know their customers, to recognize their needs, and to provide answers to their problems. Communication might also afford clients an opportunity to meet with their customers. From the knowledge about their audiences that this awareness brings, clients see how products and services could be improved to serve their audiences better. Provision of a telephone hotline that customers can call when there is a problem or an e-mail address that clients can access, brings clients into closer contact with their customers. By these means, clients can determine how, when, and where their products are being used. There is the strong possibility that this feedback will bring new uses that clients had not realized. Thus, the way can be opened for better designed products and services.

Hotlines can be used as excellent survey tools. If clients train their telephone receptionists on their hotlines to seek out in a noninquisitorial manner background information on the customer's usage and buying habits, hotlines become valuable marketing survey tools. As customer information builds up, a clearer picture of customers is formed. Trends in consumer habits appear. If the organization pays attention, clients can be prepared for these trends with new products or services to match the changing needs.

Software manufacturers have developed a cadre of "beta-users." These are software users who work with the company's software and provide feedback to the manufacturer about problems or errors in the programs. Software and computer manufacturers are also heavy users of hotlines to assist their customers should they have difficulties.

Consumer complaints can be a very effective means to gain, albeit indirectly, information from consumers. A well-organized customer complaint department provides clients with much valuable information. Problems with quality, design, or distribution can all be brought to light as the complaints are collated, studied, statistically analyzed for frequency, geographic location, and types of product breakdowns and compared with the client's own production and service records. Improvements can then be made. Customer complaints can be the single most important forerunner of "something wrong" with the products that clients have.

The sales and marketing forces must not be overlooked as tools in gathering information and providing awareness for their management. Sales personnel deal with retailers who have first-hand experience at the customer/client interface. Sales and technical service personnel also see, or should be seeing, what new products and promotional activity the competition is presenting in the marketplace and how customers are reacting to these changes.

Sales forces can be valuable as tools to gather customer information, because where they actually service retail outlets they see products and services as the customers do (and as professional audit companies do). Additionally, they see this side by side with competing products and services. Trends adopted by the competition provide a foretaste of things to come which clients should be aware of.

PREPAREDNESS

Analogies can best describe the concept of preparedness clearly, even simplistically:

- If it is necessary to travel down a poorly lit street at night and alone one does not walk close to the entrances of buildings and darkened alleys. Where possible, one arranges to have company on the journey, keeps to the middle of the street, and carries a flashlight and some protective device such as a siren alarm or pepper spray.
- Householders away for extended periods of time leave timers on lights, arrange with neighbors to clear their porches of telltale leaflets and newspapers, to mow or water their lawns, to clear snow away, and to move their cars up and down their driveways to simulate a presence in the house.
- Communities organize neighborhood watch groups to inform on unusual activities and suspicious people.
- People watch their diet and exercise to stave off diet- or weight-related ill health.
- People save for "a rainy day."

Preventive action is taken based on the anticipation of "something" happening. These are simply common sense preventive actions any foresighted individuals should take. One tries very simply to reduce the odds or opportunities for something calamitous to occur. Where one cannot avoid a potentially dangerous situation, one prepares oneself for this encounter in order to deter or to have control of the risk.

Police departments have developed emergency response teams, SWAT teams, to deal with dangerous life-threatening situations. While no normal organization requires such a SWAT team, it is not too far-fetched for clients to have a group within their organizations that becomes a repository, a central clearinghouse, for information gleaned from all sources described in the previous sections. This group keeps its hand on the data and interprets it for management to base its decisions on.

Clients must develop their own versions of SWAT teams, rapid response teams, that have, in addition to their regular duties, the task of digesting information fed in from their feedback mechanisms in academia, in government, in their trade organizations, and from the marketplace. A digestion of this information is then communicated to their management, who can anticipate problems and plot strategies for reasoned responses to changes going on in their environments. For this a degree of flexibility is required.

The above could be accomplished in a fairly simple manner. For example, attendees at trade shows, conferences, and meetings should be obliged to prepare a report of the critical activities at these, complete with all trade literature, samples, preprints, and other hand-outs. In addition, they should provide a list of all contacts made. Certainly, the least that should be required is a verbal report to senior management of important events, those that drew the most attention, at the shows or conferences. Those attending training courses should provide a report on the substance of their sessions. Sales personnel should be encouraged to gather marketplace information and report developments regularly and routinely to management.

Management must learn to harvest the information that is available. Encouragement of staff to report back items of interest they see, novel developments they encounter in their travels, activities of their competitors, remarks in trade association meetings made by government officials, all must be gleaned. The information is there and clients must develop the skills to reap it.

In the food industry it is good sense, indeed required by law in many countries, to have a recall program in place. The program describes a response system to a crisis of public health significance that may occur with a company's products in the marketplace. The recall team is headed by a coordinator who is usually the technical director and frequently acts as the spokesperson for the company when communicating with the media. Support comes from the shipping, sales, and marketing forces who can trace faulty product to wherever it has been shipped. Sales people clear store shelves. The coordinator prepares clear statements, frequently with the assistance of a public relations consultant, alerting the public to the hazard. This team practices with simulated drills. Its purpose is to protect the public, contain any hazard, and initiate damage control.

The SWAT team described above can be likened to this recall team but with a much less dramatic mandate. The rapid response team to glean information to assist management is an even less dramatic version of the recall team. It is a team representing different systems within and without the client's organization, who have been brought together to collate, organize, and analyze information for a client that may have some impact on the client's activities now or in the future.

This need not be a highly formalized group. In one small company, the president called his vice presidents in for a meeting after each and every trip any of them had made. They described their observations and were queried by their colleagues. Trips to trade shows brought together all the attendees for a bull session on the latest developments.

Awareness of trends allows clients to be prepared. Preparedness through preventive action is a means to reduce crises arising from change. Preventive action is self-protection. The impact of crises resulting from change can be moderated or controlled through a program of awareness. This will reduce the need for outside intervention by consultants.

Let it be perfectly clear that no one can predict crises stemming from acts of vandalism or terrorism, such as, for example, that which was sparked by the deliberate tampering with retail meat products by deluded animal rights activists who claimed they had poisoned turkeys prior to the Christmas season. However, the information-gathering team, by being aware through newspapers and trade associations that such terrorism was a fact of life and very likely to be succeeded by copycat performances, might very prudently rehearse similar "what-if" situations.

PLANT AND PRODUCT SECURITY

Developing a system for plant security will reduce the potential for vandalism by outsiders gaining access to the plant or to offices or laboratories where sensitive files, product designs, or financial records may be available. Systems employing cross-checks should be established to limit access to sensitive documents and to prevent their removal by unscrupulous employees. Where the protection of high technology premises is necessary, a very sophisticated security system must be in place and these are best supplied by professional security firms.

The safety of key personnel should be assured as far as possible. Even so simple a precaution as preventing either key personnel, or key personnel from the same department, from traveling together can prevent a calamitous loss of skills. The crisis that this would bring can be mitigated by prudent planning.

Product should also be secured, and this is best done through coding. Sometimes this coding will be very obvious as it is with food and pharmaceutical products or electrical appliances, or it may be more subtle as with microchip components. Tamper-proof or tamper-evident packaging can be used to discourage product sabotage.

Identification of employees in distinctive ways, e.g., color-coded work uniforms, makes it clearly recognizable both who the workers are and whether the wrong workers are in a particularly sensitive department where they should not be. Such color-coding certainly does make visitors or intruders stand out. There are other means of restricting access with keys, identity cards, or pass codes.

Preventive Maintenance, Product and Brand Integrity Systems

Preventive maintenance programs in manufacturing operations will reduce crises caused by equipment breakdowns, contaminated or defective products, or employee injuries. Keeping machinery in working order allows product specifications to be met consistently and where time-sensitive materials are processed, this is important in preserving quality. The amount of nonstandard product reaching the customers is reduced, as is the need for any product recall. Where clients supply parts which may later prove to be substandard, clients can possibly face serious repercussions and the loss of a major customer.

Concern in social matters will reduce problems within the organization and within the community. For example, safety equipment for workers in hazardous work areas will minimize long-term disabilities and injuries due to accidents. In addition, the need for lawyers and labor negotiators to advise in possible litigation can be minimized. Prompt attention to waste management and waste disposal, effluent control, and control of noxious vapors will reduce complaints and avoid visits from environmental authorities. By being a good corporate citizen, the client avoids resorting to outside resources to resolve issues that could have been resolved more readily before they became problems.

A sound quality control (quality assurance, product integrity, total quality management, call the systems what one will) system designed to maintain quality from raw materials or parts through to finished products is essential to maintaining standards of safety and performance. By specifying standards that must be met for each step in processing, crises caused by poor or malfunctioning product can be reduced. This keeps the goodwill of customers.

An effective research and development department also helps to reduce the need for consultants through the careful design and testing of new products for reliability, safety, and quality prior to their release to the public. Such activity has the added advantage that it promotes a sense of self-reliance within the client's organization. The sales department can sell with the confidence that they have a good product. By having good quality and reliability designed into products, the risks of product liability losses are diminished.

FURTHER CONSIDERATIONS

Tasks for farming out to consultants should be confined to those arising from some very specific need which cannot be met with internal resources. Such tasks must be necessary for the welfare of the clients' organizations, their customers or their staffs, and their communities.

By avoiding assigning unnecessary or trivial tasks to consultants, a reduction in their use can be made. If consultants are kept busy with trivial or unnecessary tasks simply because they are on a retainer, then it is past time to review the need for that relationship. A careful scrutiny by clients of the tasks they assign to their consultants will demonstrate many ways to reduce the need for consultants.

Consultants should not be used for frivolous or silly reasons. The silliest reason that I have encountered for hiring a consultant was the following: "We hired him because he is very popular and therefore he must have something important to say." This particular consultant had been written up in several newspaper and magazine articles, been interviewed on radio and TV talk shows, and was enjoying great success making extraordinary claims for his new consumer research technique for successful product development.

The foregoing is not so rare an occurrence as it may appear. Henry Mintzberg, a noted and respected management consultant (quoted in *The Financial Post,* June 10/95 by Kathryn Leger), minced no words in blasting a trend he sees in management styles espoused by management gurus:

> "Faddishness (Re-engineer, Empower your employees, Be ready for chaos, Crazy times for crazy organizations) is really killing management because people apply things without thinking. Everyone is so obsessed with being current."

If clients are attracted to consultants because they are trendy, then consultants with good self-promotional skills will always be needed. Being current, trendy, or fashionable are not valid reasons to resort to consultants.

Consultants should keep low profiles and cause as little disruption as possible when on their client's premises. Quite unlike Shahin's parody of a consultant (1995), the consultant should not appear as a super deluxe top-of-the-line car "on cruise control." Unfortunately, many do go out of their way to create such impressions but, then, many clients are impressed by such behavior.

Unless there is a compelling reason, such as some extraordinary economic or other advantage to having a consultant on a retainer, clients have no need for keeping consultants once their projects have been finished. A consultant fills a need. When the need has been satisfied, the consultant ought to disappear.

The key phrase is, of course, "once the need has been satisfied." Where a need continues or develops out of the previous projects that have been undertaken, then a continuing or long-term need for a consultant, perhaps, a retainership, may be justified. That justification must be continuously evaluated as the client's needs change. Retainers for consultants are a tacit admission that the client's organization is not yet a self-contained one.

The use of consultants represents a business expense. The costs for their services can become a not inconsiderable expense for both small and medium-sized companies.

Consultants must always be regarded as necessary evils: evil because the use of a consultant invariably means an intrusion into the orderly affairs of a company, an unexpected expense, or the need to remedy an unforeseen mistake or crisis in a product, in production, or in marketing; and necessary because the skills of the consultant are required to resolve the crisis expeditiously. Consultants must never become a crutch necessary to the future development of the growth of their clients.

Clients ought to carefully examine their reasons for using consultants. Then they must proceed with measures to counter these reasons. Then, clients can be truly their own master. Baden-Powell, founder of the Boy Scout movement, provided the Scouts with their motto — "Be prepared." When queried what they should be prepared for, his answer was "for all things." Would that all companies, organizations, or people requiring consultants had adopted this motto for their mission statements. Had they done so, the occasions for their need for consultants would drop drastically.

11   The Future for Consultants and Consulting

Progress might have been all right once, but it's gone on too long.

Ogden Nash

The real problem is what to do with the problem solvers after the problems are solved.

Gay Talese

The future is like heaven — everyone exalts it, but no one wants to go there now.

James Baldwin

CONSULTING IS NOT A NEW PHENOMENON

The diversity of services that consultants offer is perhaps a modern and novel twist. The numbers of consultants might also be astonishing, but consulting is not a modern activity. The large number of consultants is likely a direct result of the many individuals experimenting with consulting as a means of self-employment. The variety of services is fueled by their attempts to find a niche for their particular talents. A brief review of the history of science reveals that consultants, certainly not by that name, have played important parts not only in major events in history but also in the daily lives of people almost since the beginnings of history. The central figures in whatever drama was being played out on the world's stage have always seen a need for advisers or for expertise of some nature. The once much sought-after Delphic Oracle in Greece is such an example.

There are other examples throughout history. Regiomontanus (1436–1476) was called from Nüremberg where he was working to advise the Church on the reform of the calendar that was desired (Singer, 1959). Charlemagne (A.D. 742–814) had a counselor, Alcuin of York, who was a government adviser (or consultant) to Charlemagne (Lamb, 1963). Similarly, one recognizes Aristotle (384–322 BC) as a government adviser to Alexander of Macedon, better known as Alexander the Great (Singer, 1959). Later, there was Archimedes (287–212 BC), with his superb ability to apply his scientific skills to practical problems, for example the development of Archimedes' screw to raise water for irrigation. He also advised Hiero, who wished to determine whether the crown that had been made for the gods on Hiero's orders was truly all gold or whether it had been admixed with silver by the goldsmiths. Craftsmen were imported from the European continent (an early example of outsourcing?) to glaze the windows of a monastic building as early as the seventh century (Gies and Gies, page 68, 1994).

Fredrick Accum (1769–1838), a leading figure in applied chemistry, was a consultant by any definition of the word. His services were employed in many fields of industrial chemistry (Farrer, 1996). He applied the principles of chemistry to the detection of adulterants in food and applied food analysis to the regulation of the food industry. Besides the impact he made on the safety and purity of food, Accum consulted for a soda manufacturer, the pottery industry, the gas-lighting industry, and for town governments who wished to promote their mineral waters. According to Farrer, by 1820 Accum had become a very popular figure as a consulting chemist.

Throughout history, rulers, generals, the guilds of medieval Europe, and companies have all sought the advice of experts. In earliest times, people called upon an augurer who consulted the entrails of an animal for advice as to the best time or best methods to use to undertake some venture. Augury as practiced on animals or as divined by how bones fell when tossed in the air are practices, among many other forecasting practices, that have passed out of favor for advising. Nonetheless, the methods of today's augurers (consultants) can be equally bizarre and mysterious to their clients. Indeed, some methods, particularly statistical methods in consumer research, have become so arcane as to be understandable only to the select few who practice them.

People still seek advice by resorting to others, no longer called augurers but now called demographers, to predict how different segments of the population will behave. They consult statisticians who advise investors what financial markets might do in the future after analysis of very complex economic indices and formulas. There are also the futurists who study trends worldwide (Toffler, 1970; Kahn et al. 1976; Naisbitt, 1982). From their observations of trends, the futurists attempt to describe probable scenarios for future developments. Companies, governments, and individuals use this knowledge in planning their strategies for the future.

If history teaches anything about consultants, it is that they have always been sought by governments, by industries, by organizations, and by individuals for the skills, expertise, and technologies these consultants possess.

Today that need has been formalized as companies advertise the post of consultants to keep on staff to advise their clients. *The Globe and Mail*, Canada's national newspaper, published (February 7 and 10, 1997) several advertisements for consultants: there were a number of judicial information positions for the Ontario provincial government; several in computer operating systems for UNIX, NT, and OS/400; and another in business administration to report to a president. The needs are in the newer technologies and sciences of computers, information handling, and management. Demands for management consultants are advertised for in *Oxford Today* (9, No. 2, 9, 53 Hilary Issue 1997). The demand for consultants is neither far from diminishing nor confined to North America. There has been, and will continue to be, a need for consultants as advances are made in technology, in the arts and sciences, and in the fields of sociology. That is easily predicted.

While many may feel as Ogden Nash has written that progress has gone on for far too long, nevertheless it will still go on producing problems or opportunities for which many will need assistance.

CONSULTING'S CHANGING FACE

Throughout its long history, consulting has changed in very subtle ways. Its future will in no way mirror what it once was nor what it has become today. For consultants, the future will not be an exalted heaven as Baldwin describes and certainly many consultants will be loath to go there. Many, indeed, will not be able to go there with the services they currently offer. These changes are apparent as follows:

- First, the marketplace for consulting itself is being altered in many ways. For one, consultants will narrowcast their skills even further rather than broadcast them as they have.
- Second, the consultants, themselves, are being forced to change by these same developments. Advances in communication, information retrieval, and other fields of technology are narrowing the gap in access to knowledge between client and consultant. Consultants will require more training to keep ahead of their clients.

Changes in these areas will shape the future of consulting and of the consultants plying the trade.

The consultant and consulting, the activity, will be affected by the same influences in the consulting marketplace. To evaluate the differences time might make in their natures, some effort must be made to separate one from the other.

CONSULTING: THE ACTIVITY

The list of contents of *The Montreal Professional Review* (Volume 1, No. 1, 1996) demonstrates the great diversity of consulting activities that are available. Using a variety of names, to wit consultants, advisors, service providers, counselors, and specialists, the publication describes:

- Legal consultants
- Training and development consultants
- Consultants for the World Wide Web
- Investment counselors

- Health counselors
- Business advisors
- Financial planners
- Communication specialists

Some of these activities, for instance, World Wide Web consultants, were unheard of a few years ago. Legal consultants, on the other hand, must be very old or else how can Shakespeare have Dick the Butcher comment, "The first thing we do, let's kill all the lawyers" (*Henry VI,* Act IV, Scene 2, ln 86) be understood. Obviously, lawyers for legal consulting date back several hundred years.

Diversity of services is certainly prevalent. A radio talk show host recently interviewed a woman who described herself as a stress consultant and counselor, for example. Consultants are active in fields never heard by Regiomontanus a few hundred years ago. This diversity requires a closer look.

A GROWING DIVERSITY OF ACTIVITIES AND NICHE MARKETS

More people are presenting themselves as consultants, and competition for clients has forced these people to find unique niches for their widely and wildly diverse array of skills. The range of skills can go from the sublime to the ridiculous. For the sublime, there is the following:

- Legal services
- Life styles
- Management
- Business

- Financial services
- Environmental services
- Health services
- Labor

- Communications
- Computerization
- Sciences
- Consumerism

and so on. Each of these subjects in this far-from-complete list can be broken down further with the result that a number of subfields can be found. Financial services, for example, can be further subdivided into such specialized topics as:

- Investment counseling
- Taxation advising
- Bankruptcy
- Public offerings

- Pension planning
- Accounting
- Mergers and partnerships
- Forensic accounting

and on and on. Each subtopic will have its own consultants. The health services, for example, can be split up into consultants who are:

- Nutritionists
- Exercise physiologists
- Personal coaches
- Ergonomics specialists

- Dietitians
- Athletic psychologists
- Trainers

Dividing the sciences would reveal many more pigeon-hole categories.

For the ridiculous, there are the gift consultants, clothing consultants (how to dress for power), party consultants (how to give parties to impress customers), and the lawyer who specializes only in lawsuits involving animals.

There are consultants who consult for other consultants. For example, there are new-product development specialists whose expertise is primarily in the development of special dietetic foods and who advise (consult for) consultant dietitians who, in turn, advise those patients who have unique dietary needs or simply have weight problems. As another example, financial counselors advise their clients on investments. Some do not research the stocks they sell; instead they buy their financial information and data on the companies they promote from other specialists (consultants) who provide, collate, and research investment information. (This is further reason for the client to inquire, during early negotiations with the prospective consultant, who will carry out the work.)

Specialist skills have even been marketed to their old companies by the entrepreneurially inclined who were downsized. They have come back to work on a short-term contractual basis. The result is consulting or outsourcing — whatever one wishes to call the activity. A variety of skills are available and these skills can be packaged by enterprising people to service clients in unique niche markets. For example, the health sciences can be split into:

- Nutrition consultants who provide advice to clients on disease control and health management through nutrition.
- Personal consultant trainers expert in kinesiology for athletes striving to improve their performance in some sport.
- Personal coaches for those who are simply concerned for their health or recuperating from some illness.
- Stress counselors called in by clients concerned with the health of those in high-pressure jobs within their organizations.

Similar divisions of skills could be made in other fields to demonstrate the creation of niche markets.

There is an element of a Catch-22 here. Companies downsize. Getting down to their core business creates a vulnerability in some areas of their business — stress, for example. A profusion of skills is made available that is packaged by many of the outplaced employees who then promote themselves as consultants. Other individuals with special skills see possibilities to offer their skills to potential clients. The abundance of consultants with such diverse skills encourages consultants to promote themselves even more intensely and to specialize more narrowly to be able to promote the difference they offer.

In a competitive marketplace, clients seek every opportunity to excel. Consultants promote themselves as able to assist clients to excel. The diverse skills offered by consultants present potential opportunities to explore new technologies, to introduce more efficient operating systems, and to restructure their organizations. What these companies cannot perform in-house, they outsource to this new breed of consultants. It becomes an almost self-contained, self-feeding mechanism.

Outsourcing is a well-established business activity, and downsizing is still proceeding unabated. Indeed, so popular has outsourcing become that it is very likely that contract work will be the *modus operandi* in the workplace. Outsourcing will become a rival to full-time work. This will make future prospective job-seekers package their skills and training to compete as consultants, by either joining consulting firms or as individuals starting their own businesses.

In the future, consultants with these packaged skills will be vying intensely with one another to get the contracts resulting from the growing trend to outsourcing. They will become, in essence, another service supplier competing with all other suppliers. Consultants, to be able to compete effectively, will need to be not only in the vanguard of new technologies, but they will need to hone their marketing skills to get those contracts that are available.

Downsized companies are frequently and unfortunately unprepared for the unexpected. And the unexpected still occurs with disconcertingly, unexpectedly, irregular regularity, causing new opportunities for consultants.

Crises and the opportunities they can bring will not diminish in the future. They are more likely to increase with the complexity of today's lifestyles. They will arise from very unusual sources stimulated by new issues and unexpected needs in society. For example, no one anticipated the furor over PCBs and other ozone-depleting chemicals. They were safe, said the experts, before scientists discovered the danger to the ozone layer. Instantly, a new area for consulting opened up as companies sought alternatives to PCBs and safe disposal techniques.

Future results should be interesting. One can bet the rent money that niche markets within niche markets will be found, and consultants will themselves require the skills of other consultants. For instance, consultants will need to call upon those who can advise them on improving their marketing techniques. They will need help devising their Web pages. They will need those consultants who are expert in the new technologies to train them. Consultants to consultants may even become a new industry. In time there may even be courses in universities on consulting as a new profession.

Problem-solving, once a native skill of consultants, is currently in danger of becoming formalized. New methodologies for problem-solving are being developed, and the sacred domain of the consultant will become a common ground and no longer a unique skill. New skills must be developed to replace the old time-worn methods.

There is a major downside to this ever-finer specialization respecting the diversity in fields of consulting. Consultants are becoming experts in areas of trivia. They are developing a mastery of the inconsequential. However, if their clients wish to buy...

Communication and Computer Sciences

Computers have altered the face of consulting by giving new tools to the consultants and also to their potential clients. These tools have sped communication worldwide, permitted desktop publishing, created software that permits rotatable designs of the most complicated structures, or allows complete statistical analyses to be carried out, plus other features, and created a new arena for consulting activity: information retrieval. If consultants can find essential information on the Web so can their clients.

These skills acquired by consultants and available to clients create a problem for consultants. They must be able to do more than their clients. They will have to become more adept in the new technology or develop new niches for their computer skills. This requires time and training.

But whatever else computer and communication technology have brought, they have provided a new opportunity for consultants and consulting — security. Security of communication and security of confidential databases is fast becoming a major problem. Hackers for reasons either of devilish amusement, simple nuisance value, or for purposes of theft, have found it a challenge to break into so-called secure systems. A new reason for the employment of consultants has been born to combat these acts.

GLOBALIZATION

Globalization of business activities and markets has forced companies to recognize that no matter how desirable their products or services are, they cannot suit all the market segments for all peoples of diverse cultural backgrounds in all geographic locations. Companies require information and guidance on such topics as:

- The social customs and etiquette of entering into business negotiations with foreign business people. That is, cross-cultural training is necessary to help clients avoid corporate blunders with foreign customers.
- Legislation in foreign countries governing labeling, advertising, safety standards, licensing, taxation, or business practices. This may also include advice on those unwritten protocols of doing business in foreign countries.
- Market intelligence about consumers, their demographics and psychographics, in foreign markets. Clients need to know how to make desirable products for these peoples.
- Marketing procedures, the nature and identity of the competition, how pricing structures are established, and data on competent distribution channels in these foreign markets.

Consultants with the above expertise will have to package themselves to sell their skills to foreign clients.

The globalization of business activities cannot be denied. At the same time, there are no global products (or services) that can satisfy the tastes, customs, and needs of customers without some modification in the products being offered. People in foreign lands must have products that satisfy their needs and that respect the legislated and religious laws of the lands in which these products are to be distributed. Products must be redesigned for the geographic areas they are to be used in, the conditions these impose on the products, and how people in these areas will use the products. Information on the environmental conditions in different seasons in other countries influences the packaging of products or helps to decide whether temperature or humidity control is necessary for protection of quality or for the proper functioning of a product.

Globalization has not been without its disadvantages: it brought increasing government intervention into people's daily lives as countries sought to protect their industries through restrictive tariff regulations and trade practices. But this increase in intervention has also been, and will continue to prove to be, a lucrative field for consultants to assist foreign clients through the morass of government legislation. They will need to either up-grade their knowledge of foreign legislation or develop alliances with lawyers expert in such legislation.

Global warming has even been touted as a factor in producing opportunities for consultants. Clients need knowledge about the changes that global warming might bring to be able to include these in their long-range planning. Weather can affect marketing programs, agricultural supplies and economic conditions in clients' immediate environments and in their more far-flung markets.

SOCIETAL FACTORS

A good example of how social issues created a need for consultants occurred in Canada. In the province of Quebec the issue of pay equity arose: that is, equal pay for equal work. Of course, this raises the confusing issue of how one equates jobs involving different skills. An article in the newspaper was headlined, "Equity was also a boon for consultants" (Scott, 1996). Companies, in the face of this pending legislation, were forced to turn to consultants to determine what the criteria for comparing jobs equitably were. How is the work of a teacher, predominantly a female role, compared with that of a school janitor, a predominantly male role, or either of these jobs compared to that of a nurse, again a female role usually, but with a degree of higher skills and responsibility? Here in the problem of work/pay equality, the social and legislative issues forced many companies, government bodies such as school boards, and trade unions to seek guidance from "work" experts. But there were economic repercussions from this dilemma of assessing pay equity. After all, equity evaluations had to be made in such a way as to keep wages down in order for the government to avoid inflationary pressures! Thus the single issue of pay equity brings forth social consultants (work experts), labor experts (negotiation consultants), and economic experts to advise the various parties.

There are other issues of a social nature that require the advice of experts (consultants). Discrimination in the work force, palliative care for the terminally ill or those chronically in pain, the use of placebos in medical research, sexual harassment in the workplace, all introduce problems in ethics or sociology. For example, the use of marijuana is illegal. It is used to ease the pain of terminally ill cancer patients. Acceptance legally for this humanitarian use crosses into the realms of legislation, medicine, and ethics. Legal, security, medical, and ethical consultants get involved.

Activity worldwide relating to social issues shows no sign of abatement. In fact, there is ample evidence that it is growing not only for local issues but on an international scale. Clients look for assistance to avoid giving offense by their products, their product names, their advertising, or their behavior in foreign markets.

The Consumer

Consumers are changing. They are becoming more sophisticated and demanding. This change is not a uniform one occurring with the same momentum in all countries. Many markets, especially in third-world countries, are moving slowly from production-driven markets and economies to consumer-oriented ones. Such changes, and the opportunities they present, require the expertise of consultants to guide clients wishing to enter these markets. Clients need to understand the shopping and retailing habits but also to know consumer habits and social mores in these foreign countries as the switch from product-oriented to consumer-oriented markets is made.

Legislation, demanded by consumer advocates both to promote better nutrition and to provide consumers with nutritional information, has been promulgated. The result was nutritional labeling. This provoked a need for professional nutritional advice. Again, consultants — nutritionists, analysts, and labeling experts — jumped to advise food processors. The result has been consulting analytical laboratories specializing only in nutritional work.

Legislators, under pressure from advocacy groups enact legislation that can change the way certain business can be conducted, can place an embargo on the importation of certain goods, set workplace standards for safety, define employer/employee relationships respecting sexual harassment or unlawful dismissal, and so on. Each enactment may be cause for hiring a consultant. For example, if a food ingredient is proscribed, food manufacturers then scurry to reformulate products or to find a suitable substitute. A consultant in formulation development may be required.

Environmental Activism

Environmental concerns raised by citizens forced governments into legislation that punishes polluters and encourages recycling. The new laws created a need for ecological and environmental impact studies. Consultants specialized in these areas were required. This concern for the environment has spawned new industries based on the science of ecology, for example. There is a need for people with knowledge and experience in waste management techniques, such as waste reduction, by-product utilization, recycling, gas production, composting, and even green manuring to reduce urban garbage accumulation or to utilize it. A new discipline of environmental decontamination technology has developed and with it there has been code-veloped a cadre of this technology's own consultants. The need to contain and clean up oil spills, a comparatively new disaster with the advent of super tankers, resulted in specialists who can deal with these catastrophes. A similar need to quench oil well fires produced its own specialists.

Each advance in technology, each new development, will create its own environmental impact. The plastic revolution brought great advantages as well as a material that is practically nondegradable. The nuclear age brought the need to find ways to safely transport, process, and store radioactive wastes. Consultants will be required to provide expertise to blunt these impacts.

People Movements

The mass movements of people as tourists, refugees, or migrants moving in search of work, has exposed people in many countries to new foods and flavors. As people move about they bring with them their cultural habits. One of these is their foods and food cultures. Companies, especially food manufacturers, hasten to satisfy the needs of these immigrants and introduce these newcomers to local products. Consultants with experience with the new customs, especially in the use of their new foods, in their preservation and knowledge of their nutrition, find they are required to help manufacturers develop new uses for these traditional products and preserve their desirable qualities.

Ease of travel has revealed to tourists the delights of many tropical fruits and vegetables. Tropical countries are eager to take advantage of these new interests in their agricultural products for commerce. The need for consultants arises in several quarters. The following series of events is a most common one:

- The delicate fresh qualities of these tropical fruits and vegetables must be preserved during storage, transport, and retailing in foreign countries. For this, the expertise of food scientists is required.

- If markets for these exotic products are developed, then agriculturalists and agronomists will be required in the tropical countries to assure that there will be a safe, regular, and plentiful supply of product.
- All the foregoing will require a business infrastructure to support it (management consultants, venture capitalists).

Travel, then, can be a stimulus to the need for consultants whether it is recreational or involves mass movements of people in critical situations.

Social Activism

Activism on the part of the public, a direct result of the more educated, socially aware, and sophisticated customer, has required clients to seek, for example, advice to redesign advertising campaigns to avoid chauvinism, sexism, age bias, and racism or to simply avoid demeaning stereotypical images. Social activism has also had an impact in the workplace. Companies have had to seek the advice of social scientists to cleanse their organizations of any biases or inequalities and to train staff, especially managerial staff, regarding sexism and harassment in the workplace. Activism can be the driving force to protect the work environment, but it can have an uglier side, militant activism leading to terrorism:

- Antiirradiation groups mobilize to overturn store shelves displaying irradiated foods.
- The random poisoning of Tylenol™ several years ago killed several people.

All these acts, and many others that have been perpetrated, gave impetus to ways to make products more secure, to protect the public, to educate consumers, and to protect brand images. This requires the efforts and skills of several different consulting activities to respond quickly to the problem. However, such terrorism will become more sophisticated in the future and will require ever-more sophisticated techniques to combat it. Computer viruses require computer consultants to devise "firewalls" to stop them.

All the foregoing points clearly to how the activity, known broadly as consulting, has been changing and will continue to be changed by as yet unforeseen circumstances in the future. The *need* for the services that consultants provide will not change or even abate. The services will change to meet the need and the diversity of services and products offered will grow as complexity grows in the workplace and in social concerns. Advances in the applied sciences in general will change the tools of how consulting is practiced.

THE CHANGING FACE OF THE CONSULTANT

The consultant, that stand-alone individual with a jack-of-all-trades knowledge, is fast disappearing, although there will certainly always be individual consultants whose skills stand out from others. They will be shortlived. So too, but at a slower pace, is the high-profile consultant disappearing. Technology is moving so rapidly that any consultant's skills will become *passé* within two or three years. The consultant whose expertise is based primarily on long experience and varied skills cannot survive in today's climate. Self-promotion cannot save the big-name consultancies. They cannot maintain expertise in all the skills that will be required in a niche market, because there is too much fragmentation of skills.

Consultants of today will be forced to devote a considerable portion of their time to constantly upgrading skills or reorganizing their companies to offer newer technologies to clients. The latter will mean that networking with those with the skills will become imperative, and consultants will move gradually from being largely solo performers to being members of a more broadly based network.

Students fresh out of college have highly specialized skills in newer technologies. Their weakness lies in their lack of interpretive experience, in their inexperience in analyzing problems, people, and business activities. However, such skills can be introduced in college courses through case studies, seminars led by nonacademic executives, and with more cooperative programs with industry or even with consultants.

NETWORKING

In earlier chapters networking was discussed as a characteristic of many solo consultants. That is, they have, through necessity, been forced to forego their independent status and join alliances with other consultants with other skills. The network then represents diverse skills capable of undertakings much beyond the skills of any individual in the network. Stratecon EuroBEST is one such alliance of consultants working in the food field (Anon. 1994). Several individual consultants, all specialists in different fields and living in different parts of the world, have pooled their resources. Together they represent a formidable consulting force in food technology and food business development.

Such networks can compete with larger, more formally structured consulting firms. Their advantages are lower overhead and greater flexibility. They can provide a wider range of services by their ability to co-opt individuals with the necessary expertise to the network for any undertaking. At the close of the project, the network disappears, as it were. They exist only when the need for them arises. These alliances can be very loose arrangements frequently based, literally and figuratively, on a handshake between the participants. Other alliances, however, can be more formal partnerships. How they are formulated is unimportant. It is the resource base that is created for their clients that is important, not how their organization is structured. Clients seeking consultants will find that these networking alliances will become more the norm in the future. Those that evolve into partnerships may become the future large, all-purpose consultancies of tomorrow.

What might the future of retainerships be? The solo consultant will become a thing of the past, an anachronism in today's world. Consequently, it will be inevitable that retainerships that clients may have had with an individual consultant will also disappear. They will certainly change at the very least. These will be replaced with either a network or a "technical clearinghouse dispatcher" in place of the individual.

The network will hold the retainership and not any individual consultant within that network. The needs of the client will be supplied by that individual within the network with the necessary skills. Communication between a client and the network would be through that consultant whose specialty most closely matches the client's interests at that time.

The technical clearinghouse dispatcher would work much like the network above except that it would be the client who maintains the network. Clients would have resource persons on staff among whose responsibilities would be that of dispatcher. These persons would maintain lists of consultants (individuals, companies, networks, etc.) with expertise in a variety of fields. They would keep up-to-date dossiers of literature describing the skills and accomplishments of each consultant on the list and references the dispatchers have investigated. This is a formalization of the business cards kept individually by many clients and discussed earlier in the chapter on finding consultants.

When an outside resource is needed by a client, the dispatcher responsible for this clearinghouse of technical skills would refer to the list of approved consultants. The most suitable would be contacted for further discussions.

TODAY'S TOOLS

Networking provides individuals with common interests within some society an opportunity to meet, to discuss mutual concerns, to socialize, and to exchange ideas. However, computers with e-mail and advances in communication technology (faxes) made networking possible for even wider audiences of individuals with common interests. E-mail has proven a most effective tool for clients to interface with consultants.

These advances in communication technology have greatly altered the way information can be transferred, stored, and retrieved. Consultants can provide their clients with better service, but there is another side to these developments. They have also enabled clients to access these same databases. This access puts a client on an equal footing with the consultant respecting the availability and interpretation of knowledge. This becomes a two-edged sword: the client is, or could be if advantage is taken of the new technologies, as well-informed as, even better informed than, the consultant.

The result is obvious. Consultants must not only keep ahead of their clients' skill levels, but they must also become more adept at using the newer procedures to provide more sophisticated services, i.e., to supply something clients cannot provide themselves. Consultants must be self-controlled and self-directed enough to be continually learning and training in the newer technologies and their applications. Not only must consultants keep ahead of their clients, but they must also surpass the skills of the new graduates educated in the newer technologies who appear in the marketplace each year.

Competition from universities and university–industry–government consortia will grow much stronger and more professional in the future. The pressure on universities to seek funding and other means of support (shared use of industrial equipment and facilities, for example) from industry will become irresistible.

Further competition to consultants is provided by industry. Sandwich courses permit students to gain experience and apply their training to assist industry with its problems. These students enter the work force able to supply their employers with work experience, knowledge of the new technologies, and analytical skills. Consultants in the hotel/restaurant field, for example, might find themselves competing with graduates who have experience in every job in the hotel/restaurant industry, frequently gained in several different countries. They are formidably trained people with multilanguage skills who will take their place in industry and will prove to be powerful competition for consultants to match.

These courses provide potential clients with a body of skilled, business-wise employees knowledgeable about, and trained in, the newer skills that consultants may have to scamper to acquire. This competition can be very heady rivalry indeed. The competition posed by these students will force consultants in the future to possess at least equivalent skills. They must show clearly to their potential clients what advantages there are to using their services. To do this, among their other needs, they will require promotional skills.

The result is a challenge to the consultant and a boon to the client. The level of managerial skills of the recent graduates who are hired by clients will have an impact on the caliber of consultants. The consultant must become more versatile and more resourceful. Managers are more experienced and smarter: consultants must be more adept, experienced, and even smarter. The new environment will require an entire remake of the consultant of today.

The client, because of the greater competition afforded by the academic sector, will have a greater selection of consulting services to choose from. This competition should open the door to highly competitive bidding with cheaper prices prevailing. Clients will need to apply greater discriminatory skills in selecting the consulting services that will be best suited to their needs.

Consultants will be best suited to apply their skills in future in those branches of consulting that academics and universities cannot profitably (in an academic sense) pursue in depth. For instance, consultants must avoid the basic research areas. Consultants serve their clients best in areas of application, in problem solving, in projects involving a broad range of disciplines, that is, where marketing skills, data on customer psychographics, new product development, knowledge of foreign legislation pertaining to labeling, standards, etc., and export markets are needed. Projects that are multidisciplined involve flexibility, travel, connections, and versatility. They involve putting together bits and pieces from many branches of the hard and soft sciences. These are the branches of consulting that must be exploited by tomorrow's consultant.

CONSULTING IN THE FUTURE

It is a very safe prediction that there will be a continuing need for consultants. History confirms this. They will deal with the changing technologies, social customs, and new legislation that will inevitably come. New industries are being continually developed, and these will require their experts, specialists, and consultants. New social issues will emerge that will tax the skills of governments and industry alike, and "the experts" will need to be called in for consultation.

But consultancy and the consultants who practice this will change. Today's consultant will not exist as this person has been known. In place of the individual consultant, there will be the consulting network — a formally or informally organized network designed to serve very specific needs, reflecting both expertise in specialized technologies and geographical distribution of the skills. The consultant of the future, will be a member of such a group.

The results of all this for consultants are:

- There will be a growing multitude of consultants who will act both individually and collectively through networking alliances.
- There will be a terrifying fractionation of the services and products they offer. Their fields of expertise will become more diversified, and they will specialize in niche markets that they will develop from their new expertise. They will be highly knowledgeable in narrowly specialized technologies, skills and sciences. This narrowness of focus will force them into alliances in order to manage projects requiring diverse skills.
- They must follow their clients into foreign markets because of globalization if they hope to keep these clients, and conversely, must be prepared for competition from foreign consultants who, in their turn, are following their clients.
- Consultants in the future must be trained in the newer technologies that their clients are exposed to or even already using. They must keep ahead of their clients and will therefore need to spend more time learning the new technologies.
- They must become more competitive and devise new promotional techniques to develop client/consultant bonds. The competition will come both from within their own countries but also from without as foreign consultants see the opportunities available.
- They will be resourceful and innovative — the ultimate attributes of the consultant — through instant access to equally skilled partners around the world.
- They will have well-developed conceptual skills, be comfortable with the bizarre, and eclectic in their interests, seeing in the unusual and seemingly inconsequential the exciting uses and applications to unusual problems that clients might bring.

The jack-of-all-trades individual consultant will disappear but not that individual's ability to adapt widely disparate skills, arts and technologies to the resolution of a client's problems and needs. This ability will become the new "flying-by-the-seat-of-one's-pants."

Competition will be keen, even cutthroat, as consultants are forced into developing niche markets requiring their highly specialized skills. This will force more promotional activity either through greater efforts at networking or more blatant publicity and advertising campaigns.

To accomplish all this, the consultants of the future will themselves have to consult other consultants for development of promotional and marketing skills. This brings the story full circle: consultants will form alliances with other consultants to complement their own skills as they try as networks to be service providers.

Tuller (1992) provided his description of a future for consulting. His future included some predictions similar to those described in this chapter. He did introduce some very interesting new concepts, however. He predicted:

- More regulation of the consulting industry through licensing at either the state or federal level.
- Certification by the granting of degrees in consulting after the successful completion of graduate work.
- Training schools for technical consultants.

Any attempt to predict the future more closely than that presented above is impossible. My own interest in the history of food science and technology has resulted in a collection of old cookbooks and texts on food technology, and clippings from newspapers, magazines, and journals for historical references in foods.

What is amusing reading in all these references are the attempts made by some of the authors in this collection to predict what will happen next in their particular field. None can be accused of skill or accuracy in clairvoyance. Nor do I claim any aptitude for seeing into the future beyond what has been prompted by current events and suggested in this chapter.

"The best thing about the future is, it comes only one day at a time."

Attributed to Abraham Lincoln.

References

Akre, E., Green politics and industry, *Eur. Food Drink Rev.,* 5, Winter, 1991.

Anon., Guidelines for the use of consultants by World Bank borrowers and by the World Bank as executing agency, The World Bank, August 1981. ISBN 0-8213-9000-7.

Anon., A growing partnership with industry, U.S. Government Printing Office: 1993 – 706-542.

Anon., IFTers form consulting network to serve industry worldwide, *Food Technology,* 48, 10, No. 12, 1994.

Anon., Andersen Consulting faces $100m damage claim, © 1995, Lafferty Publications Limited, International Accounting Bulletin, April 19, 1995a.

Anon., The liability monster, © 1995, Lafferty Publications Limited, Management Consultant International, April, 1995b.

Anon., United States: BCG and Figgie drop lawsuits, © 1995, Lafferty Publications Limited, Management Consultant International, June, 1995c.

Anon., IFT's 1996 classified guide, in *Food Technology,* 49, December, 1996.

Anon., Here's what to know when hiring a consultant, *The Globe and Mail,* C4, March 14, 1997.

Bagnall, J., Just what the doctor ordered: cooperation leads to bio-medical breakthroughs, *The Gazette,* Montreal, A13, April 24, 1996.

Baird, B., News of industry, *Food Technology,* 51, 13, No. 8, 1997.

Barwell, I., The real test for technology: can local manufacturers use it?, *Ceres,* 16, 35, No. 1, Jan. – Feb., 1983.

Bishop, R. A., The elements of project analysis: a stocktaking, *Ceres,* 15, 30, No. 6, November–December, 1982.

Biss, C. H., Coombes, S. A., and Skudder, P. J., The development and application of ohmic heating for the continuous heating of particulate foodstuffs, in *Process Engineering in the Food Industry,* Field, R. W. and Howell, J. A. eds., Elsevier, London, 1989, 17.

Bradshaw, P., Selling consulting services, *Piedmont Airlines,* 77, 78, 81, March, 1987.

Bruce, H., Your gain, my pain: downsizing has a downside, *The Gazette,* Montreal, B3, May 15, 1996.

Bush, P., Expert systems: a coalition of minds, *Prep. Foods,* 158, 162, No. 9, 1989.

Camp, R. C., *Benchmarking: The Search for Industry Best Practices That Lead to Superior Performance,* Quality Press and UNIPUB/Quality Resources, 1989, serialized in *Quality Progress,* 61- 68, Jan.; 70-75, Feb.; 76-82, Mar.; 62-69, Apr.; 66-68, May, 1989.

Carty, A., Convocation Speech, Carleton University, June 14, 1997, Personal communication.

Chianello, J., Intel now judged on damage-control speed, *The Financial Post,* p23, December 14, 1994.

Coghlan, A., Prof. Snooty and his pals pick up the pounds, *New Scientist,* 147, 6, No. 1985, 8 July, 1995.

Connor, D. and Davidson, J. P., *Marketing Your Consulting and Professional Services,* John Wiley & Sons, New York, second edition, 1990, chap. 22.

Cox News Service, Red hot chilis may increase cancer risk, *Chicago Tribune,* News section, p4, February 26, 1994.

Danzig, M., Potential pitfalls of Industry-University Cooperative Research Centers, *Food Technology,* 41, 103, Dec. 1987.

Desowitz, R. S., *New Guinea Tapeworms & Jewish Grandmothers: Tales of Parasites and People*, Discus Printing, Avon Books, New York, 1983.

Farr, D., High pressure technology in the food industry, *Trends Food Sci. Technol.*, 1, 14, 1990.

Farrer, K., Fredrick Accum (1769–1838)–consultant and food chemist, *Food Science and Technology Today,* 10, 217, No. 4, 1996.

Fuller, G. W., *New Food Product Development: From Concept to Marketplace*, CRC Press, Boca Raton, 1994, 116.

Gay, K., Outsourcing can be effective — if it's done right, *The Financial Post,* 24, April 12, 1996.

Gies, F. and Gies, J., *Cathedral, Forge and Waterwheel: Technology and Invention in the Middle Ages*, HarperCollins, New York, 1994, 68, 78.

Giese, J., Technical centers facilitate food product development, *Food Technology*, 51, 50, June 1997.

Hammer, Margareth, Why projects fail..., *Ceres*, 26, No. 1, 32, Jan.-Feb., 1994.

Herrod, R. A., Industrial applications of expert systems and the role of the knowledge engineer, *Food Technology*, 43, 130, May 1989.

IFST(U.K.), Code of professional conduct & professional conduct guidelines, October, 1991.

Ip, G., Outsourcing becoming a way of life for firms, *The Globe and Mail*, October 2, 1996.

Kahn, H., Brown, W. and Martel, L., *The Next 200 Years: A Scenario for America and the World*, William Morrow and Company Inc., New York, 1976.

Kay, E., Managing trauma in real life, *Globe and Mail Report on Business*, 13, No. 5, 82, November, 1996.

Kenward, M., Is there anybody there?, *New Scientist*, 133, No. 1805, p 62, January 25, 1992.

Kiernan, V., Seductive software leaves psychology tests null and void, *New Scientist*, 154, No. 2081, 5, 10, May, 1997.

Krueger, B. and Walker, C., The University of Nebraska's Food Processing Center, *Food Technol.*, 41, 99, Dec. 1987.

Lamb, H., *Charlemagne: The Legend and the Man*, Bantam Pathfinder Editions, Bantam Books, New York, 1963.

Leger, K., Re-engineering management gurus, *The Financial Post*, 19, June 10, 1995.

Livesey, B., Glitch doctor, *Globe and Mail Report on Business*, *14*, No. 5, 96, November, 1997.

López-Carrillo, L., *A Case-Control Study of Chili Pepper Consumption and Gastric Cancer in Mexico*, a Ph. D. thesis presented to the Department of Epidemiology and Public Health, Yale University, 1993.

Mahoney, P. J., Essay: Time to unshackle U.S. competitive strengths, *Scientific American*, 262, 136, May, 1990.

Mason, M. E., Potential benefits to the food industry of Industry-University Cooperative Research, *Food Technology*, 41, 105, Dec. 1987.

Matson, J. V., *Effective Expert Witnessing*, Lewis Publishers, Boca Raton, 1994, 34.

McCormick, C., Dollars for scholars, *The Gazette,* Montreal, F8, April 1, 1996.

McFarland, J., Canadian trainers wise up to U.S. market, *The Globe and Mail*, B15, Dec. 10, 1996.

McLellan, M. R., An introduction to artificial intelligence and expert systems, *Food Technology*, 43, 120, May 1989.

Milner, B., WorldCom wins costly battle for MCI, *The Globe and Mail*, B1, November 11, 1997.

Morand, P., Bridging the gap between universities and industry, *The Financial Post*, July 5, 1995.

Naisbitt, J., *Megatrends: Ten New Directions Transforming Our Lives*, Warner Books, Inc. New York, N.Y., 1982.

Pierce, F., Silence of the experts, *New Scientist*, 152, No. 2058, 50, November 30, 1996.

Ramsay, L., Who's accountable for the results of consulting work?, *The Financial Post*, 48, September 15, 1994.

Robbins, M. P., *The Cook's Quotation Book: A Literary Feast*, Robert Hale, London, 1987.

Rossen, J. L. and Solberg, M., Rutgers University's Center for Advanced Food Technology, *Food Technology*, 41, 100, Dec., 1987.

Rush, P., No flies on this seminar participant, *The Financial Post*, July 17, 1982.

Scott, S., The path to pay equity, *The Gazette,* Montreal, October 12, A1, A18, 1996.

Shahin, J., They're heeeere, *American Way*, p 42, 44, 45, December 1, 1995.

Singer, C., *A Short History of Scientific Ideas to 1900*, Oxford University Press, 1959, 196.

Snow, C. P., *Science and Government*, Harvard University Press, Cambridge, 1961, chap. IX.

Stackhouse, J., Watch what we do not what we euphemize, *The Globe and Mail Report on Business Magazine*, 19, December, 1991.

Swartzel, K. R. and Gray, D. O., Industry-University Cooperative Research in agriculture and food science: North Carolina State University's Center for Aseptic Processing and Packaging Studies, *Food Technology*, 41, 96, Dec., 1987.

Toffler, A., *Future Shock,* Bantam edition, Random House Inc., New York, 1971.

Tuller, L. W., *Cutting Edge Consultants: Succeeding in Today's Explosive Markets*, Prentice Hall, Englewood Cliffs, N.J., 1992.

Walters, S. G., Improving U.S. world competitiveness through Industry-University Cooperative Research, *Food Technology*, 41, 94, Dec., 1987.

Weiss, A., *Million Dollar Consulting: The Professional's Guide to Growing a Practice*, McGraw-Hill, Inc., New York, 1992.

Index